THE INTERNATIONAL LAW OF PEACE

LIONEL M. SUMMERS

1972 OCEANA PUBLICATIONS, INC.

Dobbs Ferry, New York

To

Marjorie Whiteman

and

William W. Bishop Jr.

For whose accomplishments in the
field of international law I have the
most profound admiration.

Library of Congress Cataloging in Publication Data

Summers, Lionel Morgan, 1905–
  The international law of peace.

  Bibliography: p.
  1. International law. I. Title.
JX3180.S77I57   341   72–4367
ISBN 0-379-00133-0

Manufactured in the United States of America

FOREWORD

106939

"The United States Government does not lie or intentionally mislead." There was a roar of incredulous laughter from the Washington sophisticates of the cocktail circuit at the stupidity of this punch line from the graying raconteur. His story was that of a young man in the Department of State charged during World Was II with drafting third person notes to the Minister of Switzerland who represented German interests in the United States. The occasion was one in which the young man, out of patriotic motive but contrary to the fact, sought to portray an incident in a prisoner of war camp as not in violation of the Geneva Prisoner of War Convention. The stern admonition came from his superior, a foreign service officer who has long since moved into, and out of, the ambassadorial ranks.

Professor Lionel Summers has, in his words, "unabashedly" approached the subject of the law of peace from "quite a personal standpoint." Thus encouraged, I reminisce in a personal way on national credibility.

If this book were about the laws of war, discussion of the credibility of sovereign states might be irrelevant. But in a book about the laws of peace, words like credibility and honesty are significant and related to law.

As a young college student I was enamored with the idea that if states were to adhere to the same standards of morality as men, wars might be avoided. Later on I thought that World War II, Korea, and Vietnam knocked that idea out of my head. Now I am not so sure. And I suspect the generation which will use this book is not so sure either.

It has been a long time since we have been reminded of the morality story about George Washington who, as a child, could not tell a lie and confessed he had chopped down the cherry tree. One might find parallels in President Eisenhower's admission of responsibility for the Gary Powers U-2 overflight of the Soviet Union, and President Kennedy's acceptance of responsibility for the Bay of Pigs. But I suspect the Eisenhower and Kennedy incidents do not carry the same moral connotation as the cherry tree story. Honesty became a virtue only because we got caught and the cover stories had been blown sky high. It is possible that lack of credibility is the fate of a great power. England in the days of empire was "Perfidious Albion" and the assurance of innocence by Foreign Minister Gromyko at the time of the Cuban missile crisis was not a model of credibility. But the thought flashes across my mind that credibility may be a characteristic of a great power that remains great, and lack of credibility may be a sign of weakness and possibly disintegration.

It might not be a bad idea for statesmen dealing with each other to

iii

keep their mouths shut or tell it like it is. It surely would be a welcome change if more nations had the reputation for not lying or intentionally misleading.

It's too much to expect, I suppose. But there may be hope in the work of men like Professor Summers and his students. They conceive international law to be an instrument to help make states honest, to keep them that way, and to provide, by precedent and practice, some minimal standards of international behavior, without which the future is gloomy indeed.

When I joined the Office of the Legal Advisor of the Department of State in the 1940's, I had the quaint idea that it was our duty as lawyers to advise the Secretary of State of what the law was, and thereafter American policy was to be formulated within the metes and bounds of the law. It did not occur to me that a policy might be formulated and the international lawyers then brought in to make the best possible legal case in support of what the policy-makers were determined to do anyway. It may have been the naiveté of youth. I read the volumes of former State Department Legal Advisor, Charles Cheney Hyde, in which he presented international law "chiefly as interpreted and applied by the United States" to mean that he was first a lawyer, second a lawyer in the Department of State, and third, maybe a policy-maker if there were a close legal question involved. Professor Hyde as Legal Advisor to the Department of State, was not "house counsel," as is the case today. I doubt there is much hope for law as a means of helping maintain peaceful relations when house counsel is called upon to provide a legal basis for policy decisions already made.

Law should be the foundation for policy decisions and not a scaffold which Mr. Webster defines as "a temporary or movable platform." Professor Summers' book is no scaffold.

March 20, 1972   Carl Marcy
Washington, D.C.

                                            Chief of Staff,
                                            United States Senate
                                            Committee on Foreign
                                            Relations

CONTENTS

PREFACE

There have been innumerable books published - some quite recently - on public international law. While some are less technical than others, only a very few are designed primarily for use by beginning students unacquainted with legal terminology and processes, or for use by a layman not seeking to acquire a technical grasp of the subject.

It is with such a student or layman in mind that I have written this book, trying to explain the international law of peace in simple terms. (Someone else can write on the international law of war.) I am unabashedly approaching the subject from quite a personal standpoint and am illustrating points from my own prior experience as a Foreign Service Officer, an Assistant Legal Adviser to the Department of State, an Agent of the United States before an international commission, the United States Member on another such commission, and a participant in both bilateral and multilateral international negotiations. In drawing upon my personal experiences, I am not trying to write my memoirs. I am only trying to inject a human element by looking at international law through the eyes of an individual who has, for many years, had to grapple with actual problems.

The book consists of the actual text, footnotes, a fairly extensive bibliography, and a series of hypothetical problems to text the ingenuity of students. To one of the problems, I have added the complete text of an extradition treaty - partly because it is relevant to that problem, and partly because nowhere else in the text have I given an example of a complete treaty. Since crime control is such a pressing issue at the present time, I thought that a treaty on extradition would probably be more interesting than other treaties. Moreover, any of my readers contemplating a bank robbery may be interested, since Brazil used to be a haven for bank robbers. Now that there is an extradition treaty, the potential bank robber may be discouraged from making the attempt, and I would therefore have done my bit toward promoting law and order.

In preparing the present volume, I had the great assistance of friends and colleagues who read the text and furnished me with many comments that saved me from outright mistakes or clarified ambiguous meanings. Any errors that are left are my own. I am particularly grateful to:

Mr. Clarence E. Birgfeld, F.S.O. (Ret.)
Mr. Charles Bevans, Asst. Legal Adviser on Treaty Affairs, Department of State
Prof. Wm. W. Bishop, Jr., University of Michigan, formerly Editor

in-Chief of the American Journal of International Law
Hon. Hardy C. Dillard, Judge of the International Court of Justice
Prof. Wilbur Dorsett, Rollins College
Dr. Paul F. Douglass, Prof. Emeritus, Rollins College; former Adviser to Syngman Rhee
Major General Palmer Edwards USA (Ret.)
Prof. S. Houston Lay, California Western University
Mr. Eric Lindahl, F.S.O.
Mr. Kyle Mitchell, F.S.O. (Ret.)
Mrs. Lewis Parker, F.S.O. (Ret.)
Prof. Rufus Smith, F.S.O., (Ret.), Rollins College
Mr. George Spangler, former Asst. Legal Adviser for Claims, Department of State
Prof. Richard N. Swift, New York University
Mr. Ralph Townley, United Nations Secretariat
Mr. Howard Van Zandt, Vice President, I.T.T. in Japan

With care and patience they examined the first draft, either in its entirety or with particular reference to their special competence. In addition to furnishing me with comments written or oral, they encouraged me to proceed in the preparation of the text.

I also had the valued assistance of four of my former students - Mr. Charles Draper, Mr. Thomas du Pont, Mr. Robert Glass and Mr. Stephen Johnston - in doing much of the preliminary research on which the initial version was based.

Moreover, I could never have finished the volume without the excellent secretarial, research, and editorial assistance of Mrs. Carlton Colyer, Mrs. Marilyn Ross, and Mrs. Daniel Linhart.

I also owe a large debt to the staff of the Mills Memorial Library at Rollins College for their unfailing assistance. Such assistance included finding where I put things (which requires the talent of Scotland Yard), reading my handwriting and, in general, helping in every manner possible.

I am also grateful to Mrs. Helen Philos of the American Society of International Law, who was of invaluable help in checking the bibliography and making suggestions to render it more useful.

Last but not least, I shall always be thankful for the strong support and understanding of my wife Lucy and my daughter, Natalia Brennen.

Grateful acknowledgement is made for permission given to quote from books, periodicals and individual letters. Specifically, thanks are extended to the following organizations and individuals for permission to reproduce the quotations appearing on the pages of the text shown opposite their respective names, as listed below. The texts themselves are identified in the footnotes, so that for the sake of brevity they are not described fully at this point.

Princeton University Press   Page 2, 3

Before closing this Preface, I want to express my frustration that time does not stand still. Between the time the text was set in print and the time that this book will appear, new events have or will render some of the conclusion subject to reexamination. Fortunately there are not too many, as international law does not change that quickly. Moreover, in some instances, the lasting impact of the new events is hard to determine. It does seem clear, however, that President Nixon's visit to China will necessitate a reexamination of the concepts of recognition. For example, will the People's Republic of China be able to sue in the courts of the United States?

INTRODUCTION

The first question to ask is,"What is International Law?" Generally speaking, international law can be defined as the law that governs the relations of states. International law is sometimes also referred to as public international law to distinguish it from private international law.

As the distinction between public and private international law is not quite the same in the United States, Great Britain and the other common law countries as it is in Europe, it may be well to devote a few paragraphs at this stage to summarizing the Anglo-Saxon and European interpretations of these two terms. Otherwise the reader, chancing upon a continental text, could understandably be confused.

As far as the Anglo-Saxon common law countries are concerned, private international law is the same thing as conflict of laws which is that branch of jurisprudence which determines which law is applicable to a particular situation when there is the possibility of several laws being pertinent. Let us assume that an American citizen met a Brazilian coffee dealer in Kingston, Jamaica, and arranged for a shipment of coffee to be delivered in Morocco. Later there is an argument about the contract. The two parties had not indicated in the contract which law should apply, so that in the event of a suit, brought possibly in still another state, France, for example, the judges must determine whether the law to be applied is Brazilian, Moroccan, Jamaican, American, or French.

The illustration relates to a business transaction. There are also many instances where conflict of laws situations arise in personal matters. For example, is a divorce granted in Mexico to citizens of the United States and France good in France and the United States? The subject of conflict of laws can present many fascinating problems. It is, however, a topic which is outside the scope of this book.

The continental lawyers believe likewise that conflict of laws is a part of private international law. However, they consider that problems of nationality, particularly those stemming from the interpretation of domestic laws concerning nationality, also fall within the orbit of private international law. In contrast, in the common law countries, the subject is usually treated as part of public international law.

Finally, the laws governing the status and rights of aliens, e.g., the rights to acquire land, to inherit property, to engage in the professions, are deemed by the European jurists to be part of private international law. Their common law counterparts, on the other hand, consider this phase of the law merely to be a part of the domestic law unless, of course, the rights of the alien are guaranteed by treaty or the treatment of an alien constitutes a violation of international law.

1

While speaking of the differing meaning attributed to public international law, it should also be mentioned in passing that extradition, that is, surrender of a suspected or condemned criminal by one state to another, is considered by the European jurists to form a separate branch of the law --penal international law--whereas common law jurists include the subject under public international law.

There has been considerable argument in the past whether international law--and from now on I will be speaking only about public international law as envisaged by the common law countries--is a branch of the law at all. Austin, a well-known English jurist of the last century, argued that law could be law only if it could be enforced by a sovereign authority; and that, since international law did not have such an authority behind it, it lacked the characteristics of law in the strict sense of the term. The simple answer to that argument is that international law does in fact exist and is applied daily in innumerable instances throughout the world. It is quite true that there have been many violations of international law in the past and that doubtless there will be grave breaches of that law in the future. Nevertheless, on a day-to-day basis, the network of treaties and customs which constitutes the main basis of international law is relied upon heavily to provide the machinery whereby an interdependent world can continue to exist. The view of a distinguished American diplomat, George Kennan, who is keenly aware of the limitations of international law are pertinent. He decries an unwarranted reliance on that law to solve all problems and yet pays tribute to international law as the bulwark of international relations, saying:

> "No one who has spent many years of his life in practical contact with the workings of international affairs can fail to appreciate the immense and vital value of international law in assuring the smooth functioning of that part of international life that is not concerned with such things as vital interest and military security. In my own case this was brought home in a most vivid manner, for during the second World War my own personal safety and that of a hundred and twenty-nine other official internees in Germany came to depend very largely, over several months, on such protection as international law could afford. In general, I think, you will find that foreign offices and professional diplomatists are very much attached to international law as an institution, and cling to it as one of the few solid substances in their world of shifting, unstable values."

Even in the case of flagrant breaches, lip service is now paid to international law which may be evidence of some progress. In 1914 when Germany brutally invaded Belgium, the German Chancellor Von Bethmann-Hollweg cynically stated that the treaty with Belgium, guaranteeing her neutrality, was a scrap of paper. In 1939 Hitler, with all his disregard of world opinion, went to elaborate lengths to try to prove that Poland had attacked Germany. There is no indication that he really persuaded anyone, but at least even Hitler felt that he had to justify his conduct and could not merely classify an international agreement as a scrap of paper.

At the same time that the innate strength of international law is recognized, it must be admitted that it has its frailties and sometimes suffers from its own supporters. Kennan, in the paragraph following the one just quoted, seems to imply that one of the problems of international law is the unrealistic zeal of some of its advocates, saying:

> "But it is important to the efficacy of international law itself that we should not overstrain its capabilities by attempting to apply it to those changes in international life that are clearly beyond its scope of relevance. I am thinking here of those elementary upheavals that involve the security of great political nations. The mark of a genuine concern for the observation of the legal principle in the affairs of nations is a recognition of the realistic limits beyond which the principle cannot be pressed."

Sometimes impracticality is compounded by a lack of knowledge of the actual workings of international law in practice and the relationship of that law to social factors. A well-known internationalist jurist has gone so far as to say in a fairly recent book review that "scholars in international law are largely impervious to the new ideas that have developed in the neighboring disciplines of the social sciences and contemporary philosophy."

As a converse to the lack of practical knowledge of the academician is the appalling ignorance of the theory and practice of international law displayed by diplomats who should be among the first to understand its intricacies. Moreover, the Legal Adviser's Office of the Department of State, which should be in the forefront of the promotion of international law, has been accused of trying to promote policy and to buttress political positions rather than analyzing the law.

An even more serious handicap to the development of international law is the ingrained problem of a multinational jurisprudence including the difficulty of effecting changes to meet new conditions. In ordinary law, changes are made through the growth of customs, legislation, judicial decisions having the force of law, and sometimes, the invocation of fictions. To what extent can international law use these same methods? Customs do come about as the result of new concepts adopted by the community of states. Occasionally a new concept or custom will be adopted quite quickly. Thus the universal lack of objection to spacecraft voyaging for peaceful purposes through outer space over the territory of many nations seems to have created a new custom which distinguishes air space from outer space and permits the use of outer space without hindrance from the countries whose territories

lie underneath. By the same token there seems to have been general acceptance of the doctrine first propounded by President Truman in 1945 that a
state bordering on an ocean had a right to control the exploitation of the
mineral and other wealth of the continental shelf adjacent to its territory.
At present there is a convention on the subject but the convention, signed
in 1958, essentially codified an already existing practice. These two instances are, however, more the exception to prove the rule than the rule
itself, for the development of custom in international law is generally a
slow and laborious process. It is likely to be even slower as the community
of nations increases in size.

There is, needless to say, nothing to compare exactly to legislation
in the international field. The nearest approximation is the broad international treaty which either codifies existing practice or establishes new
rules. It would be idle to deny the existence of any number of such treaties
and conventions. In the aggregate they constitute a very substantial quan-
tity of treaty law. Nevertheless, the negotiation and ratification of a treaty
is generally a far more difficult process than the enactment of domestic
legislation, particularly when a number of nations is involved. When a nation, or a state in a federal union, sees that a problem exists and needs to
be remedied, the legislature can take appropriate action relatively swiftly.
In international law change usually cannot be effected without infinite toil
and struggle.

The jurisprudence of a nation is constantly enriched by the decisions
of its courts. Admittedly the binding value of a judicial precedent is greater
in the common law countries than in ones where the civil law prevails.
Nevertheless, even in the latter the decisions of the highest courts are given
respect and attention and mold the character of the law. In the international
scene quite a different situation prevails. There is only one true international court in the world, leaving aside the rather specialized courts of the
European Communities and the European Court of Human Rights. Unfortunately the International Court of Justice has not had too many occasions
to render decisions as nations have been reluctant to submit their disputes
to that body. There have also been some arbitral tribunals, but they have,
particularly in the post-World War II period, been few and far between.
As a consequence international jurisprudence contributes relatively little
to the development of international law. In fact, most of the contemporary
decisions on international law are rendered by national courts.

Fiction is another method used both in Roman and English law to
circumvent traditional law that has outworn its usefulness but which is difficult to change directly. In general, its aim is to provide equity in an otherwise inelastic situation by postulating facts not subject to challenge. I think
one of the best examples of the use of fiction in the present day, even though
it is not labeled as such, is the decree of President Bourgiba of Tunisia
prohibiting plural marriages. President Bourgiba was faced with the fact
that the Koran specifically permits four wives and that according to devout
Moslems, the Koran is holy writ which cannot be altered. Hence, he did

not feel that he could propose a law which would run diametrically contrary to the Koran. Instead, he relied upon another provision of the Koran which in effect states that each wife must be treated equally. Seizing upon that provision, he stated in legislation that "the polygamist can never treat equally all of his wives." While the law does not say so explicitly, economic difficulties undergone by the poor probably hinder the equal treatment of wives. Now this may be true with regard to the average inhabitant of Tunisia where poverty is widespread. Nevertheless it certainly is not true with respect to a wealthy merchant or banker who could unquestionably, at least from a monetary standpoint, provide quite well for four wives or even more. Yet the wealthy banker is prohibited from challenging the assumption that he cannot provide for a plurality of wives and must accept the fiction that his means are insufficient for the purpose.

In international law there is seldom any reference made to fictions although, as I will explain later, there are two or three instances where concepts very akin to fictions are used to achieve a desired result. Those instances are the exception.

In summary, it is not surprising that international law, with a few notable exceptions, moves slowly and ponderously to keep current with the changing conditions of the world. Nor is it surprising that it is sometimes behind the times. The present lag is undoubtedly accentuated by the speed of technical change, by the emergence of new ideological and social concepts and the plethora of new ecological problems which threaten the world. Even domestic law has a hard time following the twists and turns of new developments and satisfying the demands of both conservative and liberal factions. It is wholly comprehensible that international law is in a state of flux as it adjusts to new realities. Nevertheless, when one considers the handicaps and limitations of international law one is rather amazed at the strength of its bonds.

Chapter I
THE DEVELOPMENT OF INTERNATIONAL LAW

International law as we now know it is relatively new. This is not to say that some of the basic processes of international law do not have their roots in antiquity. The first development of the nation-state was accompanied by embryonic attempts to enter into treaty relationships and to send and receive diplomatic missions. One of the early treaties usually mentioned in the histories of international law is an accord between Ramses II of Egypt and Hattusili II, the King of the Hittites in 1291 B.C., which provided for an alliance and for extradition.

The emergence of the Greek city-state naturally gave an impetus to the development of what might be termed international law concepts even though those concepts applied only to the Greek community. The rest of the world was considered barbarian. About the only contact that the Greeks had with the "barbarians" was through trade and war. In the Peloponnesian Peninsula, however, there was a great deal of intercourse between the Greek city-states and institutions began to arise that have their counterpart today. Thus one city-state would request a citizen of another city-state to act as the patron and protector of the citizens of the first residing or traveling in the second. He was called a "proxenoi." The affinity to the present consular officer is obvious.

When the Greek civilization was absorbed into the Roman empire, the development of international law between nations was suspended for the good and simple reason that the Romans controlled virtually all of the known Western world. Hence in the era of the Roman Empire it was Roman and not international law that was applicable. Naturally there were empires, kingdoms and tribes on the borders of Rome such as the Parthian Empire and the German tribes with whom the Romans were in constant battle. From time to time they might exchange envoys, particularly to treat on questions of war and peace. Nevertheless, international law was not a necessity in the day of the Pax Romana except for such limited purposes as the status of ambassadors. At the same time the Romans did develop certain concepts that had a compelling influence on future international law. Such development was indirect and was effected through the Roman law itself.

At the beginning of the Roman state, Roman law was based essentially on the Twelve Tables and on rather primitive concepts of jurisprudence suitable to a small and insulated nation. As Rome grew and became the center of empire, it soon became manifest that the old Roman law which the Romans applied among themselves could not be applied to the thousands

6

of Armenians, Gauls, Iberians and other non-Romans who flocked to Rome. Yet these individuals had to have a law that could be applied to them. A Roman official known as the Praeter Peregrinus was appointed to act as a magistrate for foreigners. In the course of time, a law which was based on the consensus of the laws prevailing in the various parts of the Roman Empire was developed for application to foreigners. It was known as the jus gentium or law of the people. Before long this law, since it was deemed to be universal and in a sense the distillation of legal wisdom, because intertwined with the Stoic philosophy, which looked to a divinely inspired natural law, a law suggested by the reasonableness of nature, and which appropriately was called the jus naturale. These concepts became a compelling force in the development of Roman law and naturally found their echo in Justinian's Code, which was compiled in the Eastern Roman Empire by the great Byzantine Emperor Justinian well over a century after the fall of Rome.

After the fall of Rome in the last half of the fifth century came the long decline into the period of the Dark Ages. Even then there were elements which sought to preserve law and order. As had just been stated, the Emperor Justinian in the Eastern Roman Empire compiled the Justinian Code. In Rome itself the Pope tried to mitigate the horrors of war and endeavored to bring some spirit of conciliation into the thinking of the people. It cannot be said that the efforts of the Pope were very successful. Part of this lack of success was probably attributable to the fact that several of the Popes were scarcely paragons of virtue themselves and their authority was often weak. It is interesting though that the Popes did strive to reduce war by pressing for periodic truces and by trying to outlaw certain weapons as being too horrible to use. Among them was the crossbow, which nowadays seems rather harmless compared to napalm and the atom bomb.

The coming of the Renaissance and the gradual emergence of civilization brought a revival of the study of law. In particular Roman law was subjected to intense study in the Italian city of Bologna by the so-called Bologna glossators. Heavily influenced by the concepts of the Roman law, international law likewise became the subject of interest. As stated by Garrett Mattingly, a well-known historian of the Renaissance: "In what we call the international law of the fifteenth century Roman law was the most important element, the warp on which the legal garment of the great society was being constantly woven."

Among the early writers were the Spanish theologians, Suarez and Vitoria, who devoted many pages to a consideration of what was and was not a just war. Alberico Gentili, another writer of note whose name is always included among the fathers of international law, was an Italian jurist who had emigrated to England and was teaching at Oxford. Gentili wrote on the laws of war, basing his book to a considerable degree on the observation of the practice of states.

The great father of international law was Hugo Grotius, who wrote in the first part of the seventeenth century. In his De jure belli ac pacis he drew together the threads of Roman law, natural law, and the practice of states interlacing them with his own views. Looked at from the present viewpoint his book is rather lopsided in the consideration of some topics and is a far cry from a present synthesis of international law. Nevertheless it constituted a gigantic step in the establishment of international law on a scientific basis.

Grotius was followed in turn by a host of writers who enlarged upon and embellished his ideas. Some preferred to take their inspiration from natural law, others from the observation of the practice of states. Still others combined the two methods. It is not worthwhile trying to note all of these numerous writers. The only one who deserves special mention is a Swiss writer who wrote in the eighteenth century. That writer, Emmerich de Vattel, was widely read in the United States and his book, written in French--Le droit des gens--was well known to the founding fathers of America. As will be seen later, some of his ideas still constitute the basic theory of the responsibility of states.

While the writers were explaining and analyzing the principles of international law and trying to establish that law on a scientific basis and even before, other events were likewise contributing to the development of that law. One of the most important was the rise of the mercantile city-state and in general the revival of commerce. As a consequence it became necessary to have laws and rules governing maritime commerce and the law of the sea. They were embodied in several codes and tables usually issued by a maritime state or by a group of states. Among the most famous were the Tables of Amalfi, a little Italian town south of Naples which in the Middle Ages was a leading maritime city; the Hanseatic Code published by the Hanseatic towns of North Germany; the Rolls of Oleron, Oleron being a small island in the Bay of Biscay; and the Consulato del Mare published in Barcelona. Much of what was contained in these various tables and declarations is not international law in the present sense. Nevertheless, in some respects they are surprisingly modern. In the Rolls of Oleron, compiled by Eleanor of Aquitaine from existing judgments, occurs a ruling on the duty of a master to his seamen. It reads:

> "Maryners bynd them with theyr mayster and any goo out withoutte leve of the mayster and drynke dronken and make noyse and stryfe so that any of them be hurte, the mayster is not bounde to cause them to be heled nor to purvey ought for them, but he may well put them out of the shyp (and hyre others in their place, and yf any coste more than the maryners put out, he ought to pay yf the mayster finds anything belonging to him). But yf the mayster sende them in any erande for the prouffyte of the shyppe, and that they shuld hurte theym, or that any dyd greve them, they ought to be heald at the costes of the shyppe. This is the judgment."

The size of the nation-state also created problems that had to be met through the establishment of institutions analagous to the ones that presently exist. Thus it became clear that temporary missions could no longer serve the purpose of providing for the continually expanding relations of the states and that permanent missions would have to be created. Quoting again from Mattingly: "the first resident diplomatic agent of whom we have any published mention served Luigi Gonzaga, 'Captain of the People of Mantua,' at the Imperial Court of Louis the Bavarian before 1341." Naturally as a concomitant to the developing relations of states and the burgeoning of commerce and trade there came into existence a network of treaties.

Another factor that was to influence the development of one rather peculiar international law practice, extraterritoriality, was the establishment of trading centers, first by Italians and then by other nationalities, in the Levant. Generally speaking, the rulers of the Byzantine Empire or of the Muslim domains in Asia Minor were content to let the foreigners take care of their own affairs so long as, of course, they paid the taxes and were not a source of trouble. Hence they permitted the foreign colonists to designate a magistrate among their midst, who was called a Consul and who administered justice among his co-nationals in accordance with their own laws. Thus was born the concept of extraterritoriality which was to have such far-reaching effects in the later centuries in Asia and Africa.

It seems incredible that a sovereign would be willing to permit a whole group of aliens to operate under their own laws independent of the jurisdiction of the State. One reason was that at that time there was the general belief that an individual carried his own law with him. Conversely the concept of the supremacy of the territorial law had not yet been thoroughly established. In fact, a rather curious remnant of that belief lingered on into the late eighteenth century in the first Consular Convention negotiated by the United States immediately following its independence. In a convention with France, French and American Consular Officers were given the right to settle disputes between their co-nationals.

Another element contributing to the rise of extraterritoriality was that most of the territory where it was practiced lay under the dominion of the Muslim rulers whose basic law was Islamic. That law being a religious law is, by its very essence, inapplicable to non-believers. The question as to the law which should be applied to non-Islamic sects in the Muslim empire had been raised in the very early days of the caliphate, and a precedent had been established to permit them to apply their own laws-- at least in civil matters. According to one Arab jurist:

> "Muslim occupation of Jerusalem, Omar, the Second Rightly Guided Caliph, improved the Muslim treatment towards non-Muslims. He permitted them to use their own laws as regards acts of worship and personal status. The non-Muslim religious leaders were allowed to exercise judicial

<u>powers and to enact legislation</u> covering acts of worship,
marriage, divorce, inheritance and other matters covered
by their religion. (Underlining supplied)

This benevolent and lenient attitude on the part of the Ca-
liphs was not beyond the scope of the jurisdiction of Muslim Law, since the Quran said: 'Let the People of Gospel
judge by that which <u>Allah</u> hath revealed therein' and 'if then
they have recourse unto thee (Muhammed) judge between
them or disclaim jurisdiction.' Thus, Muslim Law provides for the competence of non-Muslims within Muslim
territory to settle their own disputes with regard to acts
of worship and personal status."

While the Islamic Law did not forbid the application of penal sanc-
tions to non-Muslims, it was not too bold a step to allow officials of a foreign settlement to apply both civil and penal law. Such permission was embodied in a series of agreements between nations trading with the Levant
and the Levantine powers. These agreements were arranged by chapters
(capitulos) which gave rise to the term "capitulations." In other areas of
the world the term extraterritoriality was used. The whole system nevertheless had its roots in Asia Minor.

In the course of time the capitulations and the principles of extraterritoriality were imposed upon one nation after another--China, Japan,
Thailand, Ethiopia and many more. Moreover while the original capitulations were agreed to at the beginning on the basis of equality and as a means
of promoting justice (one of the most important treaties was between Francis I of France and Suleiman the Magnificent) they degenerated into a mechanism whereby the West could take advantage of its strength and power.

Capitulations and extraterritoriality are no longer in existence although the United States claimed extraterritoriality rights in several countries for a number of years after the end of World War II. They have, however, left behind a legacy of bitterness and hatred which has poisoned the
air today. One of the legitimate grievances of Red China is the abuse of
extraterritoriality by the Western powers in the last century and the beginning of the present one.

While capitulations and extraterritoriality in their original form
have disappeared under the impetus of anti-colonialism and the rising
strength of the non-Western world, some of the principles involved have
found a new abode in the status of forces agreements under which thousands
upon thousands of members of the armed forces are able, to some degree
at least, to exempt themselves from local jurisdiction. This is a topic too
complicated to discuss in a brief survey of the history of international law.
It will be commented upon more fully in later pages.

As we enter into the modern age, roughly marked by the advent of
the American and French Revolutions and the rise of industrialization,

international law starts developing at a faster pace. There are several reasons to account for this relative surge. One is that the world was becoming more and more closely knit. It is true that in 1789 the world was still far away from the jet age. Nevertheless, there was commerce between Europe and the Americas and throughout Europe, and the fast American clippers were going as far as Canton, China, to trade furs and ginseng for the silks and spices of the Orient. A good instance of how international institutional law was developed is furnished by the increasing attention paid by the governments to the exchange of mail. For a long time the postal system had been the prerogative of sovereigns and had operated on a rather hit or miss basis which in many respects was inferior to the system developed in Roman days. It literally took less time in Roman days for a letter to reach England from Rome than it did some eighteen centuries later. It was obvious that something had to be done, for mail was one of the instruments of commerce. There were a number of agreements and finally, shortly after the middle of the nineteenth century, the Universal Postal Union was created. The development of the telegraph and the necessity for providing international control for radio communications stimulated the same process.

The examples just given serve to show how the push of industrialization, the demands of commerce, and in general the growing interrelationship of the world necessitated a network of agreements and the establishment of international organizations large and small. Another factor which undoubtedly had its influence in international law and was responsible for many of the treaties negotiated in the last century was the rise of humanitarianism.

It would be idle to argue that humanitarianism has always progressed on an even keel. The barbarous atrocities of Hitler and the current massacres of innocent men, women and children in large parts of the world from Indonesia to Nigeria show that the tenets of humanitarianism are not always observed. Nevertheless if we look at the situation as it existed, let us say at the end of the Napoleonic wars in 1815, and as it exists today, it is obvious that progress has been made and that on the whole, the world is moving in the direction of concern for the individual.

England has always been considered to have been in the forefront of humanitarian action, yet in 1815 the conditions of the working classes in England were absolutely deplorable. Slums, excessive hours of work, lack of any care for workmen, silicosis in the mines, all made the life of a working man intolerable. It was not until 1819 that England passed a law outlawing the employment of children under nine years of age and prohibiting older children from working for more than twelve hours a day. The discipline in the British fleet was brutal, enforced by floggings and hangings. In the army the conditions were not much better. Until Florence Nightingale raised a hue and cry following the Crimean War little attention was paid to the plight of the poor soldier wounded in battle or overtaken by disease. On an international scale it took a vivid description of the suffering of the wounded following the battle of Solferino in the second part of the century to galvanize the world into the creation of the Red Cross. In the British colonies slavery still persisted and engaging in the business of the slave trade was considered to be perfectly consonant with high standards of morality. Oswald, the highly respected British plenipotentiary who helped negotiate the treaty of peace with the United States in 1783, had an interest in the slave trade.

Equally abhorrent were the efforts of England to force opium on China. In other respects also, the prevailing morality was brutish. Prize-fights resulted in the killing or maiming of the participants; there was little protection for animals and public executions were joyous days of celebration for the whole population except, naturally, the victim.

Britain has been cited as an example of the lack of humanitarianism because of the very fact that it was more advanced than most countries, and a budding humanitarianism had started to take root in the eighteenth century. In other areas, the situation was even worse. In the United States the indiscriminate killing of the Indian and the preservation of slavery constitute a blot on our history. In Russia serfdom was not abandoned until 1861 and pogroms were frequent.

Gradually there was an awakening of conscience and acts that would have been looked upon indifferently in an earlier era began to be criticized. The Red Cross Convention came into being in August of 1864 which provided at least some amelioration for the sick and wounded in time of war. The Red Cross Convention was in turn followed by a series of international treaties designed to stop the narcotics trade, to eliminate the traffic in women and children, and to promote other social measures. Today this growing tide of humanitarianism has been responsible for the approval by the United Nations of a series of conventions on economic and civil rights. They will be referred to more fully later.

Along with this growth of multilateral treaties designed to provide for greater cooperation and to eliminate some of the strident evils such as the slave trade, there was a great increase in the number of bilateral treaties between nations, covering virtually every subject under the sun, from commerce and trade to arbitration. Arbitration, particularly as an arm of international law, achieved prominence in the last century. Starting in 1794 with the Jay Treaty between the United States and Great Britain, provision was made by the United States for a whole series of arbitral tribunals whose function it was to decide disputes on the basis of law. The high point occurred in 1899 when, at a conference called at The Hague by the Emperor of Russia, the nations agreed to establish the Permanent Court of Arbitration. The name was somewhat of a misnomer since the convention signed by the parties essentially provided for a panel of jurists who could serve when called rather than for a permanent court. It nevertheless was a stride forward, making inevitable the day when there would be a genuine World Court.

Coupled with the concrete steps taken by the various nations to implement international law and to create rules by which the nations could abide was a continuation and growth of the earlier studies on international law, not only by individual jurists, but by well-known associations such as the International Law Association.

To summarize, there were a whole host of factors working toward the creation of an international law--technological developments, humanitarian impulses, the interdependence of the world, the rise of arbitration, the interest of academicians. There were, of course, and still are serious gaps. Nevertheless progress was being made and, in my opinion, continues to be made.

Chapter II

THE SOURCES OF INTERNATIONAL LAW

The word "source" can have varying meanings. In a bibliographic sense it is used to refer to an erudite text, including a learned text on international law, constituting a well of information.

In international law the expression "sources" usually has a broader connotation. The term refers to the contributing factors that have molded or are continuing to mold that law and on whose basis the present law can be determined. Among them are treaties and other international agreements, customs, court decisions and generally accepted legal principles.

In stipulating what legal factors the International Court of Justice should apply in making decisions, that is, to what sources it should look, Article 38 of the Statute of the Court says:

> "1. The Court, whose function is to decide in accordance with international law such disputes as are submitted to it, shall apply:
> a. international conventions, whether general or particular, establishing rules expressly recognized by the contesting states;
> b. international custom, as evidence of a general practice accepted as law;
> c. the general principles of law recognized by civilized nations;
> d. subject to the provisions of Article 59, [Article 59 in effect provides that decisions of the courts shall not constitute binding precedents] judicial decisions and the teachings of the most highly qualified publicists of the various nations, as subsidiary means for the determination of rules of law."

Actually only a moment's study will reveal that there is a considerable degree of overlap between the various factors. Thus a convention can be a codification of existing customs rather than an innovation in the law. The decisions of judicial bodies and the writings of publicists, that is, experts, are not going to be based on arbitrary concepts. They will, instead, as will be discussed more fully later, be predicated upon existing legal landmarks. The days when a Grotius could practically create international law largely on the basis of his own reasoning have long since disappeared. The overlap can be made clearer if each of the "sources" is analyzed and explained.

14

International conventions in Article 38 mean international agreements of any type. There is a plethora of terms used to designate international agreements: treaties, conventions, pacts, protocols, charters, statutes, exchanges of notes, and so on. Generally speaking, although not always, these terms correspond to particular types of agreements. Treaties are rather solemn instruments, such as Treaties of Peace, of Alliance, and of Friendship, Commerce and Navigation. Conventions--as applied to particular agreements and not in the generic sense used in Article 38 --are agreements of a more technical nature. Actually some of them may be more important than treaties. Ready examples that come to mind are the conventions on the laws of war, the conventions on the law of the sea and consular conventions. (The latter juxtaposition of terms is particularly unhappy since the average person thinks of a consular convention as a meeting of consular officers accompanied presumably by the traditional whoopee that accompanies conventions. I can speak from experience as I have had the occasion to work on several consular conventions to the bafflement of my friends, who thought I was arranging a consular gathering. And to confuse the picture further I did, in my capacity as Supervisory Consul General for Japan, request the consuls in that country to meet in Tokyo. We were, however, very careful to call the meeting a conference and not a convention.) A pact is a solemn and unfortunately sometimes rather meaningless undertaking--such as the Kellogg-Briand Pact of 1928 outlawing war which did little to stop Hitler or anybody else. Protocols are usually addenda to treaties such as a protocol providing for the compulsory settlement of disputes arising under the treaty. But this is not invariable. There have been some highly important separate agreements designated as protocols. Charters and statutes usually have reference to the constitutional documents of international organizations. Even here, however, there may be exceptions. The document creating the League of Nations was a Covenant. Exchanges of notes are more informal arrangements effected by the exchange of correspondence between two governments.

In the United States we have somewhat the same difficulty of terminology by including among the "treaties" requiring submission to the Senate for its advice and consent all sorts of agreements that are not called treaties by name.

However, so long as everyone is aware that the terms are not used literally no real harm is done.

Custom is another old and established source of international law covering many fields. Until quite recently diplomatic privileges and immunities were almost entirely--there were a few exceptions--governed by custom. Now the subject has been codified into a convention negotiated in Vienna in 1961. Consular privileges and immunities were regulated by a large number of bilateral conventions and in their absence by custom. A convention was all to the good as it was generally more precise than custom. Nevertheless a convention was not actually needed to permit consuls to operate. I functioned quite adequately and happily in Japan without the benefit of a convention. Since then one has come into force. I venture to guess that the lives of my successors have not been materially altered.

Custom consisting of a "general practice accepted as law" as distinguished from usage is usually slow in building. One traces the origin and development of custom in antecedents showing a consistent line of accepted practice through the course of the centuries. Nevertheless, as stated in Chapter I, certain customs such as the right to transit the outer space lying about national territories and the right to claim rights in the continental shelf, have grown up very rapidly.

Customs can also be eroded away by new practices. Not too many years ago there was a rather general agreement that the limit of the territorial sea was three marine miles. Now, as the celebrated Pueblo incident demonstrated, we are willing to concede a claim of a state to a much wider area of water adjoining its coast.

In addition to being established by long continuing practice, custom can also arise from the widespread acceptance of treaty stipulations. As between the parties to a treaty, the treaty itself governs. A treaty may in addition establish a custom that becomes in time binding on parties that never signed the treaty. For example, if the major maritime nations agreed in a treaty to a particular course of conduct at sea, the other nations of the world might be hard put to go counter to the precepts established by that agreement which in the course of years solidify into a binding custom.

Probably the most difficult factor or source to grasp and the one least readily used by the courts is "the general principles of law." It was inserted originally into the statute of the first world court to give the judges an additional basis on which to render opinions, and to prevent cases being dismissed on the ground that there was not any applicable law.

In many respects the concept goes back to the old Roman idea of jus gentium--the law common to all nations. In international law general principles of law have been applied, for example, to determine that undue delay in bringing a claim bars that claim on the analogy of the domestic statutes of limitations. General principles have also been invoked in some other relatively restricted instances.

Actually the full potential of the concept has never been really employed. It is not always easy to make an analogy between international and domestic law. There is always the difficulty of determining what, in a given situation, is the law common to all nations. I believe nevertheless that the effort of developing "general principles" is worth making and that far more study should be given the question than has been given to it so far. Possibly a better understanding could be achieved if general principles were divided into these relating to substantive law that governs the legal merits of a problem and establishes rights, procedural law that concerns the ways and means whereby a substantive right can be vindicated and damage law that determines the amount of compensation owing for an infraction. The latter two may be particularly important for there is by now quite a bit of substantive international law and it is not so necessary to fill in the nooks and crannies. Besides, substantive international law often poses problems that may have little relation to domestic law.

From my own personal experience I have found international procedural law to have as many holes as Swiss cheese. As United States member on the United States Japanese Property Commission I wished on more than one occasion to be able to apply the general principles of law on procedural matters. In one instance my dilemma was resolved because the case was settled. Possibly a brief mention of the problem I encountered will help illustrate my concern. In the case to which I refer an American oil company had some of its small tankers operating in Japanese waters seized in prize by the Japanese authorities when Japan and the United States went to war.

By the end of the war the vessels were either sunk or badly damaged. The oil company submitted a claim against Japan on the basis of Article 15 of the Treaty of Peace which provided that Allied property losses in Japan arising from the war should be paid for by the Japanese government. The Japanese countered by pointing out that there was another Article in the Treaty of Peace which permitted the review of prize court judgments. The oil company through the Agent of the United States admitted this to be so but contended that it could choose which remedy to pursue and that it had chosen to claim compensation.

In many ways the situation had all the characteristics of cases involving the election of remedies. (If a man is injured in an industrial accident can he elect to sue or must he claim workmen's compensation?) Could this doctrine be applied to international law on the basis of general principles? And if it could how could one be sure that the jurisprudence of the world was in accord on the election of remedies? I found virtually nothing to help me. Fortunately, as I have said, the case was settled so I was relieved of resolving the problem.

In another case the testimony of the witnesses taken over a considerable period of time and relating to past events proved to have many contradictions. My colleagues thought that those contradictions vitiated the case. I, on the contrary, thought that it showed the essential honesty of the witnesses since it was quite obvious that they had not been rehearsed to tell the same story. In essence I believed that contradictions, in testimony relating to events that had taken place several years before, so long as they did not affect a really major issue, could be expected and in a sense added to the veracity of the presentation.

I searched everywhere for some precept of evidence rooted on domestic law that would, like a saying of Confucius, suggest that "men who all say same thing not necessary truthful."

I want to hasten to make clear that in looking for such a universal precept I was not trying to slide Anglo-Saxon rules of evidence into international procedures by the back door. Heaven forbid when one considers that the authoritative American text on evidence--Wigmore on Evidence-- covers nine long volumes of technical discussion. I did think nevertheless that it might be highly appropriate to introduce into international litigation some of the basic guidelines governing the evaluation of evidence as applied by domestic courts.

I do not know what the answer is. Possibly it lies in the increased study of the subject aided by computers such as the one that now exists at the World Peace Through Law Center in Geneva. In Tokyo I had relatively limited facilities so that a pertinent precedent could easily have escaped me.

The same is true on the law relating to damages. There has been a thorough three-volume work written on damages in international law. New problems, however, keep rising on which international precedents alone shed relatively little light.

I have deliberately directed more attention to the general principles of law than to conventions and customs partly because the general principles are harder to understand and the field for their application has not been fully explored and partly because I will refer to conventions and customs far more in later chapters than to general principles.

One thing that does seem to be clear is that general principles yield to established international law in case of conflict. Probably every system of jurisprudence holds that duress vitiates a contract. But a peace treaty imposed by a victorious power on the vanquished is not illegal because the treaty was signed under compulsion even though from a propaganda stand-point much may be made of the fact of compulsion. An illustration is the unremitting campaign of Hitler against the Treaty of Versailles. Notwithstanding all his fulminations and a certain sympathy for Germany, no reputable international lawyer thought the treaty invalid.

The writings of publicists and judicial decisions once more overlap the other sources. Publicists, a quaint expression at best, are innumerable. Individually they can range from persons who write one insignificant article to men of great learning who produce fundamental texts on international law or on certain branches of that law. Collectively they include members of learned groups who collaborate to produce studies on the whole or part of international law. Around the 1930's Harvard sponsored a group selected from the professional and academic circles and from the Department of State to prepare suggested codes on various aspects of international law together with comments. More recently the American Law Institute has compiled a Foreign Relations Code. Generally such groups are unofficial. The International Law Commission of the United Nations plays, however, a definite official role in the codification of international law.

Whether the publicist can be individual or collective, whether he be superficial or erudite, the text--unless it is a mere compilation of existing treaties, decisions or previous publications--is likely to be a narrative record of international law as it is rather than the exposition of a theory about what might be better law. There may be some of the latter in a text as every author likes to make suggestions which he believes will lead to improvement. Nevertheless a text that emphasizes theory and recommendations and is deficient in recording practice will find it difficult to obtain general acceptance and will not be used to any extent by practitioners.

Hence the texts are likely to be primarily a reasoned comment resting on an analysis of pertinent conventions, statutes, court decisions and customs. As a consequence a text is useful to the International Court of Justice or for that matter to any other court as a summary of relevant conventions, customs and general principles rather than as an independent source.

To a large extent the same is true of court decisions whether national or international. They are not based upon what the jurist thinks should be the law but on what the law is as best he can ascertain. No jurist could ignore a pertinent treaty just because he disapproved of its terms.

The practice of referring to earlier decisions is looked upon with particular favor by Anglo-Saxon jurists who have been trained to follow judicial precedents--the doctrine of stare decisis. Nevertheless even a continental lawyer will be glad to find a case in point to give him assurance that he is following the right path. To my mind the best statement on the value of precedents is found in a decision of the Anglo-Japanese Property Commission. The Commission said:

> "The issue has already been considered by the United States-Japanese Commission which has given a considered determination of the point in its decision No. 4, dealing with some ten claims then pending before it...."

. . . . . .

> "This decision was given on the Treaty and the Law now before us, after a very full and thorough consideration of the factors involved. We are, of course, not bound by that decision and are quite free to reach a different conclusion if we think the U.S.-Japanese Commission was in error, but judicial comity and the desirability of certainty and consistency in the interpretation of Treaties and the Law, which has led to the establishment of the principles of stare decisis in so many countries, clearly indicates that we should not take a different course unless we have strong and cogent reason for dissenting from the view of the Commission which has just completed its work. Having carefully considered the arguments put before us and whilst acknowledging the force and weight of much of the argument advanced by the Japanese Agent, we, nevertheless,

do not find sufficient reason to differ from the view taken
by the U.S-Japanese Commission...."

There is one large difference between a text writer and a jurist on
a court or commission. The text writer does not have to resolve concrete
cases to which there is no ready answer. He may point out uncertainties
in the law but he is not under a pressing obligation to offer a definitive solution. A jurist, on the other hand, may have to determine a case on which
the law is quite ambiguous. In deciding a case he resolves the ambiguity
and to that extent adds to international law instead of merely restating existing rules.

The task of a jurist in reaching a decision is by no means a simple
one. In a personal letter to me Judge Dillard said:

"Most people seem to think that the law is or ought to
be pretty certain and that all the court need do is to 'apply' it to the facts. They do not realize how subtle and
difficult it is to determine which facts are significant and
why; nor do they sufficiently realize that the law is couched
in the kind of rhetoric that is by no means self-revealing
but invites recourse to 'the felt necessities of time and
place.'"

Because of that difficulty there are so many split decisions in both
international and domestic courts, with judges sometimes disagreeing acri-
moniously. Our own Supreme Court is a constant example of how the members of the court view the same problem from differing viewpoints. Even
though a decision is not unanimous it still constitutes an addition to international law. And, even if it breaks new ground, it is part of the continuance of the law. The jurisprudence of the past will necessarily have a part
in its formation.

In summary, international courts will rely on conventions, customs
and general principles. In trying to determine what they are they will consult texts and earlier decisions. In some cases decisions which plow new
ground will have a validity of their own.

Section I of Article 38 quoted previously is followed by a short Section 2 reading as follows: "This provision (Section L) shall not prejudice
the power of the Court to decide a case ex aequo et bono, if the parties
agree thereto."

What this means is that if the application of the strict letter of the
law would result in injustice or uncertainty, the court may be permitted to
determine the case on the basis of what is right and reasonable. In a few
instances a court has been authorized to decide on an ex aequo et bono basis in boundary disputes when the documents establishing the titles were
in indescribable confusion and it would have been fruitless to apply strict
law which might have had the undesirable result of dividing a village in half.

Actually there have been very few cases decided on this basis as nations are understandably reluctant to give such a wide authority to an international tribunal. Recently, however, one of the conventions on the law of the sea-- the fishing and conservation of the living resources of the high seas--provides for a method that is certainly akin to the ex aequo et bono method. Article 9 states that:

> "Any dispute which may arise between states under Articles 4, 5, 6, 7 and 8 [all of which in one form or another relate to conservation] may be submitted for settlement to a special commission of five members."

The language of the convention in Article 10 then lists the criteria for determining the issues which criteria are primarily scientific rather than legal.

Under no circumstances should ex aequo et bono be equated with equity, although this has been done. "Equity"as used by American lawyers is essentially an Anglo-Saxon concept that grew up side by side with the common law and operated to mitigate some of the harshness and rigidity of the latter law. It also has the broader meaning of justice and fairness. In this sense it does play some role in international law and decisions.

In the Agreement for the Settlement of Disputes Arising under Article 15(a) of the Treaty of Peace with Japan, Article V provided: "Each commission created under this agreement shall determine its own procedure, adopting rules conforming to justice and equity."

Neither my fellow commissioners nor I took this to mean that our commission could adopt rules that would disregard the law. What it meant --or at least what we thought it meant--was that the Commission should give weight to equity in drafting rules, and inferentially in reaching decisions. If in a given case the law was quite clear it would have to be abided by even if the results might not produce equity. Where, however, as is so often the case, the legal factors point to more than one acceptable solution, equitable considerations should swing the balance. In other words injustice should, wherever possible, be avoided. This is a far cry from ex aequo et bono. I believe this is in keeping with the views of other commissions.

Chapter III
THE CONTRIBUTION OF INTERNATIONAL ORGANIZATIONS
TO INTERNATIONAL LAW

International organizations, in the present connotation of that term, are of relatively recent vintage. Nevertheless, their contribution to the development of modern international law has already been substantial and is bound to increase in the future. Some of the more important aspects of that contribution, such as the codification of international law, will be discussed in other chapters of this book. It may, however, not be amiss to make an overall, if necessarily summary, survey of the role played today by international organizations in promoting the law of nations.

As I have just indicated, international organizations are largely a phenomenon of the present age. To be sure, all sorts of plans and ideas had been advanced in the past for international cooperation and world or, better said, European government. Among them was the Great Design of Henry IV of France, which is actually attributable to his astute Minister, the Duc de Sully. The Great Design, which assumed final form in 1638, envisaged a federation of fifteen states of Europe with a general council or senate. While the idea was projected in the interests of peace, one of its principal aims was to humble the House of Austria, so that it was not entirely altruistic in motivation.

Others voicing suggestions for world government and international collaboration in the century and a half that preceded the watershed of the American and French revolutions were Jeremy Bentham, Emeric Crucé, Hugo Grotius, Immanuel Kant, William Penn, Jean Jacques Rousseau, and the Abbé de Saint-Pierre. Even though none of the plans was ever implemented, the fact that so many eminent philosophers and statesmen were interested in the subject was a portent of things to come.

Following the French Revolution, international organizations began to come into their own. At the beginning, primary stress was placed on bilateral international organizations constituted for a specific purpose and for a limited period. Arbitral commissions such as those created under the Jay Treaty of 1794 between the United States and England come to mind. Nevertheless, the concept of a grouping of states to preserve the existing order and further peace was not entirely overlooked. The Holy Alliance proposed by Alexander I of Russia was, in many respects, a lofty and inspiring document which expressed some of the basic principles that later found their way into the Covenant of the League of Nations and the Charter of the United Nations.

To a very large degree the Holy Alliance remained a pious aspiration. Of more practical significance was the loosely established Concert

22

of Europe that endeavored to regulate the affairs of that continent. It was initiated by the Treaty of Chaumont of March 1, 1814, and confirmed by Article 6 of the Quadruple Alliance. The article read:

> "To facilitate and to secure the execution of the present treaty, and to consolidate the connections which at the present moment so closely unite the four sovereigns for the happiness of the world, the high contracting parties have agreed to renew their meetings at fixed periods, either under the immediate auspices of the sovereigns themselves, or by their respective ministers, for the purpose of consulting upon their common interests, and for the consideration of the measures which at each of those periods shall be considered the most salutary for the repose and prosperity of nations, and for the main-tenance of the peace of Europe."

As the century advanced there was an obvious need for the consti-tution of international organizations to deal with technical and humanitarian problems. As pointed out in Chapter I, among the earliest and best known was the Universal Postal Union, created at a Congress convened in Berne on September 15, 1874, to bring order out of chaos in the postal services. The United States had dipped its toe into the gathering waters of interna-tional organizations a little earlier. In a treaty with the Sultan of Morocco signed on May 31, 1865, the United States and a number of other powers agreed to maintain a lighthouse off Cape Spartel. The lighthouse still blinks at the maritime traveler as he approaches the entry to the Medi-terranean from the Atlantic, although by now Morocco has assumed its up-keep.

The impetus towards international organization was given a push by the two Hague conferences of 1899 and 1907 and the creation of the Perma-nent Court of Arbitration discussed in Chapter XVII. Although that impetus was abruptly halted by the coming of World War I, the end of that war saw the constitution of the League of Nations which functioned in the inter-war era.

At present the focus of activity is in the United Nations and its fam-ily of related organizations. In addition there are a number of intergovern-mental organizations which are not affiliated with the United Nations, some of which, such as NATO, CENTO, SEATO, COMECON, the OAS and the OAU, are of considerable importance, particularly from a defense or re-gional standpoint, or both.

In the last available Year Book of International Organizations (the 12th edition, 1968-1969) a tabulation is made of 229 intergovernmental organizations, not counting bilateral ones. Of these, 67 are stated to be dead or inactive, which means that there were 162 multilateral interna-tional organizations functioning in 1968-1969. Probably by now there are more. Some of them, as has been stated, are of considerable importance. On the other hand, some appear to be rather restricted both in scope and in the area in which they operate. Just for example, the International Moselle Company has only 3 participating members. Similarly, the Organization of Senegal Riparian States has only 4 countries composing its membership.

Complementing the intergovernmental organizations there are a host of private international organizations which sometimes, nevertheless, have government support and work in conjunction with intergovernmental organizations having the same interests.

According to the same Year Book there are 2,188 non-governmental organizations of which 674 are dead or inactive. This means that there were 1,514 functioning in virtually every conceivable field. They range from entities having wide interests and many members to organizations of rather limited scope. (I am not an ornithologist and I know nothing of Esperanto, but I am inclined to believe that the impact of the Esperantist Ornithologists' Association, which is one of those listed, might be rather circumscribed. If I am wrong, I tender my apologies here and now.)

The contribution of international organizations to international law takes various forms. Mr. Constantin A. Stavropoulos, the Legal Counsel of the United Nations, has dealt forcefully with the importance of the United Nations in fostering the development of international law in an article on that subject. His comment on the scope and effect of resolutions is particularly interesting. Because of his official position and intimate knowledge of the subject, that comment is well worth quoting. He says:

"The Organization established by the Charter [of the United Nations] --itself a treaty as lawyers like to point out --consists of a series of organs which hold regular meetings to discuss matters of international concern and where nearly all States are now represented. A mechanism thus exists which, whatever its inadequacies, regularly formulates collective views with respect to virtually every topic of interest to States. The major development in international law which has occurred during the past 25 years has been the creation and operation of this machinery, and it is to this that international lawyers all over the world now turn their attention, as well as to the most basic features of international relations, namely, the existence of independent States. The United Nations does not, of course, except within certain limited fields chiefly concerned with its own internal operations, have direct powers. The most characteristic product of discussion in United Nations organs is the adoption of a resolution. Taken that, in the first instance, the powers of most United Nations organs are purely recommendatory, and having in mind the principle of State sovereignty, it is difficult to categorize the effect of such resolutions and to accommodate them in the traditional pattern of law-making instruments. The theory on the matter is disputed and raises questions of great difficulty. Nevertheless, the regularity of meetings, such as the annual sessions of the General Assembly, the persistence of certain issues, and the process of aligning Members' views on a given topic, has resulted in a situation in which resolutions, most notably those of the General Assembly, have come to play a substantial part in determining State practice in international law and in the creation and interpretation of international legal obligations. The effect of a resolution may vary from case to case and even from State to State, but it seems undue conservatism to suggest that Assembly resolutions have not, in fact, become one of the principal means whereby international law is now moulded, especially in those instances, ranging from the Universal Declaration of Human Rights of 10 December 1948 to the Declaration on the Granting of Independence to Colonial Countries and Peoples of 14 December 1960, where the resolution has enjoyed the support of virtually all States Members, both at the time of its adoption and subsequently." (Underlining supplied)

The effect of a resolution is probably greater when it purports to interpret an existing principle in international law rather than to establish a new one. Even in the latter case, it is obvious that the consensus of the States gathered together in the United Nations will be greeted with great respect and that if the consensus is virtually unanimous it would probably be not too much of an exaggeration to say that a new rule of international law emerges. Nevertheless, it would be hazardous in the absence of an authoritative interpretation to state exactly the legal effect of a resolution. For example, at the 24th General Assembly a resolution was approved preserving the seabed of the high seas from appropriation and exploitation pending the establishment of an international regime to control such exploitation in the interests of mankind as a whole. Specifically, the resolution declared that:

"... pending the establishment of the aforementioned international regime:

(a) States and persons, physical or juridical, are bound to refrain from all activities of exploitation of the resources of the area of the sea-bed and ocean floor, and the subsoil thereof, beyond the limits of national jurisdiction.

(b) No claim to any part of that area or its resources shall be recognized."

In effect, the United Nations has adopted a rule which is quite akin to the standstill agreement relating to Antarctica embodied in a formal treaty. If some nation were to defy the resolution and proceed to exploit the seabed, it would be very interesting indeed to see whether an international court would consider it as having acted in violation of international law.

Another aspect of the contribution of international organizations to the growing network of interstate obligations are the rules promulgated by some agencies which, for all intents and purposes, have the same effect as treaties. Articles 21 and 22 of the Constitution of the World Health Organization provide a perfect example of the authority for an agency to adopt such rules. Those articles read:

Article 21

"The Health Assembly [of the World Health Organization] shall have authority to adopt regulations concerning:

(a) sanitary and quarantine requirements and other procedures designed to prevent the international spread of disease;

(b) nomenclature with respect to diseases, causes of death and public health practices;

(c) standards with respect to diagnostic procedures for international use;

(d) standards with respect to the safety, purity and potency of biological, pharmaceutical and similar products moving in international commerce.

(e) advertising and labelling of biological, pharmaceutical and similar products moving in international commerce.

Article 22

"Regulations adopted pursuant to Article 21 shall come into force for all Members after due notice has been given of their adoption by the Health Assembly except for such Members as may notify the Director General of rejection or reservations within the period stated in the notice."

WHO has, in fact, issued such regulations which thus became part of the constantly expanding web of international obligations.

In addition to adopting resolutions and issuing regulations--be it by one of the central organs or by a specialized agency--the United Nations has been responsible for the very important work of the International Law Commission, a body of twenty-five legal experts representing an equal number of states. That Commission has succeeded in preparing drafts of seven conventions codifying various aspects of international law which were submitted to international conferences at Vienna and Geneva for consideration and approval. The seven conventions consist of four on the law of the sea, one each on diplomatic and consular rights and privileges, and one on the interpretation of treaties. Each will be discussed fully in later chapters. All of these conventions have now become treaties although the number of states they bind varies from agreement to agreement.

In addition, the International Law Commission has prepared a draft convention on Special Missions. In this case the United Nations obviously did not consider it necessary to call a conference to consider that agreement but instead approved a draft prepared by the International Law Commission. Such approval was predicated on a report of the Sixth or Legal Committee of the United Nations General Assembly. Although not yet in force the proposed agreement has been opened for signature and ratification or for accession. Furthermore, the International Law Commission has prepared an agreement with regard to stateless persons which likewise has not yet come into force. It is presently working on several other problems including the thorny one of responsibility of states.

The International Law Commission is not the only organ of the United Nations concerned with international law. Legal problems of every kind and nature are referred by the General Assembly to the Sixth or Legal Committee, which considers them and makes reports such as the one approving the convention on Special Missions.

Not content with passing resolutions embodying principles of law, sponsoring codification conferences, approving draft declarations and conventions, issuing regulations, and generally investigating and reporting upon various questions concerning international law, the United Nations also promotes a better knowledge of the law by publishing international agreements binding on member states as well as a series of volumes reproducing international arbitration awards.

This short summation of the contribution of the United Nations and its specialized agencies to international law does not take into account the judicial work of the International Court of Justice, which has decided a number of cases following its institution, since World War II. That Court and its activities will be considered fully in Chapter XVII.

While the work of the United Nations and its agencies and commissions is particularly noteworthy since it operates on a global scale, other international organizations are also making contributions that should not be overlooked. Thus the European Commission of Human Rights as well as of the European Court of Human Rights have played an important part in implementing the human rights provisions of the European Convention for the Protection of Human Rights and Fundamental Freedoms signed at Rome on November 4, 1950.

Another important European international judicial body is the Court of Justice of the European Communities initially created for the Coal and Steel Community but now also used by the European Economic Community and EURATOM as well. The work of this court is particularly interesting since it has made a number of decisions, some of which are on a supranational rather than on a purely international basis.

Necessarily this is a very brief and summary survey of the role of international organizations. Moreover it ignores entirely projected plans of regional organizations for the advancement of law such as the projected Arab Court of Justice. To some extent, however, some of the gaps are filled by substantive discussions in other chapters.

Chapter IV
THE MEMBERS OF THE INTERNATIONAL COMMUNITY

The principal and traditional members of the International community are sovereign states. According to generally accepted criteria a state should possess a permanent population, a defined territory, a government and the capacity to enter into relations with other states.

At present there are 131 states in the United Nations. In addition there are some states that do not belong to that body--Switzerland because of her neutrality, Western Samoa, Tonga and Nauru, the divided states-- Germany, Korea, and Viet Nam and the mini-states of Europe--Liechtenstein, San Marino, Andorra and the Vatican City, as well as the Trucial states along the Persian Gulf and Sikkim in Asia. It has been argued that the really small states are not fully states since they cannot meet their international responsibilities. The League of Nations at one time refused to admit Liechtenstein on the ground that it could not meet the League obligations. It is somewhat questionable whether a corresponding viewpoint would be taken by the United Nations today in view of the mini-states that have been admitted. None, however, are quite as small as Liechtenstein. Moreover, the fiction held for so long that Taipeh represented all of China including the mainland, effectively barred Red China from participation for many years.

Even if Byelorussia and the Soviet Ukraine are subtracted from the list of sovereign states on the ground that they are not really independent although they are represented in the United Nations, there are around 140 states in the world today. The chances are that the number will increase as the few remaining protectorates, colonies and dependencies, the Bahamas for example, achieve independence. There will, of course, be even more if some of the centrifugal tendencies in some areas result in the creation of new nations carved out of the territory of existing ones. Quebec comes to mind.

In comparison to the number of states that existed at the beginning of this century the number is astonishing. Nevertheless that number is relatively small compared with the multiplicity of kingdoms, principalities, dukedoms and ecclesiastical possessions into which Germany and Italy were at one time divided.

Theoretically each state has exactly the same rights as every other state except insofar as it may be limited by its own agreement, as, for example, Switzerland accepting neutral status, or little Nauru, which permits Australia to manage its foreign affairs and provide for its defense.

In practice, of course, there is considerable disparity between the influence of states. It is generally conceded that the United States wields considerably more power than Mauritius. Moreover the facts of international life are recognized when only five important states are given permanent seats on the Security Council of the U.N. and in the weighted voting system adopted by some international organizations such as the International Monetary Fund.

Protectorates, colonies and dependencies used to form an important part of the international community and had limited personalities of their own. In some instances they were permitted to adhere to international agreements--particularly technical agreements--in their own right. To the extent that semi-sovereign states still exist, this is still true. Thus Antigua, Bahamas, Bermuda, British Honduras, British West Indies, Dominica, Gibraltar, Grenada, Hong Kong, and several other British possessions are listed along the entities having international agreements with the United States in the list of treaties published by the Department of State at the beginning of each year.

Closely allied to the colonies, protectorates, dependencies or other possessions of the various powers were the former mandates and the trusteeships. They originated at the end of World War I. President Wilson was opposed to colonies and did not want colonies created out of the breakup of the overseas German Empire or the southern reaches of the Ottoman Empire. Hence the lands that formerly belonged to the two empires were made mandates subject to the administration of a mandatory power which was to administer the area assigned to it as a sacred trust of civilization.

At the end of World War II the existing mandates (Iraq had become independent) became trusteeships with the exception of South West Africa. Moreover Somalia changed from the status of an Italian colony to an Italian trusteeship.

It is not very profitable to delve into the intricacies of the mandate and trusteeship system since there are only two trusteeships left--New Guinea, administered by Australia, and the Trust Territory of the Pacific, the Micronesian Islands taken over as strategic areas by the United States from Japan, the original mandatory power. South West Africa is somewhat in limbo. The Republic of South Africa, which administered the territory as a mandatory power when it was still the Union of South Africa, has argued that the mandate ended with the end of the League. In advisory opinions the International Court of Justice has held that the mandate continued. The Republic of South Africa will not agree to end its control and there the matters stand, with tempers heating on both sides and with the United Nations abandoning the effort to maintain the mandate and pressing for independence.

States of a confederation were considered to have an international personality. There are, however, no longer any confederations, notwithstanding the fact that the Swiss style Switzerland as the Helvetic Confederation, a fact brought to the attention of every visitor to Europe by the familiar

C.H. (Confederation Helvetique) appearing on automobiles registered in Switzerland.

Usually states of a federal union, as distinct from a confederation, have little or no international authority in their own right. In certain instances they are nevertheless permitted to enter into agreements with foreign political entities. Under the American constitution "no state shall, without the Consent of Congress, ... enter into agreement or compact with ...a Foreign power, "which obviously means that with the consent of Congress it may do so.

In September of 1969 Quebec and Louisiana tried to enter into a cultural agreement which also provided for the exchange of training in petrochemicals. The Secretary of State, however, judging from press reports, interposed objections.

There have been a few instances when states with the consent of Congress have entered into some agreements with adjoining political entities with regard to such non-controversial matters as bridge maintenance. Nevertheless its use in more important cases seems to have been frowned on.

Actually there is no reason why this clause could not be used in some instances to advantage. Back in the late 1940's I was negotiating a cultural convention with Italy on which agreement was never reached. One of the chief stumbling blocks was that Italy, as the protector of its emigrants, wanted Italian degrees given legal recognition in the United States for professional licensing purposes. Even if the federal government had been disposed to meet the request and felt that it could do so legally under the Missouri v. Holland case, discussed later, the states of the union would have been up in arms. I suggested, in a dispatch from the Embassy, that the treaty permit the states to negotiate this point with the Italian government. Since the Italian emigrants are concentrated in a relatively few states there need not have been a large number of agreements. I got precisely nowhere with my suggestion.

Possessing a certain amount of international standing are belligerents and insurgents. The most famous case of belligerency is that of the Confederate States of America. While they did not enter into treaties with foreign powers, they were accorded rights in the prosecution of war normally accruing to a sovereign state. Thus when the "Alabama" engaged in raiding, sometimes to the inconvenience of neutrals, she was not considered as a pirate ship. The same is true to a lesser extent of insurgency, a status just below that of belligerency.

So far the discussion of who or what constitutes an international personality has dealt with territorial entities or at least entities, such as belligerents, tied to territory. Recently more and more attention has been given to the concept that an international organization has an international personality. Obviously an international organization does not stand on the same footing as a territorial state. Nevertheless it can enter into agreements with a state, as evidenced by the highly important Headquarters

Agreement between the United States and the United Nations. Moreover the International Court of Justice has held in an advisory opinion that the United Nations could press an international claim arising out of the death of one of its employees, Count Folke Bernadotte, who was killed in Palestine while on a United Nations mission in that area. Furthermore, the Convention on the High Seas permits an international organization to fly its flag over a ship.

There has also been a school of thought--a minority school--which holds that an individual has a personality under international law. Usually the concept is stated in the technical phrase that an individual is a subject of international law and not just an object of that law.

The proponents of the theory point out that individuals have rights under many treaties, that they are subject to liabilities, as, for example, pirates who are considered to be enemies of human kind or, to use the classic Latin phrase hostes humanis generis, and that in a few instances they have been permitted access to international tribunals in their own name.

There is no doubt that an individual can avail himself of an international agreement. Thus an alien authorized by treaty to practice a profession or trade may invoke its provisions to protect his rights. Pirates have been prosecuted under the law of nations. Nevertheless, it is hard to see the practical consequences of the adoption of one theory over the other. I cannot imagine that a pirate about to be hanged on the yardarm is greatly concerned whether he is a subject or an object of international law. Nor is the privilege sometimes granted to an individual to appear directly before an international tribunal necessarily controlling. That privilege may be given to him purely as a matter of convenience.

In general, as expressed by one well-known writer, Charles Fenwick, "The argument [on the status of the individual] is obviously a highly theoretical one."

Chapter V
TERRITORY

It has been stated in the previous chapter that one of the attributes of a state is territory. Territory includes a defined land surface, inland waters, the territorial sea, and the overhanging air space. Outer space is not included judging from the fact that missiles fly over large areas without a word of protest from the governments of such areas.

In this chapter attention will be devoted to land, inland waters, and air space. The territorial sea will be considered in the later chapter on the sea in general.

How does a state acquire territory? The new nations which have been created almost exclusively out of former colonies usually come into possession of the territory of the colony they replace. Sometimes two colonies or trusteeships merge. Somalia, for example, was created out of the former British and Italian Somalilands. Sometimes the converse is true, as when the subcontinent of India was divided into India and Pakistan. In the case of the Spanish colonies in Latin America, which in one sense could be looked upon as one large colony, the new nations followed Spanish administrative subdivisions. In the case of Israel the state was predicated on the concept of a historic home in Palestine having its roots almost a couple of millenia in the past.

The main problem has been the delimitation of the boundaries of the new states. Only too often they followed the administrative subdivisions or colonial frontiers established by the ruling powers essentially for their own convenience. The lines separated tribes, often took little account of economic realities and, in general, left much to be desired. Speaking of the new African states, Prime Minister Trudeau of Canada said: "The frontiers of these countries simply retrace lines marked out years ago by colonialists, according to the fortunes of conquest, exploration and administrative whimsy." Furthermore in many instances boundaries were drawn in remote areas without adequate surveys, particularly if the boundaries were between administrative subdivisions rather than between separate colonies. In the former case the administering power might not consider an exact delineation worth the effort.

As a consequence new nations have been plagued by boundary disputes which continue to this day. In Latin America such disputes have been quite common. Recently the Queen of England arbitrated a dispute between Chile and the Argentine. In another part of the world a boundary dispute between India and Pakistan in the Rann of Kutch was also settled by arbitration.

Surprisingly enough boundary problems and disputes over the possession of coastal islands, whose existence has been known for centuries, also arise in areas where one would think the territorial questions had long been settled. Within relatively recent history the International Court of Justice resolved disputes between Belgium and Holland over a small piece of territory lying on the boundary. Moreover, in a case between England and France it decided upon the ownership of some relatively insignificant islands in the English Channel.

A factor contributing to the confusion on boundaries is that the international conferences of the past were not organized or staffed as they are at present. In negotiating the Treaty of Peace with Great Britain that followed the American Revolution, Franklin had as his only real assistant, aside from his fellow commissioners, his grandson, William Temple Franklin.

That grandson was a rather foppish young man who liked to walk a cat on a ribbon through the streets of Paris. It is fair to assume that his cat-walking activities must have interfered with his keeping of adequate records on behalf of his grandfather, for at a later date a serious controversy arose as to which map the commissioners had used in plotting the Northeast boundaries. Obviously the records had not been very well kept.

Generally speaking, rivers constitute reliable boundaries since they are easily identifiable. Usually in rivers the boundary is in the middle of the stream, but if the whole width of the stream is not navigable, then it is in the middle of the navigable channel. By following this practice each riparian state shares in that part of the river that can be used for navigation. If an island happened to be in the middle of the channel with the stream splitting on two sides, a rather unusual situation, the boundary would presumably run through the island. The question has taken on considerable significance on the Sino-Soviet border since the Russians maintain that the Chinese border on the Ussuri River is, contrary to usual practice, on the Chinese bank, while the Chinese claim that it is in the middle of the **river**. An examination of the pertinent treaties finds little substantiation for the Russian claim.

So far I have on the whole been talking about the original territory of a state when it comes into being. How does it acquire additional territory?

At the present time the problem is far less important than it used to be since, with the exception of Antarctica, virtually every part of the globe has been preempted. This does not mean that there are not changes in territory in the current epoch. It is only that they are relatively insignificant compared to the days of colonial expansion and national consolidation, as when the House of Savoy gradually acquired the whole of the Italian Peninsula and established the Kingdom of Italy or the United States became master of the whole of the American continent south of Canada and north of Mexico.

The period of colonial expansion began with the voyages of Columbus, the discoveries and settlements of the Portuguese and the almost contemporaneous push into Siberia of the Cossaks of Ivan the Terrible led by Stepan Yermak.

In the eighteenth and the beginning of the nineteenth century there was a relative lull in the onward rush of colonial empires. In fact in North America and in Latin America the process was reversed and colonies became sovereign states. It is hard to say definitely why there was this lull. Among other factors time was undoubtedly needed for consolidation and digestion. In all likelihood the incessant wars that took place in Europe in the pre-Napoleonic period, including such laborious and exhausting wars as the Thirty Years War, which brought cannibalism into Europe, drained Europe of its energies. These wars came to their climax with the Napoleonic struggles, which convulsed Europe for about two decades. The wars had their repercussions in the colonies in the sense that the nations, particularly France and England, fought over their colonial empires as well as over purely European considerations.

Following the Congress of Vienna in 1815 there was relative peace in Europe. There were wars, in fact quite a few, but none were on a continental scale. Hence the energies of the people were once again funneled into colonial exploration and the establishment of the dominance of the whites over the non-whites.

The reasons were many to account for this new push. Among them were commercialism, prodded by the industrial revolution and the search for markets; patriotism, which equated possessions all over the globe with national greatness; strategic factors, and humanitarianism. The latter seems to be somewhat misplaced in empire building. There was, however, a powerful sentiment that favored bringing Christianity and civilization to the "little brown brother" and assuming the "white man's burden."

The nations had a more restricted field in which to operate than formerly as most of the globe had been parcelled out. The Americas, protected by the Monroe Doctrine and the power of the British fleet, were no longer subject to colonialization. And large parts of Asia, such as India and Indonesia, were already under foreign control. Nevertheless central Africa was virtually unexplored and unsettled, many of the islands of Oceania and parts of southeast Asia had eluded Western domination, and China was ripe for the plucking. The biggest hunk of China was taken by the Russians, who browbeat the Chinese into giving up the Amur region and shortly thereafter the maritime provinces where Vladivostok is now situated.

Then also there was the profitable game of relieving declining colonial powers of their territories. The United States and Imperial Germany both joined in that game and acquired possessions from Spain.

Since World War II the trend has been in the opposite direction. In Africa before that war there was only one really independent state--Liberia. Egypt, although nominally independent, was still linked to Britain; Ethiopia was under the fascist yoke; and the Union--now the Republic--of South

Africa had not severed its Commonwealth ties, which were stronger then than now.

Summarizing what has been said, the transfers of territories or changes in sovereignty are not likely to be nearly as common in the future as they have been in the past. Nevertheless transfers or increases of territory may occur, so it is just as well to be aware of the methods open to states for the enlargement of their domains.

Border rectification, although theoretically only determining more precisely an imprecise boundary, may result in a state acquiring territory or at least having its title acknowledged to territory in dispute. Sometimes the area claimed is considerable in size.

A state can always purchase territory if the other side is willing to sell. Sometimes the motivation comes from the vendor anxious to sell land no longer needed. Russia, not the United States, was the moving spirit behind the transfer of Alaska. The Russian Minister used every device to persuade reluctant Senators to consent to the treaty. And it was Napoleon, not the American representatives, who proposed the Louisiana purchase. When his brothers, hearing of his decision, invaded his bathroom and expostulated with him while he was still in the bathtub, he splashed water on them, causing his valet to faint from excitement. (This is not a very strong recommendation for the sangfroid of French butlers.) Other purchases made by the United States were the Gadsden Purchase and the Virgin Islands. The United States also paid Mexico and Spain at the end of the Mexican and Spanish Wars for the areas transferred to the United States, but those transactions scarcely qualify as purchases willingly agreed to by both sides.

Land has also been acquired by a state because of the desire of an existing entity to join that state. In American history the leading example is provided by the annexation of Texas. In Italy one state after another opted to join the House of Savoy.

In recent years mergers of states have not been too successful. Several efforts to constitute a new state out of existing political entities have failed. The United Arab Republic, joining Syria and Egypt, lasted for only a few years, and the same fate befell the union of Mali and Senegal. About the only merger that seems to have survived is that between Tanganyika and Zanzibar into Tanzania. The general tendency is the other way, with centrifugal efforts dominating the scene.

Land can also be acquired by discovery and settlement and, in fact, considerable territory was acquired in that manner. There is, however--with the possible exception of some small uninhabited islands--no more territory to be taken through this method.

In the Arctic some nations have invoked the so-called sector principle whereby claims to the territory up to the North Pole are made by running lines from the Pole to the western and eastern extremities of the northern sea frontier of the nations closest to the Pole. The United States has been unwilling to accept the principle.

At the other end of the world a number of claims were made by governments to Antarctic territory, which resulted in some disputes. The Antarctic Treaty of December 1, 1959, provided that "Antarctica shall be used for peaceful purposes only." Article IV then went on to stipulate:

"1. Nothing contained in the present Treaty shall be interpreted as:

(a) a renunciation by any Contracting Party of previously asserted rights of or claims to territorial sovereignty in Antarctica,

(b) a renunciation or diminution by any Contracting Party of any basis of claim to territorial sovereignty in Antarctica which it may have whether as a result of its activities or those of its nationals in Antarctica, or otherwise;

(c) prejudicing the position of any Contracting Party as regards its recognition or non-recognition of any other State's right of or claim or basis of claim to territorial sovereignty in Antarctica.

"2. No acts or activities taking place while the present Treaty is in force shall constitute a basis for asserting, supporting or denying a claim to territorial sovereignty in Antarctica or create any rights of sovereignty in Antarctica. No new claim, or enlargement of an existing claim, to territorial sovereignty in Antarctica shall be asserted while the present treaty is in force.

For the foreseeable future, therefore, there is, in effect, a standstill agreement with regard to Antarctica.

Discovery and settlement are both essential to the acquisition of title. The settlement may nevertheless be in one location supposedly controlling a hinterland of considerable size.

A state may also acquire title by prescription, that is, by continued unchallenged use. It is quite unlikely that a whole new area would be acquired in this way today, although it might be a method of acquiring land just beyond the frontier in a remote region whose sovereign is lackadaisical in protecting its rights.

Territory can also be acquired through natural causes. If the sea or a river builds up the shore with sediment, what is known as accretion takes place and the new land belongs to the state owning the bank. Similarly a country can push out its boundaries by man-made construction jutting out into the sea.

In contrast to accretion is avulsion, which takes place when a frontier riverbed suddenly changes its course. In that case the boundary stays where it was before the river moved. The sketch below illustrates the difference between avulsion and accretion.

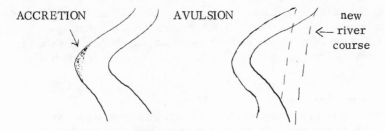

ACCRETION   AVULSION   new
                                     ← river
                                     course

The Rio Grande has been particularly susceptible to avulsion, and in the Chamizal area around El Paso avulsion created a serious controversy between the United States and Mexico that lasted for years. Now very expensive and very elaborate engineering projects have been undertaken to keep the river in its course.

In the supposedly bad old days when war was legal, nations could acquire land by conquest and their acquisitions would be recognized by the world. Usually, but not invariably, the conquest was sealed by a treaty of peace so the title of the conqueror rested on the double support of might and cession by treaty.

With the outlawing of war the taking of a neighbor's land by force was presumed to have become illegal. When the Japanese took Manchuria, Henry Stimson, then Secretary of State, refused to recognize the Japanese conquest. The pattern has not been even. A number of governments recognized Victor Emmanuel III as Emperor of Ethiopia. Following the last war the Italian and satellite peace treaties took considerable territory from the defeated enemies. (In this case presumably the war on the part of the Allies was legal since the Axis states started it, which leads to the conclusion that a victor in a war it did not commence can punish its adversary by taking territory from it.) Israel has taken considerable territory from the Arab states. And other examples could be adduced.

In a few areas of the world question has arisen as to the right of a nation to take over territory it claims it was unjustly deprived of in previous history or which naturally belongs to the national patrimony. Acting on the basis that that right exists, India took over the Portuguese settlements in Goa. Spain is claiming Gibraltar and China wants redemption of the Amur regions from Russia.

Normally land is taken in full sovereignty and for an unlimited duration. This is not necessarily always the case. There are one or two minor places in the world where two nations share sovereignty. England and the United States jointly control Canton and Enderbury Islands in the Pacific in what is known as a condominium.

There are also leased areas in the world. Britain has leased territory adjacent to Kowloon (the continental part of Hong Kong), and the United States operates the Guantanamo Bay Naval Base in Cuba and the Panama Canal Zone by virtue of perpetual leases. At the beginning of the century when China lay prostrate, Germany, France, Great Britain and Russia all had leaseholds on Chinese ports. Even without acquiring a specific territorial right in an area many powers in the past demanded and obtained spheres of influence which gave them special privileges and a kind of supervisory control over an area. Until the invasion of Czechoslovakia by the Soviets the general belief was that spheres of influence were no longer part of international life. The Russian action in Prague seems to indicate nevertheless that at least the Soviets are not persuaded that spheres of influence are a bygone institution.

A nation can also have a limited right in the territory of a state much as an individual can have a right of way across his neighbor's property. Such limited rights might be very important in providing a landlocked country with a right of way to the sea and port facilities in a harbor of a neighboring seacoast state.

Before leaving the question of the types of control or interest that one nation may maintain in the territory of another it is worth taking a look at the curious case of Okinawa or, to be more precise, the Ryukyu Islands of which Okinawa is the principal island. Under Article 3 of the Treaty of Peace, Japan agreed to any American proposal to place certain areas, including the Ryukyu Islands, under trusteeship. Article 3 then goes on to say:

> "Pending the making of such a proposal and affirmative action thereon, the United States will have the right to exercise all and any powers of administration, legislation and jurisdiction over the territory and inhabitants of these islands, including their territorial waters."

Actually the Ryukyu Islands were never placed under trusteeship, although they continued to be administered by the United States. The United States did acknowledge that Japan had a "residual sovereignty" on the islands, whatever that amgibuous phrase may mean. Recently President Nixon agreed to the return of Okinawa to Japan.

Generally speaking a nation may use its land, inland waters and air space in whatever way it wishes. It does not have to admit aliens within its border, it can prohibit unauthorized airplanes from using its air space, and can reserve to itself navigation on inland waters. It can also be a wastrel of its assets and deplete its resources.

Naturally there are some limitations on the use of land, water and air. (The sea, even the territorial sea, presents problems of its own.) Those limitations may stem from a treaty or from more or less generally accepted principles of international law that parallel in many ways the domestic laws concerning the use of land.

By treaty many states permit foreign airplanes to fly overhead and land for non-traffic purposes, that is, for refueling and repairs. Even without such a treaty a nation will not ordinarily object to an overflight by a commercial or private plane that strays over its territory because of stress of weather or a navigational error. It is true that in one celebrated instance Bulgaria shot down with heavy loss of life an Israeli commercial airliner that had inadvertently crossed its borders. There was, however, a strong outcry against the Bulgarian action.

By the same token most navigable rivers of interest to more than one state are usually opened to commerce by treaty. On the Rhine one can see the vessels of all the states through or along which the Rhine passes. Before the war the Danube was likewise open for use as an international waterway. Unfortunately the cold war has put a damper on international cooperation and the free use of the Danube has been one of the victims.

Even without a treaty there is a doubt whether an upstream state has the right to diminish radically the flow of water to a downstream state. Spain even went to far as to complain when France diverted water from a stream for hydroelectric purposes even though all the water was returned to the stream before it reached Spain. The arbitral tribunal to which the case was submitted held in favor of France, but only because Spain could not prove any damage.

The same is also true of pollution. A state is under an obligation to prevent its wastes from spilling over whether the pollution is of air or water.

A state is likewise under an obligation to prevent its territory from being used to the detriment of another. Thus it cannot or should not permit its territory to be used to mount guerrilla raids or military expeditions against a neighboring state. The neutrality laws of the United States are supposed to provide compliance with that obligation. The record of the United States has not always been clean, as demonstrated by the Bay of Pigs episode in Cuba. The Communist nations have even more flagrantly violated the rule in support of the so-called wars of national liberation.

A nation is likewise under an obligation to prohibit other activities noxious to a foreign state such as counterfeiting.

Of considerable importance is the obligation of a state to do what it can to keep a deadly disease within bounds. The World Health Organization International Sanitary Regulations among other factors provides that a state:

> "...shall take all practicable measures...
>   (a) to prevent the departure of any infected person or suspect;
>
>   (b) to prevent the introduction on board a ship, an aircraft, a train, a road vehicle, other means of transport or container, of possible agents of infection or vectors of a disease subject to the Regulations."

Some nations are also bound by treaty not to take certain action on their soil. This negative approach is usually exemplified by a promise not to fortify certain areas.

All in all one can see that while a state's sovereignty over its territory can be very extensive there are certain limitations to that sovereignty created by treaty or custom. As the world becomes more and more interdependent the likelihood is that those limitations will increase.

Chapter VI
RECOGNITION

The recognition of states and governments is clouded by a considerable degree of uncertainty and is tinged with political and practical difficulties that render hazardous the development of a logical legal pattern.

Theoretically the recognition of a new state takes place when a state already established in the international community acknowledges that a new member of that community has come into being and is entitled to exercise the privileges of a sovereign entity.

Recognition of a government is somewhat different although the recognition of a state necessarily carries with it recognition of the government then in power. It might conceivably be possible to reorganize a new state but not its government, but it is hard to see how that could be done.

The recognition of a new government is considered necessary when there is a break in the continuity of governments and a new ruling group assumes control. The change requiring recognition is almost always, if not invariably, the result of an extra-legal overturn of the existing authorities. A mere transfer of authority in accordance with constitutional practices from one political party to another does not require recognition. Not a single state "recognized" the Nixon administration when it took over from the previous Johnson administration. It was not necessary. Even when DeGaulle changed the Fourth French Republic into the Fifth recognition was not needed as the transition followed an orderly pattern with the French people ratifying a new constitution before it came into force. But when there has been a revolt and a new regime is installed the change calls for the recognition of the new regime.

The recognition of both states and of government often presents serious legal and political problems. Particular complications are engendered when the entity seeking recognition is a revolting province seeking independence or is a new government in quest of power whose ultimate success is by no means assured. The state or government against which the revolt is directed will not be any too pleased if recognition is granted the dissident faction.

The United States hesitated for a long time before recognizing the revolted Spanish colonies, although part of the hesitation stemmed from the fear of alienating the Spaniards during the delicate negotiations that led to the cession of Florida to the United States and the delimitation of the western frontier. If any foreign state had recognized the Confederacy, Washington would have reacted violently. In more recent days few governments recognized Biafra when it was in revolt against Nigeria.

41

The same is true of the recognition of a government. An established government may be at a temporary disadvantage in the face of rebels and yet succeed eventually in quelling the rebellion. (For some time at least the theory prevailed that eventually Chiang Kai-shek might reassert control over mainland China.)

Largely because of these difficulties efforts have been made to rationalize, equivocate, temporize, or take only half measures. Thus a Mexican foreign minister developed the concept that bears his name--the Estrada doctrine--to the effect that formal recognition is not necessary when a government changes hands. Instead foreign states just pick up the threads of relations and carry on as before. This theory works quite well when the rebel government is in undisputed control. It does not work very well when there are two contending authorities both claiming to rule the country, as happened in Spain during the long Spanish civil war which terminated in a Franco victory. Which faction does one deal with?

Hence states when they are uncertain tend to grant <u>de facto</u> or factual recognition as distinguished from <u>de jure</u> or legal recognition. Supposedly this form of recognition is somewhat less than full recognition but how far less no one really knows. The pungent comment of an English writer is worth quoting:

> "But statesmen in recent times have very much desired to have it both ways. They have desired to admit that a new community is a State, for the sake of the conveniences this will bring, --the ready intercourse of commerce, the easy redress of grievances, the unobstructed access and intelligence; and at the same time they have very much desired to avoid the necessary consequence--the frank admission of independent statehood, with freedom to dispose of the State's resources, untrammelled by the engagements of others. They have therefore invented the bastard institution of so-called 'de facto' recognition, according to which they can deal with a perfectly independent community as a State while refusing to it the right of a State."

. . . .

> "This desire of politicians to create a new status of <u>de facto</u> States with truncated rights, unknown powers and undefined responsibilities, is a phenomenon of this illogical twentieth century. It would have been impossible in the nineteenth century, which had no animus against clear thinking. Anyone can see what confusion would be caused by the admission of a new class of ambiguous States. It would be impossible to know whether and for what purposes they could raise a loan, whether they could grant

concessions and privileges, whether they could grant passports and visas, how far their envoys had diplomatic prerogatives, whether they could settle outstanding disputes relating to their territories, and a host of similar matters. If it is answered that their position in these respects would be exactly the same as that of belligerent rebels, such an answer would be simply untrue. States recognized de facto have sent regular envoys; but when the envoys of belligerent rebels are received, it means that the independence of the rebels is finally and fully recognized. "

The remarks relate to the recognition of States. They are, however, equally pertinent to the recognition of governments.

Another supposed advantage of de facto recognition is that it can be withdrawn. Assertions to that effect are found in some texts. It is by no means clear, however, that most cases where recognition was supposedly withdrawn are not really instances when the new government failed to maintain itself in power and was supplanted in turn by another government or by the government it had temporarily overturned. I know of no instance when de facto recognition was withdrawn from a government that continued in authority without substantial challenge.

One concept that seems on the whole to be well established is that de jure recognition cannot be withdrawn. A quarrel can take place after recognition and diplomatic relations can be broken but the recognition subsists. The United States broke diplomatic relations with Cuba but the Castro regime still remained the recognized government of that country in the eyes of the United States.

Probably the most confused thinking of all took place during the Spanish Civil War when the British were trying to balance the probably victorious Franco with the legitimate Republican government still in control over a substantial portion of Spain. The British held that Franco was the de facto authority over that part of Spain he dominated. The result for the British courts was disastrous from the standpoint of logic, for in effect they had to hold that there were two governments in Spain.

One writer on recognition, after concluding that legally de jure and de facto recognition were essentially the same, said that they were quite different politically. De facto recognition implied misgivings. In non-legal terms the difference is the same as that between a peck on the cheek and a kiss.

I think the point is well taken, for recognition in many ways is more political than legal. Courts will always follow the lead of the political branch of the government and will never hold that a government should be recognized, no matter how much they believe this should be the case, when the executive has withheld recognition.

Still another method of reconciling conflicting claims in some instances is to recognize a rebellious faction as a belligerent which gives it certain rights under the laws of war and neutrality but does not give it the status to speak for the nation as a whole or even a portion of the country. A step below that is the recognition of insurgency. This permits insurgents to fight at sea without being regarded as pirates but does not give them the right to invoke a blockade.

Recognition can be effected in any number of ways, the essential being the intent. Usually it is done by accrediting an ambassador to the new government or by receiving an ambassador from that regime. It can also be done by congratulatory message or by any other method that conveys the intent to recognize.

Can recognition be effected inadvertently? Could, for example, an ambassador who was in a country at the time of revolt commit his government by communicating officially with the new government before his state was ready to acknowledge the change? Probably the answer is no.

The failure to recognize does not mean that the existence of the new government must be ignored. On a day-to-day basis some communication may have to be made. In some instances the unrecognized government may become a party to a multilateral treaty binding both it and the state that has failed to extend recognition. Consular posts are sometimes kept open in the territory of unrecognized governments and consuls deal on routine matters with the authorities. My father, as Consul General in Moscow at the beginning of the Russian Revolution, had to have some relations with the Bolshevik government when it moved from Petrograd to Moscow. While the United States does not recognize Communist China there have been a series of meetings between Chinese and American ambassadors, first in Geneva and then in Warsaw, letters with Chinese postage are delivered in the United States, the Chinese are met at international conferences and so on.

Presumably there is a point beyond which one cannot have one's cake and eat it too--not recognize and yet treat with a government. For example, it might be difficult for a state to enter into a treaty of commerce and navigation with an unrecognized state and still maintain that it does not recognize that state. At the present stage of the law it is hard to know where that line falls.

What has been said points up the fact that a state is not under any obligation to extend recognition. Nevertheless a failure to recognize will be construed as an unfriendly act. Hence in most instances recognition is given as soon as a state has come into being or a new government is firmly in power without trying to weigh the legitimacy or morality of its ascent to power.

This was the principle followed in the early days of American diplomacy. It found its place in the Monroe Doctrine which stated:

"Our policy in regard to Europe, which was adopted at an
early stage of the wars which have so long agitated that
quarter of the globe, nevertheless remains the same, which
is, not to interfere in the internal concerns of any of its
powers; to consider the government de facto as the legitimate government for us; to cultivate friendly relations
with it, and to preserve those relations by a frank, firm,
and manly policy, meeting in all instances, the just claims
of every power, submitting to injuries from none." (Underlining supplied.)

While only European governments are mentioned, it must be remem-
bered that at that time these were the only governments that counted. Latin
America was just emerging into independence and was receiving special
treatment, and Africa, aside from the Barbary states, was virtually unknown. In Asia, Japan was a closed island while the Celestial Empire was
older than the European states and scarcely needed recognition, either for
the Chinese state or for the Manchu dynasty. Other parts of Asia were
either relatively unimportant or were under colonial domination.

In the early part of this century, Woodrow Wilson, who tended to
look upon matters from an idealistic viewpoint, was horrified by the force-
ful overturn of the Madero government in Mexico and the brutal murder of
President Madero by General Victoriano Huerta, who succeeded Madero.
Hence he refused to recognize the Huerta regime although it was in control
of Mexico City and large portions of the country and would probably have
been successful in subduing the opposition that still remained. Huerta fell
and was replaced by Carranza, whose government was first accorded de
facto and then de jure recognition.

The great difficulty with the Wilson doctrine, if you can call it that,
is that it sets up a foreign power as the judge of the morality and legality
of the government of another state. And what is illegal and what is immoral? If a detested and cruel dictator is ousted by force of arms and a
new constitution established, is that to be condemned?

Hence the United States has been swinging away from the Wilson
doctrine and back to the old concept that a government should be recognized
when it is in fact in control and is representing the nation. The United
States has not been wholly consistent. Communist China is a glaring example, for by now even the most hardy optimists do not believe that Chiang
Kai-shek will reestablish control over the mainland.

American policy has also been influenced by the so-called Tobar
doctrine, which was enunciated by the Central American states and which
provided that governments established by unconstitutional means should
not be recognized. In many respects the doctrine parallels the Wilson
precepts. One suspects that it was primarily designed to protect established regimes in an area of constant revolutions and was not prompted by
an overwhelming concern with legality or morality. Be that as it may, the

United States has been hesitating in some instances to recognize governments when they come into power. Before affording recognition in the Central American area and by extension in other parts of Latin America, the United States has been consulting the other Latin American states and trying to promote common action. Usually the result is that the exigencies of international intercourse ultimately require recognition so that the regime is recognized after some delay. In the meantime a potentially friendly government can quite easily be transformed into an unfriendly one.

At this point it can be asked why recognition, particularly of governments, is really so important? Cannot a government subsist without being recognized?

It can, of course, subsist but it is severely handicapped. It is unable to conduct ordinary diplomatic intercourse, it may not sue in the courts of the countries that have not recognized it, and its government's acts will not be accorded the same faith and credit as are extended to the acts of a recognized government. (This latter point will be covered more fully in the later discussion of "acts of state.") Hence the importance of recognition should not be minimized.

Before closing this chapter it is necessary to speak of the admission of members or the accreditation of new governments to international organizations, particularly the United Nations since there is a tendency to equate representation in the United Nations with recognition.

The admission of a new state to the United Nations has nothing to do with its recognition by other states. As has been pointed out in Chapter IV there are a number of states that for one reason or another are not members of the United Nations. And the early history of the United Nations is replete with instances of states, such as Italy, being temporarily debarred for political reasons. Conversely the admission of a state to the United Nations does not imply recognition by all the other members. The People's Republic of Mongolia has been a member of the United Nations for some years but the United States has not recognized that regime largely because of the insistence by Chiang Kai-shek that Outer Mongolia is still a part of China.

The accreditation of governments follows the same principle. There is a great deal of loose language about the "admission" of Red China. Actually China is a charter member of the United Nations and does not require admission. It is a question of what government should represent China. If, however, the ultimate solution is to have two Chinas in the United Nations a new entity will have to be admitted.

The United States has succeeded in having the question of Chinese accreditation classified as an important question whose affirmative resolution requires a two-thirds majority in the General Assembly. The pro-Peking faction, or better said, the faction that considers it unrealistic to have Chiang Kai-shek represent the mainland, has never been able to muster enough votes so Taiwan continues to represent China. An intriguing legal possibility is that, since the Security Council and the General Assembly

have their own criteria of accreditation which are independent of each other
--although always up to this point coincidental--that Taiwan would stay in
the Security Council as the representative of China on the strength of a Chinese and possibly American veto, and Peking would represent China in the
General Assembly. The confusion that would result would probably be indescribable. At this time the whole question is receiving reevaluation
prompted by the majority vote in the General Assembly in favor of the People's Republic of China, the ping-pong visit, and the growing realization
that the present policy may not be practical. Furthermore, it is not quite
certain that the representation of China in the Security Council would be
subject to veto in that body as the question might be classified as procedural
in character.

What has been said about the United Nations is true also of other
international organizations though they do not attract as much attention as
the United Nations. It would be quite conceivable for a new state, for example, to be admitted to the Organization of American States without being
recognized by other states in that body. If British Honduras (Belize) were
to achieve independence, it is not likely that Guatemala would accord it recognition as it considers British Honduras to be a part of Guatemala.

Chapter VII
THE REPRESENTATION OF STATES

A state, like a corporation, obviously has to be represented by human beings. At home it is represented in the field of foreign affairs by its heads of state and government--king, president, prime minister, or dictator--and by the Minister for Foreign Affairs and his subordinates and, to a lesser extent, by the officials of other governmental departments. In the United States the Department of State is the Ministry of Foreign Affairs, having derived its rather misleading name from the fact that in an earlier period it also took care of some domestic functions such as the publication of laws and handling of patents. Now all the extraneous activities have been shorn away but the name remains.

Naturally the Department of State operates under the overall direction of the President, who is vested with ultimate responsibility for the conduct of foreign affairs. Moreover, particularly in recent years, a White House staff to advise and assist the President on the relations of the United States and the outside world has increased in size and importance so that rumors fly thick and fast as to the exact role of the Presidential staff vis-a-vis the Department of State. In any event, even if it is conceded that the Department, acting under the President, has primary responsibility for the conduct of foreign affairs, it is obvious that many other departments and agencies are involved.

In fact, virtually every branch of the government of any size has something to do with operations abroad. The Department of Defense maintains a million men abroad, the CIA gathers information all over the globe, the Department of Agriculture food policies affect innumerable countries, the Treasury Department is vitally concerned in the international monetary situation and the Department of Commerce promotes foreign trade. The list could be extended indefinitely. And what is true of the United States is true of other nations although on a lesser scale.

The interests of a country abroad are primarily entrusted to its embassies and consulates. The American Ambassador is the principal representative of the President abroad and all activities of official Americans are subject to his control, or at least his guidance, particularly when direction in foreign affairs is concerned. An ambassador will not be involved in the administration of the code of military justice but will be very aroused if a general in command of forces abroad starts making speeches presuming to reflect general American foreign policy.

There has been a great deal of discussion of the role of the Ambassador as sometimes he has been dwarfed and overwhelmed by an energetic general in charge of an important command or by a director of a foreign aid mission having millions of dollars at his disposal and a large and aggressive staff to do his bidding. This is to say nothing of the CIA, whose actions have sometimes embarrassed ambassadors in the past.

To strengthen the hand of the ambassadors President Kennedy issued a letter defining their role abroad. The President said with respect to the general responsibilities of an ambassador:

> "In regard to your personal authority and responsibility, I shall count on you to oversee and coordinate all the activities of the United States Government in....
>
> "You are in charge of the entire United States Diplomatic Mission, and I shall expect you to supervise all of its operations. The Mission includes not only the personnel of the Department of State and the Foreign Service, but also the representatives of all other United States agencies which have programs or activities in.... I shall give you full support and backing in carrying out your assignment."

The President went on to define the Ambassador's relations with the military in this manner:

> "Now one word about your relations to the military. As you know, the United States Diplomatic Mission includes Service Attaches, Military Assistance Advisory Groups and other Military components attached to the Mission. It does not, however, include United States military forces operating in the field where such forces are under the command of a United States area military commander. The line of authority to these forces runs from me, to the Secretary of Defense, to the Joint Chiefs of Staff in Washington and to the area commander in the field.
>
> "Although this means that the chief of the American Diplomatic Mission is not in the line of military command, nevertheless, as Chief of Mission, you should work closely with the appropriate area military commander to assure the full exchange of information. If it is your opinion that activities by the United States military forces may adversely affect our over-all relations with the people or government of.... you should promptly discuss the matter with the military commander and, if necessary, request a decision by higher authority.
>
> "I have informed all heads of departments and agencies of the Government of the responsibilities of the chiefs of American Diplomatic Missions for our combined operations abroad, and I have asked them to instruct their representatives in the field accordingly."

President Nixon has reaffirmed the role of the Ambassador as envisaged by President Kennedy in a letter also sent by him to Chiefs of Missions. While the Presidential directives have undoubtedly effected an improvement, it would be too much to say that they work in all instances and that every ambassador is always in complete control. Nevertheless, it can be said that the Embassy is the center of American representation abroad.

By the time the United States came into existence the practice of having permanent missions abroad--rather than having envoys sent on a temporary basis to perform a particular task--was well established. It was not customary, however, for all envoys, now often referred to as chiefs of mission, to be designated ambassadors. Envoys from minor countries or to minor countries were called Ministers, Ministers Resident, and Chargés d'Affaires. (A chargé d'affaires sent on a permanent basis whom Satow, a noted writer on diplomatic practice, calls a chargé d'affaires en titre, is not to be confused with a chargé d'affaires ad interim, who temporarily replaces his chief when the latter is out of the country, takes charge between chiefs of mission, or establishes a mission in a new state pending the arrival of an ambassador. In the latter case he may very likely be the Consul General formerly functioning in the area.)

The inflation in diplomatic titles which has paralleled inflation in other titles has virtually eliminated the use of a title less grandiose than Ambassador for any chief of mission. Ministers resident and chargés d'affaires en titre have passed from the picture and ministers are now only senior subordinates to the ambassadors.

When one considers that the United States did not have any ambassadors until 1893, when it was certainly a far more important nation than some of the new states today, and then had only four of them, the inflation of diplomatic titles appears silly and undignified, a scramble for empty prestige.

The tendency to call all envoys ambassadors is in keeping with the glorification of titles generally. A janitor is no longer a janitor--he is a building superintendent.

The organization of a diplomatic mission varies according to the interests of the ambassador, local conditions and size. Obviously it is a little hard to compare the American Embassy at Valletta in Malta with the Embassy in Tokyo. Nevertheless, most embassies follow a somewhat standard pattern. The Department of State even has a chart of a typical Embassy which for some reason omits the public affairs section.

Generally speaking,--with due allowance for exceptions--an Embassy consists of an Ambassador, his Deputy, known as the DCM, his immediate staff and a number of sections. In larger countries having several consular offices outside the capital, a Counsellor for Consular Affairs is supposed to act as the Ambassador's arm in coordinating the consular offices, including the Consular section of the Embassy. The sections consist of (1) the Political Section, which reports on political events, negotiates political treaties, maintains liaison with the military and performs other tasks in the political field; (2) the Economic Section, which makes economic treaties and, in general, interests itself in all economic matters of concern to the Embassy; (3) the Public Affairs Section, which seeks to promote and maintain a favorable view of the United States through cultivating the press, managing exchange programs, wooing local intellectuals, and so forth; (4) the Consular Section, which issues passports, grants visas, takes care of shipping and seamen if the capital is a seaport, protects and helps American citizens and furnishes notarial and other quasi-legal services; and finally (5) the Administrative Section, which does all the housekeeping from managing the Embassy's motor pool to maintaining payrolls (sometimes on an area basis) and making sure that the plumbing works in the Ambassador's residence. (From the standpoint of the Administrative officer's career the latter is probably the most important.) In addition the Embassy will have military attachés (naval, army and air) who maintain their own offices. Under the general control of the embassy, although not a constituent part of the staff, is the foreign aid and the military advisory assistance group (MAAG), sometimes known by another name. The latter is very often under the command of a senior officer--a major general, for example--who tends to dwarf the military attachés in importance.

The Ambassador may be a career foreign service officer or may be a person selected from the outside by the President either because he thinks he is the best man for the job or to repay a political debt.

The backbone of the staff has been composed of career foreign service officers, i.e., persons appointed under the Foreign Service Act of 1946 to serve as generalists, as distinguished from specialists, in the diplomatic and consular service. In addition there were Foreign Service Staff Officers who were career specialists who wanted to remain as such, e.g., consular or administrative specialists, and Foreign Service Reserve Officers who, at least in theory, were appointed for a prescribed period to fill positions calling for specialized experience not found in the Foreign Service. At present the plan seems to be that most officers will be Foreign Service Officers but that they will be divided into four groups specializing in political, economic, consular and administrative work respectively. Furthermore, there is a clerical staff and a large group of local employees working in subordinate capacities. In some areas such jobs as cleaning the Embassy may be contracted to a local citizen or company. Their employees are in the Embassy but not a part of it.

A colorful segment of the Embassy is the Marine Guard which guarantees the security of the Embassy.

Officers or employees of a Department other than State--such as the Agricultural attaché--are usually allocated to the appropriate section of the Embassy. They are sent out as Reserve Officers on the basis of their own Foreign Service personnel system (the United States Information Service, the Agency for International Development, both of which have a certain quasi-independence, and the Department of Agriculture all have their own systems) or by simple detail or assignments from their home service.

Very recently President Nixon has suggested a new approach to foreign aid with various offices concentrating on security, economic development, and private investment respectively. The break-up of the central agency will have its reflection in the field.

The officers, with some few exceptions, bear diplomatic titles. The Deputy Chief of Mission is a Counsellor and in large embassies is given the personal rank of minister. Two or three officers who are heads of important sections may also be designated Minister-Counsellors. (With the inflation in titles the number is increasing.) The other heads of section are plain Counsellors. Then come First Secretaries, Second Secretaries and Third Secretaries.

In a large consular section, the head will be a Consul General. He will have under him one or more Consuls and a number of Vice Consuls. Usually, if not invariably, the senior consular officers also have a diplomatic title. When I served in Tokyo I was Consul General and Counsellor and my deputy was Consul and First Secretary.

Personnel serving with the Embassy who are not part of the Foreign Service may be given the diplomatic and consular titles mentioned above. Usually, however, they are called attachés or assistant attachés. From the standpoint of rank this does not mean that they are subordinate to the other officers. A distinguished scholar might be appointed as Cultural Attaché to enhance the prestige of the United States and it would obviously be inappropriate to rank him below a young Third Secretary.

For some unknown reason there is a general impression held by many who should know better that a consular office in a city other than the capital is limited to the performance of routine consular work--passports, visas, protection, shipping and seamen, notarials--with possibly some trade promotion thrown in. Actually a consular office is a replica of an Embassy on a smaller scale, performing its functions on a local rather than a national level. And some consulates general are by no means so small. Several are considerably larger than a number of embassies.

A good deal of the time of a consular office may be spent on political or economic affairs. In some countries the economic reporting may be of high significance. If the political capital of the nation is not the same as the industrial and economic capital, e.g., Washington and New York, Rome and Milan, Bonn and Frankfurt, Brasilia and São Paulo, the reports from the latter may be just as important as the Embassy reports, if not more so.

As Consul General in Yokohama I spent relatively little time on consular affairs, which were ably handled by my subordinates. Much of my energy was taken up in representing--making speeches, attending ceremonies, etc., and trying to assess political and economic developments in my consular district.

Some consular offices are very small and are limited to certain specific tasks which can be performed by one relatively junior officer and a local assistant or two. Such posts are called special purpose posts. The United States has several in Mexico, e.g., at San Luis Potosi.

In cities where there is not sufficient work for a full-time officer but there is a need for consular service from time to time, an American businessman may be appointed as consular agent to handle such consular matters as do arise. The United States has quite a few such agents in Latin America. Other states follow the same practice but they call the part-time officers honorary consuls and sometimes select them from the local population, a practice reminiscent of the Greek proxenoi.

Needless to say, both diplomatic and consular officers have to be acceptable to the state that receives them. In the case of a new Ambassador the acceptance is sought before he is appointed and takes the form of an agreement. Subordinate personnel do not have to be accepted by a formal agreement but their names are sent to the Foreign Office. A consular officer is accepted and empowered to operate locally by what is known as an exequator. Like a bird he needs two wings, the exequator from the government of the country in which he is to operate and a commission from his own government.

There is a wide variation in the practice with regard to exequators. Some are quite formal. Some states are content with a verbal authorization that takes the place of an exequator. Some states issue exequators to all consular officers and some to the principal officer alone.

If at any time during their tour of duty representatives of a foreign state offend the local government, that government can ask for their recall on the grounds that they are persona non grata, i.e., unwelcome persons. This is now done rather rarely except in the relations between the U.S.S.R. and the U.S.A., both of which countries periodically ask for the removal of diplomatic "spies."

In addition to maintaining diplomatic and consular establishments, the United States Information Agency maintains in some countries cultural centers or other similar offices which may be located in towns where there is no other official American establishment. They offer American library facilities to the local population and generally try to promote a friendly feeling toward the United States by the people of the community.

Furthermore the Agency for International Development often maintains outposts in those areas of the country where its projects are located, some of them rather remote from the capital.

So far, we have been talking about missions to a particular state. In addition the United States maintains missions to a number of international organizations--the United Nations, NATO, OAS and others. The United States has several ambassadors in Paris and Brussels.

In addition to maintaining permanent missions to international organizations the United States sends representatives to attend international conferences or regularly scheduled meetings of international organizations, such as the annual meetings of the General Assembly of the United Nations. The latter are held in the United States but the principle remains the same. Moreover representatives of the United States, from the President on down, pay visits abroad in their official status.

It has been pointed out at the beginning of this chapter that the Department of State is not the only agency in the United States that has its finger in the foreign relations pie. Abroad the same thing is true although most civilian activities do funnel through the Embassy. The military commands are, however, quite separate and there is nothing to prevent the government from sending a purchasing commission or other group abroad. During the war years, particularly when preclusive buying to prevent stocks from coming into the hands of the Nazis as well as buying for the needs of the United States was very prevalent, American officials were to be found abroad in large numbers. In some places, such as Montreal, U.S. Customs officials provide U.S. customs clearance at the airport.

At present we also see state officials (state in this sense being a state of the union) trying to promote the products of their state. Florida, for example, has sent its officials abroad to promote orange juice. Considering that in international law there is no distinction between national and local officials, the state officials in a strict sense represent the United States, although in a limited capacity.

Finally mention should be made of the Peace Corps, to be incorporated into the Action Corps, whose members operate in many countries. They may not be able to formulate policy, but their daily actions may have a considerable influence on the attitude of a country toward the United States.

It may be seen that the United States, in one way or another, is heavily represented abroad. The charge has been made that it is over-represented and that the Embassies have become bloated out of all proportion. The Department of State, sensitive to these criticisms, has been endeavoring to reduce the size of embassies, some of which, if local employees are included, number more than one thousand. The Department of Defense is likewise reducing the size of military groups on peaceful missions abroad.

An effort has been made to give a fairly complete survey of American representation abroad. While I hesitated to spend the space on such a description, I do not think it is possible to understand some of the later chapters without such an outline.

One final note is that some governments represent other governments in third states. This is particularly true when there has been war or the rupture of relations. The Swiss have, for example, been representing the United States for some years in Cuba and trying to protect American interests. Even in times of perfectly normal relations, however, a state may request another state to undertake certain functions-- usually consular functions--on its behalf in a third state. This is entirely sensible for some of the small countries who do not have the diplomatic and consular personnel or the money to provide for representation on a worldwide scale.

Chapter VIII
PRIVILEGES AND IMMUNITIES IN GENERAL

The problem of privileges and immunities is highly technical, quite confusing, and as a consequence often misunderstood. Unfortunately it is not a subject that can be avoided as it crops up all the time and has considerable practical significance to both states and international organizations and to many thousands of individuals all over the world.

I will try to summarize in this chapter the general nature of the immunities, indicate the entities and individuals entitled to them and explain the rationale for their existence. In later chapters I will return to the subject in greater detail.

As far as individuals are concerned the principal immunities with which they are concerned are (1) the exemption, or at least the partial exemption, from local jurisdiction, both criminal and civil; (2) the freedom from the payment of at least some internal taxes; and (3) the right to import goods without the payment of customs taxes or the examination of incoming shipments. There are naturally other privileges and rights, such as the right of a diplomat, particularly a senior diplomat, to respect and to the protection of his person and property. But the exemptions from jurisdiction and taxes and duties are by far the most important. While opinions undoubtedly differ I would say that the right to import customs-free is particularly significant. As a consular officer in Japan I did not have an exemption from jurisdiction, a factor that worried me not at all. I would, however, have been quite unhappy if I had had to pay the high Japanese income tax or to buy, on the high-priced local market, the liquor I needed for the innumerable receptions I had to give in my official capacity.

Admittedly my views might have been different had I served in a country where there was real danger of arbitrary arrest and imprisonment.

Since I have stressed the importance of the exemptions from fiscal charges, it behooves me to explain a little more fully what is meant by these exemptions. Customs exemptions on imports do not require much comment as they are self-explanatory. (What is difficult to determine is who gets them and to what extent, which will be covered in a later chapter.) Exemptions from internal taxes are far more difficult to classify. A complicating factor is that different nations have varying tax systems so that comparing exemptions can be frustrating. Moreover, while it is generally conceded that no one should be exempted from service charges there is little agreement as to what is a service charge. Is a bill for garbage removal a tax or a service charge?

Generally speaking exemptions are granted from income taxes on income not derived locally; from personal property taxes, from excise taxes when the purchaser of goods or services pays the tax, and from inheritance taxes.

It is relatively easy to understand the exemption from income taxes. A representative of a foreign country should not have to pay taxes on income derived abroad. He probably has to pay his own government. If, however, a foreign diplomat in the United States makes a gain on the New York Stock Exchange or derives income from gilt-edge American securities, he should pay a tax. A diplomat should likewise not have to pay personal property taxes for rather obvious reasons.

When it comes to excise taxes the problems multiply. In many instances there is no real logic in the collection of taxes. In some cases the tax is on the manufacturer or vendor who passes the tax on to the ultimate purchaser in the form of higher prices and in others the tax is legally on the purchaser. Hence in some instances the exemption may hinge on a wholly capricious tax structure.

Another complication is the sheer difficulty of providing the exemption. If a diplomat makes a trivial purchase on which there is a sales tax, which the buyer pays, the diplomat is theoretically entitled to the exemption. Even in Washington, where the shopkeepers are used to diplomats, granting the exemption creates an extra burden on the shopkeeper. I remember being mistaken for a foreign diplomat once in Washington and asked if I wanted to claim exemption on some minor purchase--the tax was something less than five cents. I expressed surprise that diplomats claimed exemptions for such picayune sums and was told that many did. But one can imagine what would happen if a touring diplomat claimed a similar tax exemption in Podunkville.

It likewise seems unfair to levy an inheritance tax on the estate of a representative of a foreign government just because he happens to die away from his native land. Here again complications raise their ugly heads. A blanket exemption, which would be simple, does not seem warranted. If, for example, the diplomat takes advantage of his residence to make profitable speculations and increases his estate there is no reason why his estate should not pay a tax on the profits of those local speculations.

A state is naturally not interested in exemptions from criminal jurisdiction. It is, however, very interested in immunity from civil suit. It is also interested in exemptions from taxation--an embassy building could be assessed quite highly--and in exemptions from customs duties. A state imports very valuable personal property for the use of its offices including motor vehicles and furniture and supplies of all sorts and kinds. In addition a state is interested in the right to sue, which an individual usually has automatically--and the privilege of having its governmental acts given full faith and credit by the local courts and authorities.

What is true of a state is also applicable to a greater or lesser degree to international organizations. They too may have valuable property and have to make substantial imports.

Unfortunately from the standpoint of simplicity not all entities and individuals entitled to privileges enjoy the same ones. The gamut ranges from the full range of privileges to very restricted ones. At this point in this general introductory discussion all that can be done is to indicate the various categories. They are:

1. The state and its instrumentalities

2. Public corporations

3. International organizations

4. Heads of state and officials making temporary visits abroad

5. Diplomatic officers at a post

6. Consular officers at a post

7. Diplomatic and consular officers in transit

8. Other governmental officers stationed abroad

9. Representatives to international organizations or conferences

10. Officials of international organizations such as the Secretary General of the United Nations and his staff

11. Military personnel stationed abroad

The problem is further compounded by the fact that there may be variations in treatment among the personnel listed under one heading. For example, AID officers may derive special treatment by virtue of agreements between the United States and the host country not accorded to other officials. Furthermore virtually all the categories have trailing with them (1) their subordinate clerical and administrative personnel, (2) their families, and (3) their personal servants. We should not belittle the importance of the latter. If the Ambassador's master chef is arrested for speeding and put in jail on the day the Ambassador is scheduled to give a large official dinner, that arrest may result in a culinary calamity which might impair a delicate relationship.

Generally speaking there are also variations according to the nationality of the recipient. A state is generally disinclined to give privileges to aliens residing in that state. And even third party nationals imported by an embassy may not get the same treatment as nationals of the state maintaining the embassy.

It can be seen that the combinations are almost infinite. If one had a computer and took the trouble to separate each category into its various mutations, one would probably arrive at well over a hundred groups.

Just to confuse the matter further, not all states follow the same general practice. The recently adopted Conventions on Diplomatic and Consular Privileges and Immunities do try to bring some order and uniformity into the picture. But not all states have ratified the conventions. They leave a lot of questions unanswered and they relate only to diplomats and consuls although there are a great many others who claim privileges and immunities. There is, however, pending a convention on special missions which was approved by the General Assembly of the United Nations in December of 1969.

I would like to interject an assurance at this point that I am not deliberately trying to complicate the picture to confuse the reader, although I have probably succeeded in doing so. The fact is that the situation is complicated and there is no use pretending that it is not or offering easy to understand but meaningless explanations.

Possibly some help can be vouchsafed if the basic theories of privileges and immunities are explained.

Certain of the privileges are of very ancient origin, antedating the establishment of permanent missions. When a nation sent an ambassador to treat with another nation it was considered desirable for him to return with his head on his shoulders for there has never yet been an instance of a worthwhile report being presented by a decapitated ambassador. And if a nation expected fair treatment for their ambassador, they had to extend the same treatment to foreign envoys.

Hence an ambassador was sacrosanct and could not be imprisoned and harassed. And since he could be harassed by civil suits as well as by criminal suits, he was immune from them as well. Moreover it did not seem fair to tax an ambassador when he was on a temporary visit. In fact in the days of temporary ambassadors he was usually showered with gifts by the host country, a practice that proved pretty expensive with the growth in the number of ambassadorial missions.

When permanent missions were established the same principles carried over. A diplomat should not be prosecuted criminally because it would put a constraint on him in carrying out his nation's business. (This was before Mr. Hoffa demonstrated how effectively one can operate from a jail cell.) Likewise he should not be subject to civil constraint and, by the same token, not be subject to local taxes and customs excises. One of the first cases involving the principle is picturesquely described by Blackstone in his famous commentaries. He says:

> "358. (ii) IN CIVIL SUITS. --In respect to civil suits,
> all the foreign jurists agree, that neither an ambassador,
> nor any of his train or 'comites, ' can be prosecuted for
> any debt or contract in the courts of that kingdom wherein

he is sent to reside. Yet Sir Edward Coke maintains, that, if an ambassador make a contract which is good jure gentium (by the law of nations), he shall answer for it here. But the truth is, so few cases (if any) had arisen, wherein the privilege was either claimed or disputed, even with regard to civil suits, that our law books are silent upon it, previous to the reign of Queen Anne; when an ambassador from Peter the Great, Czar of Muscovy, was actually arrested and taken out of his coach in London, for a debt of fifty pounds, which he had there contracted. Instead of applying to be discharged upon his privilege, he gave bail to the action, and the next day complained to the queen. The persons who were concerned in the arrest were examined before the privy council (of which the Lord Chief Justice Holt was at the same time sworn a member) and seventeen were committed to prison; most of whom were prosecuted by information in the court of queen's bench, at the suit of the attorney general, and at their trial before the lord chief justice were convicted of the facts by the jury, reserving the question of law, how far those facts were criminal, to be afterwards argued before the judges; which question was never determined. In the meantime the czar resented this affront very highly, and demanded that the sheriff of Middlesex and all others concerned in the arrest should be punished with instant death. But the queen (to the amazement of that despotic court) directed her secretary to inform him, 'that she could inflict no punishment upon any, the meanest of her subjects, unless warranted by the law of the land: and therefore was persuaded that he would not insist upon impossibilities.' To satisfy, however, the clamors of the foreign ministers (who made it a common cause) as well as to appease the wrath of Peter, a bill was brought into parliament, and afterwards passed into a law, to prevent and to punish such outrageous insolence for the future. And with a copy of this act, elegantly engrossed and illuminated, accompanied by a letter from the queen, an ambassador extraordinary was commissioned to appear at Moscow, who declared 'that though her majesty could not inflict such punishment as was required, because of the defect in that particular of the former established constitutions of her kingdom, yet, with the unanimous consent of the parliament, she had caused a new act to be passed to serve as a law for the future.' This humiliating step was accepted as a full satisfaction by the czar; and the offenders, at his request, were discharged from all further prosecution."

Gradually two theories as to immunities grew up. The American theory seems to be that the granting of immunities, in addition to being necessary for the reasons outlined, should be considered as a reciprocal courtesy from one nation to another. On the American theory all American officers and employees in an Embassy (this would also be true of any other office) should be treated equally and be entitled to the same immunities. From a practical standpoint there is good reason for adopting this viewpoint since clerical help, who are less well paid than officers, resent an officer being given a financially valuable fiscal privilege they do not enjoy themselves. In return the United States is willing to grant similar exemptions to staffs of foreign governments. In essence it is based on the simple principle of "You scratch my back and I'll scratch yours." The trouble is that with swollen Embassies the United States has a very big back to scratch.

The other position, exemplified by the Italian stand, is that privileges will be granted when necessary to the performance of an official function. Admittedly a diplomatic officer should be permitted to bring in a motor vehicle duty free, as he needs a car to go to the Foreign Office, to attend official functions and in general to perform his duties. A clerk, however, does not need a car for such purposes. If she brings one in it is for her personal pleasure. Hence she should not have a customs immunity. But, however logical, it is difficult to explain this theory to an indignant secretary who sees her boss importing his car without difficulty. The result as we shall see is a compromise which has little intrinsic logic.

Chapter IX
RIGHTS AND PRIVILEGES OF A STATE

A state, in addition to being interested in most of the fiscal benefits which might accrue to an individual, is concerned with the right or privilege to sue in a foreign country, to be immune from suit and to have its governmental acts given recognition and validity by foreign courts.

The problem of bringing suit primarily concerns unrecognized governments. If the government of a state is not recognized by the political branch of another government, the judicial branch will not countenance a suit brought by the former. If it stays unrecognized for some time the results can be serious for it has no means of enforcing its rights. In the long period when the government of the Soviet Union remained unrecognized by the United States it unavailingly tried to enforce a contract in the courts of New York against a person who was quite clearly taking advantage of the situation in order to defraud the Soviet Union. In contrast a recognized government customarily has no difficulty in instituting suit in the courts of a friendly foreign country.

From very early times states have granted foreign states immunity from the jurisdiction of their courts. That grant was based on comity, the respect for the sovereignty of states and the expectation of reciprocal advantage. At the beginning there was some intermingling between the immunity of a state and the immunity of the sovereign, particularly in the heyday of monarchy when the ruler personified the state. In a very early case before the Supreme Court of the United States, Chief Justice Marshall went so far as to hold that an American vessel captured by Napoleon's fleet could not be recovered by its original owner when it entered an American port as the French sovereign and his property were immune from suit.

The rule worked fairly well in the past, when the operations of government were limited. As governments, particularly the communist governments, began to control every aspect of national life and to engage in all sorts and kinds of commercial activities, the old rule unduly favored the foreign state at the expense of its private competitors. If, for example, the U.S.S.R. were operating a steamship line, it could not be sued in an action based on such operations while a private shipping line carrying on precisely the same activities could be brought into court.

The Department of State took the lead and suggested to the Department of Justice that immunity should not apply when a state engaged in a commercial (that is, private) rather than governmental capacity. The Department of Justice refused to accede. What was good enough for John Marshall was good enough for it. Finally the views of the Department of State,

61

as expressed in a letter of May 19, 1952, from the Acting Legal Adviser, Jack Tate, prevailed.

Unfortunately the Tate letter and its subsequent implementation have raised almost as many questions as they have solved. In the first place, what is the line between a governmental function and a nongovernmental one or, to use the technical term, between juri imperium and juri gestionis? At present, governments are taking over more and more power. Is the operation of a national railroad governmental in character? A Belgian court has held not, but the case could be argued.

Also does one look at the nature of the institution performing the act or the nature of the act itself? If the former, nothing done by a clearly governmental institution subjects it to total jurisdiction. If the latter, the governmental character of the institution is immaterial.

When I was serving as Legal Adviser of the American Embassy in Rome shortly after World War II, I was constantly faced with the following problem. Italy looked at the nature of the act and the United States looked at the institution performing the act. Professor Perassi, the Legal Adviser of the Italian Foreign Office, would often use the example of coal for heating purchased by a consulate as a transaction subject to local jurisdiction. His argument--and there is much to be said for it--is that such a purchase is no different from any similar purchase by a private citizen, so that if there is a dispute the supplier should be able to sue the consular office or, to be more exact, the United States.

I never had the coal situation come up as an actual case. But we did have instances of traffic accidents involving embassy and consular vehicles and there was a time when a landlord in Palermo, Sicily, had the USIA quarters padlocked in a rent argument. I had to go to Sicily to effect a settlement and realized that compromise was the only possibility. I called Washington long distance with, judging from the connection, half of Palermo listening in, and obtained permission to reach agreement with the landlord, which was an inglorious but effective way out of the dilemma.

The Tate letter also stopped short of permitting the attachment of foreign government property. This renders suit in some instances highly unprofitable, which understandably brings tears to the eyes of the lawyers. Apparently, however, when the action is against property, what is known as an in rem action, and it is necessary to attach the property to obtain jurisdiction, an attachment for that technical purpose is permitted.

Naturally, if a foreign state does not object to being sued, a court can proceed with the case. Sometimes a foreign state will start the litigation and will be met with a counter claim or a set off. If the defense is based on the transaction itself, for example, if the foreign government is suing on a contract and the other side' asserts that the contract was originally broken by that government, causing damages to the defendant, that assertion can be made the basis of a counter demand. If, on the other hand, the counter demand is based on some incident completely unconnected with the original suit--supposing, for instance, that the foreign government is suing on a contract and the defendant brings out that a motor vehicle belonging to that government injured him in a traffic accident--the law is not quite so clear.

At present considerable government business is done by corporations. It does not appear, however, that this makes much difference from the standpoint of immunity. A public corporation is considered to be just as much of a public entity as an established agency of the government.

In addition to granting a foreign government immunity from suit, a state will also, generally speaking, not question the acts of a foreign government but instead give them full faith and credit. This necessarily has to be so, for there would be chaos if every governmental act were to be subject to scrutiny abroad. At this point the question of recognition becomes important. While in many respects the acts of an unrecognized government and a recognized one are treated similarly, there are nevertheless confusing differences. Hence I will try to look first at the effect given acts of an unrecognized government. Primary attention will be centered on confiscations since they are the most prolific breeders of dispute.

If a confiscation was effected by an unrecognized government on property belonging to its own nationals, the best view seems to be that the act is valid. In 1933 the New York Court of Appeals said in passing upon the confiscation of oil in the Soviet Union:

> "The cause of action herein arose where the act of confiscation occurred, and it must be governed by the law of Soviet Russia. According to the law of nations, it did no legal wrong when it confiscated the oil of its own nationals and sold it in Russia to the defendants. Such conduct may lead to governmental refusal to recognize Russia as a country with which the United States may have diplomatic dealings. The confiscation is none the less effective."

The opinion of the New York Court is not necessarily shared by all authorities. The British Courts, for example, appear to hold to the contrary.

There is even greater tendency to give credit to the acts of an unrecognized government of a routine governmental nature such as the issuance of postal money orders. Presumably the same principle would also be applied to the implementation of laws concerning family status.

It could scarcely be otherwise. If it were, all marriages celebrated in the Soviet Union during the period when the United States did not recognize the Communist regime would not have been recognized in the United States, for marriage in the U.S.S.R. is a civil and governmental ceremony. This would have meant that all children born in that period were illegitimate.

So far emphasis has been placed on acts of unrecognized governments since lack of recognition presents an additional complication. Nevertheless problems also arise concerning the effect to be given the acts of a recognized government. Generally speaking, confiscations or expropriations provide, as has been indicated already, the major disputes. They may be considered invalid, even though representing the act of a foreign government, if they (1) are against international law; (2) affect property located outside the jurisdiction of a confiscating state; (3) are against morality.

The first point is illustrated by the Sabbatino case. Shortly after the cancellation of the Cuban sugar quota, Castro, in retaliation, decided to confiscate all American properties in Cuba. At the time of the confiscation decree a vessel was loading sugar owned by a corporation, most of whose stock was American held, for shipment to Morocco. The sugar was confiscated. The Castro government was, however, just as anxious to sell the sugar as the American corporation. As the sale had been originally arranged by a New York sugar broker who was to have collected the proceeds and paid them over to the original owners, the Castro government merely had itself substituted for that owner. The sugar went to Morocco, where it presumably disappeared in thousands of Arab coffee cups. The purchaser paid the sugar broker in New York. At this point a controversy arose whether the proceeds should be paid the receiver of the original owner or the Banco Nacional de Cuba acting for Castro. The decision hinged upon whether the confiscation would be considered as an act of state not subject to scrutiny by the courts of the United States. Eventually the case reached the Supreme Court. In essence the minority of the court held that to inquire into the validity of the confiscation might embarrass the executive in any efforts it might make to reach a diplomatic settlement. It also refused to determine whether the confiscation was or was not a violation of international law. At this point Congress, led by Senator Hickenlooper, outraged by the decision, enacted the so-called Hickenlooper Amendment which provided that a court should inquire into the validity of an act of state unless specifically enjoined by the executive and must determine whether the act of state conforms to international law. Following this amendment there was further protracted litigation, the details of which do not warrant analysis. Suffice it to say that eventually a lower court held that the "confiscation"--the act of state--was against international law and therefore not to be considered effective by American courts. The Supreme Court refused to review the case and there the matter stands except for generating more and more literature.

In the United States it seems therefore established that an act of state that is considered by its courts to be contrary to international law is not controlling. Courts have also refused to enforce confiscatory "acts of state" when they related to institutions or property outside of the jurisdiction of the state taking the action. Thus property lying outside of Russia which the Soviet Government tried to confiscate was considered immune from confiscation by the New York Courts, even after the recognition of that government (the New York Courts, because of the commercial importance of New York, were the ones primarily concerned with Soviet expropriations).

A somewhat confusing element was injected when the Supreme Court of the United States upheld such a confiscation when the confiscated assets located in the United States had, by an executive agreement, been assigned to the United States by the Soviet Union in payment of claims of American citizens. A factor influencing the Court was its obvious desire not to challenge an executive agreement. Fortunately such diversions from the standard are not likely to occur very often.

A further hesitancy to recognize acts of state has taken place when the acts of state were so brazen and so contrary to morals as to make the application of the "act of state" repugnant. A good instance is provided by the Nazi decrees confiscating Jewish property. A problem arises when the property confiscated has been sold and resold and ends up in the hands of a perfectly innocent holder.

The difficulty of the situation has understandably placed the courts in a quandary. There have, however, been cases supporting the decrees, repugnant as they may have been to the judges called to pass upon the issues.

In the more ordinary exercise of its functions, particularly diplomatic and consular functions, a state is entitled to freedom of communication, that is, not to have its diplomatic pouches examined, to respect its personnel and to the inviolability of diplomatic and consular premises. There is a mistaken assumption held by many that an embassy property is a piece of the territory of the state that maintains it. That viewpoint is altogether false. If it were true a child born on an American embassy compound to the wife of a janitor or gatekeeper would be an American citizen. Likewise the United States would have jurisdiction over any crimes committed on the embassy grounds, as, for example, the assault of one waiting visa applicant on another resulting from a quarrel of an entirely personal nature. In such a case the local authorities would clearly have jurisdiction.

It is true that embassy and consular premises cannot be invaded by police and are generally inviolable. There is some question, however, whether even that inviolability applies if the police have reason to believe a crime is being committed, as, for example, forcible detention. Also if a fire broke out at night when no one was in the embassy chancery, firemen should be able to go in rather than let the building burn just because there is no one present to authorize their entry.

From the standpoint of fiscal privileges, a government is not too different from an individual. A government, generally speaking, will want exemptions from real and personal property taxes, from excise taxes and customs duties. Since a state does not die the question of inheritance taxes is not pertinent. Generally speaking, income taxes are also not pertinent, although it is conceivable that if a state held assets in a foreign country on which it derived an income it could be taxed on that income. Fees collected by a consulate, such as passport fees, are not considered income.

In the past the distinction between the state and the individual was not very clearly observed. It made little difference whether an official cable did not have to pay the local telegraph tax by virtue of an exemption granted the state or an exemption enjoyed by the Ambassador himself. In fact in some countries all imports, whether for the state, for the Ambassador personally or for members of the staff, are made in the name of the Ambassador.

With the growth of embassies the practice of lumping all privileges into the Ambassador's privileges, which worked satisfactorily in the past, has proven to be more and more impractical. Obviously there is a difference between the Ambassador and the state he represents. In Rome the Italian government, clinging to the old traditions, suggested that all Embassy vehicles be registered in the Ambassador's name. One can imagine what would happen if the vehicles were operating in a country where the owner was liable without fault. The Ambassador might be able to assert diplomatic immunity in case of a claim, but the charge would still stand against him.

The Italian Foreign Office finally consented to the issuance of ROMA licenses, that is, ordinary licenses, as distinguished from CD or Corpo Diplomatico licenses, for the vehicles in the pool and to considering their owner to be the American government rather than the Ambassador.

Generally speaking, the states of the union are reluctant to give exemptions from real property taxes to a foreign government. By the District of Columbia Code, an embassy is considered immune from local real property taxes, while property used as residences for embassy personnel is not immune. The Department of State will not even go so far as to insist that consular property must be exempt under state laws although it tries to persuade the states to provide the exemption. Nevertheless, the United States asks for exemption for staff residences owned abroad by the government. The Vienna conventions on diplomatic and consular privileges and immunities, which will be discussed more fully in the next chapter, do not change the pattern to any great extent.

On personal property the exemptions of a foreign state are not too dissimilar from those of an individual, although the nature of the property may differ. One factor that does emerge is that the tax liability of a state will differ according to circumstances. As in the case of immunity from jurisdiction, exemptions from taxation will probably not be granted to a state acting in a commercial capacity.

The same is also true with regard to customs exemptions. In that respect the Vienna convention on diplomatic relations provides specifically for the exemption of customs duties of "articles for the official use of the mission."

Chapter X
PRIVILEGES AND IMMUNITIES OF AN INDIVIDUAL
IN GENERAL

In an earlier chapter I have indicated that there are probably more than a hundred groups and subgroups enjoying privileges in a foreign country as a result of their official status. On second thought I think the figure is low. Obviously in a general text it is not possible to go into detail with regard to every group. Hence I will concentrate on (1) members of diplomatic and consular establishments and their retinues; (2) on international civil servants and (3) military personnel. There are plenty of other categories but as the Arabs say--malish.

The nature of diplomatic and consular privileges and immunities is covered at least in part by the Vienna Conventions of 1961 and 1963, which dealt with diplomatic and consular privileges and immunities respectively.

Before 1961 diplomatic privileges and immunities were governed almost entirely by established custom. There were a few agreements, particularly in Latin America, but they were not of great importance. Consular privileges and immunities were, on the other hand, governed both by custom and bilateral treaties, some of which largely restated custom. According to the Department of State List of Treaties and other international agreements in force on January 1, 1971, the United States has about 60 agreements relating to consular affairs. Some are quite old and are not responsive to present needs and some cover the subject only partially. Occasionally consular provisions are included in more general treaties. With a good many countries the United States had no convention at all. With others the convention is only of recent date--the one with the United Kingdom entered into force only on September 7, 1952, showing that nations can operate consular establishments quite successfully without the benefit of a convention, although an agreement may help to pinpoint rights and privileges.

The general nature of the exemptions enjoyed by diplomats has been indicated in Chapter VIII. There is, as has been mentioned, a considerable variation in the practice of states, particularly with regard to the privileges and immunities, if any, of clerical and administrative personnel.

The American practice on diplomatic immunities from jurisdiction was based upon a law enacted in 1790 modelled on the British Statute of Anne. That statute was motivated by the incident involving the Russian Ambassador so graphically described by Blackstone. The framework of fiscal privileges and immunities was developed bit by bit, the development being influenced by new tax concepts, the changing role of the United States in the world and other factors.

67

Actually the United States has been quite aggressive in claiming privileges for its personnel. In some instances the position of the United States is justified; in others it is, to say the least, dubious. An illustration is furnished by the use of diplomatic passports. Such passports are designed to inform foreign officials, particularly customs officials, that the holder is a diplomat entitled to privileges and immunities. But the Department of State issues passports to all Foreign Service Officers, whether or not they are holding a diplomatic position at the time, and to a considerable number of other government officials traveling abroad. In contrast the British Foreign Office does not issue any diplomatic passports. What is even worse is that the Department of State issues diplomatic passports to retired ambassadors to facilitate their private travel abroad. This appears to be a manifest fraud on foreign governments and an abuse of privileges which degrades the value of a diplomatic passport.

The Vienna Convention on Diplomatic Privileges and Immunities of 1961, to which the United States is a party, has dealt with the question of immunities in several articles. Since the Vienna convention will undoubtedly constitute the future law on the subject, and since American domestic law will be made to conform to that convention, the major provisions of the convention as they relate to privileges and immunities are worth quoting even though they are of some length. They read:

Article 23

"1. The sending State and the head of the mission shall be exempt from all national, regional or municipal dues and taxes in respect of the premises of the mission, whether owned or leased, other than such as represent payment for specific services rendered."

. . . .

Article 29

"The person of a diplomatic agent shall be inviolable. He shall not be liable to any form of arrest or detention. The receiving State shall treat him with due respect and shall take all appropriate steps to prevent any attack on his person, freedom, or dignity."

. . . .

Article 31

"1. A diplomatic agent shall enjoy diplomatic immunity from the criminal jurisdiction of the receiving State. He shall also enjoy immunity from its civil and administrative jurisdiction, except in the case of:

(a) a real action relating to private immovable property situated in the territory of the receiving State, unless he holds it on behalf of the sending State for the purposes of the mission;

(b) an action relating to succession in which the diplomatic agent is involved as executor, administrator,
heir or legatee as a private person and not on behalf
of the sending State;

(c) an action relating to any professional or commercial activity exercised by the diplomatic agent in the
receiving State outside his official functions.

2. A diplomatic agent is not obliged to give evidence as
a witness."

. . . .

Article 34

"A diplomatic agent shall be exempt from all dues and
taxes, personal or real, national, regional or municipal,
except:

(a) indirect taxes of a kind which are normally incorporated in the price of goods or services;

(b) dues and taxes on private immovable property situated in the territory of the receiving State, unless
he holds it on behalf of the sending State for the purposes of the mission;

(c) estate, succession or inheritance duties levied by
the receiving State, subject to the provisions of paragraph 4 of Article 39;

(d) dues and taxes on private income having its source
in the receiving State and capital taxes on investments made in commercial undertakings in the receiving State;

(e) charges levied for specific services rendered;

(f) registration, court or record fees, mortgage dues
and stamp duty, with respect to immovable property, subject to the provisions of Article 23."

In Chapter VII the exemptions were listed in terms of the taxes
from which exemption was granted. Here the reverse approach is adopted.
The results are more or less the same. There is also a provision exempt-
ing a diplomat from paying social security taxes on the wages of his servants if they are covered by another system.

Families of diplomats are given the same privileges and immunities by the Convention as the head of the family. Administrative and technical personnel also get the same treatment except for two quite notable
limitations. In the first place, they do not have immunity from civil jurisdiction except for their official acts. If landlords sue for rent they have
to answer. In the second place, they are allowed exemptions from customs duties only on articles brought in "at the time of first installation,"

that is, articles they bring with them personally or which are shipped to them to coincide more or less with their arrival.

From the standpoint of logic this latter privilege makes little sense, for there is no particular magic about a first installation. If a clerk cannot afford a car when she first arrives at a post but can afford it a year later, she may be precluded from importing it without the payment of prohibitive customs taxes. Moreover this limitation hits hardest those who stay at a post for a long time, as is often desirable from a service standpoint. Those who move to a new country every two years or so are not so troubled. What motivated this solution was not logic but the spirit of compromise.

Actually some of the effects of the rule are bypassed by allowing clerks to use an Embassy commissary, where goods may be brought in in the name of the ambassador or the officers as a whole, or a military commissary or PX, where goods are brought in by virtue of military status of forces agreements. Strictly speaking, under the Vienna Convention a clerk has no right to buy a bottle of bourbon at the commissary liquor store at reduced prices. Nevertheless the practice is tolerated. Naturally this places American personnel in a favorable position, as no other country has such a network of commissaries and PX's.

The Convention goes on to provide limited exemptions to the service staff of the mission, that is, domestics hired by the government, and even smaller exemptions--in fact only for taxes on their pay--on private servants of diplomats. In every case, in order to qualify for exemption the claimant must not be a national or permanent resident of the State where the Embassy is located.

There is one provision that is worth noting. It stipulates that the host state must exercise its jurisdiction over private servants in such a manner as not to interfere unduly with the functions of the mission. This would seem at first blush to cover the case of the arrested cook mentioned previously. On the other hand, since the exemption applies only to persons who are not nationals of the host state, the Ambassador's dinner would still be ruined if he had a native cook, which is usually the case.

Diplomats in transit have more or less the same privileges as diplomats at a post except, of course, that some of the exemptions are manifestly inapplicable. A diplomat in transit would scarcely be called upon to pay direct taxes any more than any other traveller. Nations, however, are not quite so ready to provide customs courtesies to a travelling diplomat as to a resident one. The United States has had some rather unhappy experiences with travelling diplomats who were not above doing a little smuggling. The convention has some general provisions on the status of travelling diplomats in Article 40 although a travelling diplomat is not defined. When I finished my tour of duty in Japan I elected to return home to Washington by quite a roundabout route, with stops along the way to visit my daughter in Ankara, Turkey, and to sight-see along the way. Was I a diplomat in transit? I do not know. Fortunately I had no trouble and therefore did not have to test my rights.

Consular officers and employees generally enjoy, as has been said, lesser privileges than diplomats. Often, however, whether by treaty or the courtesy of the host country, the fiscal exemptions are more or less the same. I noticed no practical difference whatever when I moved from the Consulate General in Yokohama to the Embassy in Tokyo.

According to the Foreign Affairs Manual of the Department of State, consular officers in the United States are exempt from excise taxes only when the tax is paid by the purchaser and the transaction is official in character. The line between official and unofficial is often difficult to draw. Is liquor bought for representation purposes considered to be for official purposes if part of the bottle is left over and the consul uses it for his personal consumption?

As a result of some of the recent consular conventions, that are quite generous to the consular officer, the curious phenomenon has arisen of consular officers having certain advantages over diplomats, at least in terms of having the privileges spelled out. This, of course, from a diplomat's exalted standpoint is shocking and blasphemous. Hence provision has been made in the Korean Consular Convention, and possibly some others, to provide against this outrageous possibility. Thus Article 14 provides:

"The provisions of Article 11, [customs privileges] 12, [tax privileges] and 13 [insurance] shall have like application to diplomatic officers and employees, without prejudice to such rights and benefits as they may have under international law."

Consuls have no exemption from civil jurisdiction and in principle none from criminal jurisdiction except, to use the terms of the Vienna Convention on consular privileges and immunities of 1964, "in respect of acts performed in the exercise of consular functions."

There has nevertheless been a gradual realization that in the interests of good relations it is inadvisable to prosecute a consul for a minor offense. As a consequence the [1963 Consular] Convention with Korea contained the following passage:

"A consular officer or employee shall, except as provided in Article 15, be exempt from arrest of prosecution in the receiving state except when charged with the commission of crime which, upon conviction, might subject the individual guilty thereof to a sentence of imprisonment for a period of more than one year."

A particular problem with regard to jurisdiction has arisen with respect to the Soviet Union. In view of the arbitrary imprisonment of Professor Barghoorn, a Yale professor who was jailed and held incommunicado on spurious charges while visiting the U.S.S.R., and the vulnerability of

foreigners to arrest generally, the United States did not want to send anyone to a consular office in the Soviet Union who might be prosecuted by the
local authorities. Hence Article 19 of the consular convention with the U.S.
S.R. provides immunity from criminal jurisdiction. The same immunity
could presumably be claimed by any other nation that was in a position to
invoke the most favored nation clause. That clause will be discussed later.

In the case of international organizations we are dealing with two different categories, not to mention subcategories. The first category consists of the members of the missions to the international organizations,
such as, for example, the British mission to the United Nations. The members of that mission have the same rights and privileges as the members
of the British Embassy in Washington. (In the case of members of the U.S.
mission to the United Nations, the circumstance that they are operating in
their own country precludes them from enjoying diplomatic privileges.)

The officials and employees of the United Nations and of other international organizations, that is, those in the Secretariats, have privileges
that are somewhat more limited than those enjoyed by their diplomatic counterparts. The former do not pay income taxes, they are given customs
exemptions on first arrival and they are, in the words of the pertinent
American legislation, "immune from suit and legal process relating to acts
performed by them in their official capacity ...."

In the days before the cold war the problem of criminal jurisdiction
over the military was fairly simple. In an occupied country the laws of
war applied. In allied countries the troops were subject to the discipline
of their own commanders. Thus if an American soldier with the American
Expeditionary Force in World War I had raped a French woman he would
have been court-martialed by an American military tribunal.

In the case of a warship visiting a foreign port the guidelines were
never absolutely clear. Generally speaking, sailors who had misbehaved
ashore were returned to their ships by the local police, although if an offense were particularly blatant the local authorities might take control.

These rather free and easy principles, designed to operate in war-
time when the prime consideration was the cohesiveness of the military
force or in rather limited situations such as visits of warships to foreign
ports, became manifestly inapplicable when sizeable contingents were
stationed on foreign soil in time of peace for an indefinite period of time
and warships were based on foreign naval stations. In that situation the
local population would obviously resent having a considerable number of
persons immune from local jurisdiction. On the other hand it was desirable
to permit the military to try offenders in the case of offenses that did not
concern the local population. One solution might have been to permit the
military to try all offenses committed on base and the local authorities all
offenses committed away from the base. This was not a very good criterion,
however. If an American sergeant had a quarrel with a native laborer working on the base and killed or injured him, the local government was very
much concerned. If on the other hand one American killed another American

while on an expedition in the desert, the local authorities could well leave
the punishment to the military.

As a consequence a somewhat ingenious scheme of overlapping jurisdictions was incorporated into the NATO Status of Forces agreement and
into a number of similar agreements.

In essence the Status of Forces agreement provides that the state to
which the troops belong, that is, the sending state, will have <u>exclusive</u>
criminal jurisdiction over offenses against its military law that are not punishable by the law of the host state, that is, the receiving state. Desertion
or failing to obey orders are good examples. The Statute of Forces agreement goes on to provide that the receiving or host state shall have <u>exclusive</u>
jurisdiction over offenses against its law punishable by its law but not by the
law of the sending state. Since the military code of justice is very wide
it is a little difficult to think of a case involving a violation of local law that
would not also be a violation of military law, at least as far as the United
States is concerned. A stringent security law of the receiving state might,
however, be violated by a soldier without running afoul of his own military
code.

What this means is that in most cases (the cases in which neither
state has exclusive jurisdiction) both receiving and sending states have con-
current jurisdiction. It then becomes important to determine, in case of
conflict, which state has primary jurisdiction, that is, which state has the
first call to try the offender. The Status of Forces agreement provides that
the sending state shall have primary jurisdiction over offenses solely against
the property or security of the sending state or against the person or property of another member of the Forces or a civilian attached to the Forces
and over offenses "arising out of any act or commission done in the performance of official duty." The receiving state has primary jurisdiction
in other instances. A simple example is where a soldier assaulted a local
civilian in a bar in town.

In the event a state not having primary jurisdiction nevertheless wants
it for local reasons (a brawl between two soldiers in a public park, although
not affecting anyone else, might have created such an unfavorable local impression as to make the authorities of the receiving state anxious to step
in for the sake of domestic public relations) it can request the other state
to give sympathetic consideration to yielding jurisdiction.

Considering the number of troops abroad and considering that the
Status of Forces agreements do create a modified and limited form of extraterritoriality, it is surprising that they have not created more difficulties than they have.

It would be a mistake, nevertheless, to consider that all is always
precise and serene. The Girard case in Japan clearly illustrates the contrary.

Private Girard, whose mental I.Q. obviously left something to be
desired, was assigned to guard duty at an American target range in Japan.
The target practice had been impeded by Japanese scavengers who tried to

realize what profit they could from picking up used shells and bits of metal. At the time of the incident giving rise to the case target practice had been suspended with Girard and a buddy guarding the equipment while the other soldiers went away. An old Japanese woman came on the field to scavenge metal.

According to some accounts Girard actually urged her on. He then loaded an expended cartridge case in the grenade launcher of his rifle and fired it in the direction of the old lady. There is no indication that he intended any physical harm. Instead he apparently wanted to amuse himself by frightening her as a cartridge case fired in this manner makes a weird and terrifying noise. He was only indulging in a macabre and senseless humor in keeping with his mentality. Contrary to his expectations the cartridge case hit the old lady and killed her.

At this point the indignation of the Japanese broke loose. The Army wanted to exercise jurisdiction over Girard on the ground that it was an offense in the performance of official duty. The Japanese, quite rightly in my opinion, contended that although he might have been on official duty while standing guard, the shooting of an innocent person was scarcely an act done in the performance of official duty.

The case was very badly handled by the military and threatened to become a major issue in Japanese-American relations. The Army finally ceded jurisdiction on the ground that it gave sympathetic consideration to the Japanese demand for jurisdiction rather than on the basis of the Japanese having primary jurisdiction. The Japanese, so long as they had Girard, were satisfied.

When Girard was delivered to the Japanese, all the bleeding hearts in the United States rose to complain that this poor, innocent boy was being delivered for trial without any of the American constitutional guarantees to safeguard him. A case was brought in an American court to prohibit the military authorities from handing Girard over to the Japanese. The litigation was of such importance and prompt action was so imperative that the Supreme Court called the case up from the lower court, bypassing the usual appeals, and decided it against Girard.

As it turned out the sentence meted out by the Japanese was quite light. In prison he was allowed to receive visits from his Japanese girl friend "Candy". When he was released after a short stay in prison he married Candy and returned to the United States. Experience has shown that in other countries as well, a G.I. might fare better in a foreign court than in an American military court.

At the time the Status of Forces agreements were negotiated it was thought that the military could try offenses committed by members of what is called "the civilian component," which means the families of the military and civilians with armed forces, such as school teachers in the Armed Forces schools. In the course of the years two wives of military men, one in Germany and one in Japan, shot their husbands evidently having concluded that this method was far speedier and more efficient than a divorce. The military authorities endeavored to try them but on appeal to the Supreme Court, the Court held that the code of military justice did not extend to civilians. As far as I know they have lived happily ever after. At the present time the local courts are given jursidiction over crimes committed by dependents.

While the exemptions of criminal jurisdiction of military personnel are fairly extensive the corresponding civil exemptions are restricted, being confined to "the enforcement of any judgment given against him the member of the Armed Forces in the receiving state in a matter arising from the performance of his official duties."

From a fiscal standpoint the military have limited privileges. They are not subject to income tax on their pay, they do not have to pay personal property taxes and their stay in the receiving state will not be construed as establishing a residence or domicile for the purposes of taxation. They can import personal effects and furniture for the length of their stay. They can also bring in motor vehicles but cannot dispose of them without authorization.

There is also a provision stipulating that a force. . .

> "...may import free of duty the equipment for the force
> and reasonable quantities of provisions, supplies and
> other goods for the exclusive use of the force and,
> in cases where such use is permitted by the receiving
> State, its civilian component and dependents.

I have spent three chapters on privileges and immunities -- more time than I have spent on any other topic. In a few instances I have approached the same subject from different viewpoints, at least partially for the sake of emphasis. The subject is of immense practical importance to the state and to the individuals enjoying immunities whose number, by the time one includes the military and their dependents, runs into the millions. Besides, even if a person has no immunities himself he had better know what immunities are possessed by the organization or individual he is dealing with. If one rents an apartment to a diplomat one would do well to know what are the chances of collecting -- which may be nil -- in the case of default. In fact I regret that time does not permit me to go into the question further, to give added examples, and to examine the privileges of some of the groups I had to pass over.

Chapter XI
JURISDICTION AND EXTRADITION

Speaking loosely, jurisdiction is the right of a state to impose its authority on organizations and individuals and to require compliance with its laws. Jurisdiction has many meanings depending upon the context in which that term is used. For instance there can be tax jurisdiction--the right of a state to enforce its fiscal regime. Civil jurisdiction is quite important, that is the right to exercise control over personal matters such as marriage, divorce, adoption and so on and the right to have its courts or other authorities pass on the innumerable disputes between private parties that give rise to litigation. Generally speaking this type of jurisdiction concerns private international law or conflicts of law rather than public international law. Obviously a misuse of jurisdiction giving rise to a palpably erroneous and unfair decision against an alien can evoke international protest. Likewise an arrogation of jurisdiction that is completely unjustified might be questioned. For example, a divorce mill established purely and simply as a means of making money out of foreigners anxious to obtain a "quickie" divorce might well be considered as an abuse of rights. Also certain immunities from civil jurisdiction as pointed out in the previous chapter do affect public international law. But the ordinary disputes relating to civil jurisdiction do not interest states and therefore fall, as has just been said, under private international law.

When I speak of jurisdiction in public international law and in the sense used in this chapter, as distinguished for example from the jurisdiction of the International Court of Justice, I am talking almost exclusively about criminal jurisdiction -- the right of a state to try and punish an offender against its laws or the laws of nations. (The American Constitution specifically gives Congress the power "To define and punish Piracies and Felonies committed on the high Seas, and Offenses against the Law of Nations.

As is true with regard to other aspects of criminal law there is a continuing effort to achieve a balance between protecting society and the state, and safeguarding the individual. Obviously it is desirable not to let crime go unpunished. Yet should that laudable end permit a nation to seize and try a passing tourist merely on the ground that he was alleged to have committed a crime in another state which had so far gone unpunished? In such a case, the accused might be confronted with an unfamiliar legal system administered in a language he did not understand, and be unable as a practical matter to produce distant witnesses, so that he would be handicapped in establishing his innocence. It might be better to forego trying to assume jurisdiction which could result in an erroneous conviction.

Hence there is a constant effort to reconcile different theories and practices to achieve maximum justice and fairness. Concepts change over the years and different nations have varying viewpoints. By now, however, certain fairly well accepted international law rules concerning the exercise of criminal justice have been agreed upon by the majority of nations.

Sometimes nations, particularly the Anglo-Saxon nations which are scrupulous in the protection of the individuals (too much so the critics of the Supreme Court maintain) do not go as far as they are permitted to go by international law. Thus any analysis of the scope of jurisdiction in an individual case should take into account both international law and domestic practice.

There is very general agreement that a nation can punish crimes committed on its soil although there are, as has been pointed out in previous chapters, immunities from local jurisdiction such as those enjoyed by diplomats. The Fourteenth Amedndment of the Constitution specifies that "all persons born or naturalized in the United States, and subject to the jurisdiction thereof, are citizens of the United States and of the State wherein they reside." (Italics supplied.) It has been interpreted to exclude children of diplomats born in the United States on the ground that they are not subject to the jurisdiction of the United States. This necessarily means that the parent diplomat is likewise not subject to the jurisdiction of the United States.

Actually this use of words is not strictly correct. A diplomat is exempt from suit in the local courts but is not exempt from jurisdiction in the sense of being free to violate the laws of the host state.

A crime committed by him is just as much of a crime as one committed by anyone else. If his government waives his immunity (an individuals cannot waive his own immunity since it might not be in the national interest to permit a waiver) or if he loses his diplomatic position or returns to the country where the crime occurred after the termination of his mission, he can be prosecuted. Moreover an offense by a diplomat can lead to a request for his prompt recall and disgrace which in some cases may be punishment enough.

The United States Foreign Service Manual specifically admonishes American diplomats that they must abide by the local laws.

There is a question as to when a crime is committed on a particular territory. The classic example is of a man who shoots a rifle across the border and kills or wounds a person on the other side. In such a case both border states would have jurisdiction as the act took place in both states. Presumably the same principle would apply to any crime originating in one country and having its effect in another whether the nations are border states or geographically separated. If a man in Japan were to send his wife in the United States some delicious roasted caterpillars which he had first thoughtfully soaked in arsenic he could be prosecuted both in Japan and the United States. Difficulties increase when the crime is not quite so tangible and clear as murder or attempted murder. An individual harmed by a slanderous or libelous statement can sue in the civil courts and recover damages. In addition the accuser may be criminally liable. The intervention of the state is justified on the ground that the libel or slander can lead to a breach of the peace which the authorities are bound to preserve. A person may be responsible for a criminal libel when he is not for civil libel. Truth is always a defense in civil libel--it is not in criminal libel. In the old and simple days when the common law was in process of formation, a man going out in the market place and stating that Mistress Dogood had been a prostitute might well have started a rousing fight which would have disturbed the King's Peace. The fact that Mistress Dogood might have been a prostitute before she became married, settled and a pillar of the community is irrelevant.

From an international law standpoint the slandering or libelling of a person in one state by another person in an adjacent state may have the same legal effect as shooting a bullet across a boundary. Today with the press, the radio and TV not limited in their coverage to their state of origin all sorts of problems can be envisaged. In an early case involving only the printed word a Mexican was libelled by an American who published his libel in Texas. It was, however, circulated in Mexico. The American was incautious enough to go to Mexico where he was promptly jailed. The incident gave rise to a long, heated and inconclusive correspondence between the American and Mexican governments with the American government maintaining that Mexico had no jurisdiction since the libel was not published in Mexico.

I am not too sure that the United States would take the same position today. Aside from cases of libel and slander the American government is undoubtedly interested in protecting consumers against fraudulent advertising claims. Suppose a station from Mexico advertised a drug known to have deleterious effects which was sold illegally and under the counter in the United States. Would the United States have power to punish the advertiser if he happened to cross the border?

Also suppose there were a perfectly outrageous claim for a legitimate drug, for example, that aspirin cured cancer. Could the individual who made the claim in another country knowing that it would be heard in the United States and might mislead gullible listeners, be punished by the United States. I do not know but I think so.

By common agreement vessels are considered to be territory of the state whose flag they fly, at least for purposes of criminal jurisdiction, so that a crime committed on board a vessel is punishable by the authorities of the flag state. The problem could become difficult if a crime were committed on a vessel flying the flag of convenience, as for example, the Liberian flag, when the vessel never put into a Liberian port.

I asked Liberian Services, Inc., what would happen in such a case and received the following reply:

"In answer to your inquiry as to jurisdiction and punishment of crimes aboard Liberian vessels on the high seas, it should be made clear that the Republic of Liberia is, of course, fully prepared to enforce its laws in cases properly subject to its jurisdiction, wherever occurring.

As you suggested, there are some practical difficulties where crimes are committed by nationals of States other than Liberia aboard Liberian vessels at great distances from Liberian ports. However, surprising as it may seem, there have been very few such instances. These have all been investigated and in the main dealt with by Liberian authorities. In two or three cases, where quite serious offenses were involved, Liberia has (when requested) voluntarily relinquished jurisdiction to the State of which the parties involved were nationals or to the State whose domestic peace and tranquility was consequently disturbed--usually in the port at which the vessel called immediately following the offense.

It should be pointed out that difficulties of enforcement are by no means limited to vessels of Liberian registry and the differences, if any, at any given moment are at most only ones of degree."

The jurisdiction is not absolute, for when a vessel is within internal waters of another state that state can take jurisdiction over a crime committed aboard. The general rule is that the shore state will not take jurisdiction unless the crime disturbs the peace of the port. It is a little hard to say precisely when the peace of the port is disturbed. Obviously if the cook takes a meat cleaver and with loud and raucous shouts pursues the first mate over the deck until he manages to split his skull the peace of the port is disturbed. But if the same cook were to put an overdose of sleeping pills in the first mate's soup so that he quietly passed away in his cabin during the night, would the peace of the port be disturbed? I think the answer is yes for the very gravity of the offense would be considered to be a disturbance of the peace of the port. In one case Chinese sailors smoking opium in their bunks were considered to have disturbed the peace of the port although there was no evidence of any actual disturbance.

For a long time there was debate as to jurisdiction over crimes committed on an aircraft. Now there is general agreement to consider the aircraft similar to a ship so as to permit the state where the aircraft is registered to assume jurisdiction over crimes committed aboard.

So far, at least to my knowledge, there have not been any instances involving jurisdiction over crimes committed under the sea on the continental shelf beyond the territorial sea. With the prospect of small communities being established under water to exploit the resources of the sea the problem is bound to arise sooner or later. My guess is that the state controlling the continental shelf would have jurisdiction but in the absence of precedents I can only speculate.

A state can also exercise jurisdiction in the case of a crime against its security or well-being taking place abroad. Thus if a counterfeiting ring in Marseilles manufactured and circulated counterfeit American dollars, the government of the United States could prosecute in the courts of the United States any member of the counterfeiting gang who was found later in the United States.

Likewise a nation can punish its own nationals for crimes committed abroad although the Anglo-Saxon states do not, generally speaking, take jurisdiction over a crime committed by one of its nationals abroad. The reluctance to exercise jurisdiction is predicated upon the feeling that the crime should be punished where it takes place where witnesses are presumably available to both the prosecution and the defendant.

Still another basis for criminal jurisdiction is what has been somewhat inappropriately called the theory of passive personality. Under that theory a state can punish an offense committed abroad if the victim of that offense is a national of that state.

The passive personality concept does not find universal acceptance in international law. The Permanent Court of International Justice sidestepped the issue in the well-known Lotus decision. In that case a French steamer collided with a Turkish vessel resulting in the deaths of several Turkish sailors. The French vessel put in at a Turkish port and the Turks arrested the French officer of the watch on the ground of manslaughter. The French government protested the jurisdiction of the Turkish courts and the case was taken to the Court. The Turks attempted to justify jurisdiction on the passive personality theory. The Court in a divided opinion permitted Turkey to take jurisdiction but based its decision on the fact that the deaths occurred on a Turkish vessel which was assimilated to Turkish territory. It specifically stated that it did "not think it necessary to consider the contention that a state cannot punish offenses committed abroad by a foreigner simply by reason of the nationality of the victim." On this point the court reserved its opinion.

Lastly jurisdiction is sometimes based on the universality principle. The most common example of that is piracy over which crime any state apprehending the pirates has jurisdiction. There have, however, been suggestions to extend that principle to any other crimes that might otherwise go unpunished. For example one suggestion is that it apply to a crime "when committed in a place not subject to the authority of any state and the alien is not a national of any state." Since there are very few such places, possibly an uninhabited rock or some ice floe, the universality principle has a rather limited application and is not of prime importance. Nevertheless it cannot be overlooked completely.

Generally speaking jurisdiction is exercised within the territorial boundaries of the court or other cognizance of the case. There are nevertheless exceptions.

In the previous chapters on the development of international law and on the immunities from jurisdiction, I have mentioned the question of extraterritoriality. I pointed out that it owed its origins, to a considerable degree at least, to the necessity of coping with inapplicability of Moslem law to infidels. Later the same principle under the name extraterritoriality was imposed by the Western states on the weaker states of the Orient, the Middle East and Africa. There was some justification for the Western demands for extraterritoriality.

The incident that generated the American demand for extraterritoriality in China is illustrative. An Italian seaman named Terranova, aboard an American vessel, was strangled by the Chinese authorities as punishment for accidentally causing the death of a Chinese woman. There is no doubt that Terranova was put to death without adequate trial, in a brutal manner, and without justification considering that the death of the woman was an unfortunate accident and was totally unpremeditated.

Unfortunately the western powers abused the right of extraterritoriality and extended it in an unwarranted manner. Part of that abuse stemmed from the desire of the missionaries to protect their converts. According to one Far Eastern historian:

"... the[missionary] soon extended his immunity to his Chinese converts. If a convert got into difficulty with the authorities, the missionaries intervened on his behalf, sometimes vigorously. Or if a convert got into trouble with other Chinese (which could easily happen, since his going over to the foreign missionaries was considered a betrayal of his kind), the missionary also intervened. In that case, too, he went to the mandarin and asked for official support for his protégé. And the mandarin usually thought it wise to give it, no matter where the right and wrong lay. This was more commonly resorted to by the Catholics than the Protestants, but it was common enough to both. As a result not only foreigners came under the protection of extraterritoriality but Chinese who had missionary protection. In many communities therefore Chinese official authorities could not exercise jurisdiction over all their own people. Another result, of course, was that it put a premium on becoming a convert to one Christian denomination or another and led to an increase in the number of converts, sometimes without much regard to religious conviction. Communities could thus be split, with a small minority enjoying special privileges and immunities, and this in turn produced a great deal of ill-feeling and resentment on the part of the others, especially among the more educated."

Extraterritoriality has by now vanished in its original form. Nevertheless, as indicated in an earlier chapter, its complete disappearance is

quite recent. For several years after World War II money was appropriated by the United States for the administration of extraterritoriality in
Egypt, Morocco, Ethiopia, and Oman. Moreover the rather elaborate provisions of American law concerning extraterritoriality were not repealed
until 1956.

In its heyday, extraterritoriality was a very significant factor in our
legal system. The law authorized the execution of offenders and some, in
fact, were put to death. Today the main carry-over from extraterritoriality is the qualified right given the military authorities of a sending state
to try to punish their own personnel.

A less important carry-over is the right of a consular officer to take
disciplinary action against seamen aboard merchant vessels of his country's registry. Today, in a few busy ports, the Coast Guard has a Merchant Marine Detail which, along with its other duties, investigates disciplinary problems aboard American ships so that, by virtue of close co-
operations between the two agencies, there is seldom need for duplicate
investigation and action by a consular officer. Even without the Coast
Guard, the consul's duties are far less onerous than in the past. Good
living conditions, union protection, and other factors have reduced the
number of disciplinary cases a consul or, for that matter, a master of a
vessel, has to contend with in a normal situation.

In essence while extraterritoriality is gone, its vestiges--and the
status of forces agreements are very important vestiges--are still with
us. Moreover the memory of the abuses of extraterritoriality lingers on.

I have mentioned before that one of the aims of the law is not to permit crime to go unpunished. Nations have worked out all sorts of arrangements for surrendering persons accused of crime to the state claiming the
right to exercise jurisdiction.

Sometimes the arrangements are quite informal and are not sanc-
tioned by any treaty agreement. The United States and Mexico have a working arrangement whereby alleged criminals wanted by one country who have
fled to the other country are escorted to the border by the police of the
latter and by a coincidence are met at the border by an official welcoming
committee.

Occasionally a nation will be willing to surrender a wanted criminal
through extradition proceedings without requiring that there be an extradition treaty between the two states.

Normally, however, extradition is effected in accordance with an
extradition treaty which specifies the offenses for which extradition can be
requested and prescribes the procedure to be followed. The United States
has extradition treaties with a very large number of countries.

Usually a crime has to be of some significance to warrant extradition and has to be a crime under the laws of both states. (A waitress who
appeared topless against the law could not be extradited if she went abroad.)
Moreover political crimes are not extraditable. Furthermore, few states
are willing to permit the extradition of their nationals.

There are, however, a large number of offenses for which extradition lies. In the 1961 treaty with Brazil--given as an annex to one of the problems' in the appendix, there is a listing of thirty-four crimes from murder to procurement.

When a state requests extradition it has to establish that there is a probable basis for the charge. In this respect an extradition hearing is like a grand jury proceeding which does not pass on the guilt or innocence of the accused but merely on the good faith and apparent merit of the complaint. The request is made through diplomatic channels and the Department of State in the United States can have a voice in determining whether extradition should be granted or withheld for political reasons. In a case involving the former dictator of Venezuela, Perez Jimenez, the defense was made that his use of the treasury constituted an "act of state." The court said that his activities in amassing a fortune were no more an act of state than a case of rape.

Jurisdiction is an important phase of the law and is likely to become more and more important as the number of states--that is, the number of jurisdictions--increase; new areas for exploitation like the moon and the bottom of the sea are opened up; and ever more numerous populations travel increasingly throughout the world.

Chapter XII
NATIONALITY OF INDIVIDUALS

A national of a state owes allegiance to that state and in return is entitled to its protection and to be considered a member of the national community. Nationality is the link between a state and its citizens or subjects. The latter two terms are often used interchangeably with the word "national." In the United States and its territories everyone who is not an alien is both a citizen and a national except for the inhabitants of Swain Island and American Samoa who are only nationals. Since they are relatively few in number and since the rights of citizenship, as distinguished from the rights of nationality, have only an internal meaning under the Constitution, I will, in the interests of simplicity, concentrate exclusively on citizens and nationals. "Subjects" are persons owing allegiance to a ruling monarch. From the standpoint of international law there is no difference between an American citizen and a British subject.

To my mind nationality should be considered from the viewpoint of domestic law, international law, and the rules whereby a particular nationality is proved.

Obviously a thorough discussion of the domestic law of nationality should cover the laws of some one hundred and forty nations. Equally obviously it is not possible to undertake such a discussion in a general text. Hence I will analyze only the American law of nationality. In the course of that analysis I hope, however, that the general principles relating to nationality may emerge.

American nationality can be acquired in a number of different ways --by birth in the United States if not born to a diplomat, by birth to an American father or mother if the residence requirements have been fulfilled, and by naturalization. The current law on the acquisition of nationality by birth constitutes part of the Immigration and Nationality Law of 1952. As amended it appears as Section 1401 of Title 8 of the United States Code. The most important clauses of that section warrant quoting:

> "(a) The following shall be nationals and citizens of the United States at birth:
>
> (1) a person born in the United States, and subject to the jurisdiction thereof;
>
> . . . .
>
> (3) a person born outside of the United States and its outlying possessions of parents both of whom are citizens of the United States and one of whom has had a residence

in the United States or one of its outlying possessions, prior to the birth of such a person;

. . . .

(7) a person born outside the geographical limits of the United States and its outlying possessions of parents one of whom is an alien, and the other a citizen of the United States who, prior to the birth of such person, was physically present in the United States or its outlying possessions for a period or periods totaling not less than ten years, at least five of which were after attaining the age of fourteen years: Provided, That any periods of honorable service in the Armed Forces of the United States, or periods of employment with the United States Governmnt [sic] or with an international organization as that term is defined in section 288 of Title 22 by such citizen parent, or any periods during which such citizen parent is physically present abroad as the dependent un-married son or daughter and a member of the household of a person (A) honorably serving with the Armed Forces of the United States, or (B) employed by the United States Government or an international organization as defined in section 288 of Title 22, may be included in order to satisfy the physical-presence requirement of this para-graph. This proviso shall be applicable to persons born on or after December 24, 1952, to the same extent as if it had become effective in its present form on that date. " (Underlining supplied)

The law at first blush seems needlessly elaborate. The earlier laws were actually much simpler. They varied from time to time but shortly after the beginning of this century they stabilized to provide essentially that American nationality could be obtained by birth in the United States, by birth from an American father, by a woman's marriage to an Ameri-can citizen and by naturalization. In those placid days the family was con-sidered a unit, all of whose members should possess the same nationality. Women were unimportant in terms of transmitting nationality.

Two factors worked against these simple concepts. The first was the equal rights for women movement which did not take kindly to a woman automatically taking the nationality of her husband and looked askance at the idea that only the father could transmit nationality. The other factor was the growing realization that in some instances nationality was being transmitted from father to son to grandson while the family continued to live abroad and were American in name only. It is true that the law pro-vided that the "rights of citizenship shall not descend to children whose fathers have never resided in the United States." Residence, however, was not defined, and Americans residing in an extraterritorial community such as Turkey were deemed to retain their American domicile so that the link to the United States could, in many instances, still be tenuous.

Hence the more modern legislation provided that a parent must have resided in the United States a certain time, and must have had more than a casual link with it before he could transmit his American nationality to his progeny. Moreover, if one of the parents was an alien, the links of the American parent had to be particularly strong.

In an earlier version of the present law it was stipulated flatly that an American parent with an alien spouse could not transmit his nationality to his child unless he had lived ten years of his life in the United States, five of which had to be after the age of fourteen. This was meant to insure that he knew something of the United States at an age of relative maturity. If a person left the United States at age ten and married an alien his links to the United States were considered to be too tenuous to permit nationality to be transmitted. The framers of the law overlooked one important situation. Suppose Joe Doakes, as American as apple pie, born and raised in the heartland of Iowa and belonging to a family that had been American for generations, went into the army on his eighteenth birthday and was promptly shipped to Japan. In Japan he meets and marries the beautiful and feminine Suzuki-san. Nine months later Joe Doakes, Jr., makes his appearance. His father left the United States before he was nineteen so it was mathematically impossible for him to have lived in the United States five years after the age of fourteen. Joe Doakes learns he cannot register his son as an American citizen. By the time the same thing happened to a number of servicemen Congress was ready to act and to include the provision now in the present law that service in the Armed Forces is the same as residence in the United States.

Nationality can also be acquired by naturalization. In a case where new territory is acquired the inhabitants are usually given the right to determine whether they will keep their old citizenship or acquire the citizenship of the new state. The last time this happened as far as the United States is concerned was when the Virgin Islands were acquired from Denmark in 1917. Sometimes the new citizenship has to be positively requested. In other instances the citizenship of the new state is automatically conferred on the inhabitants unless they elect to keep their old allegiance. The end result is the same.

Since America was the land to which emigrants flocked it was natural that the United States favored the right of expatriation, that is, the right to renounce nationality. Obviously it was undesirable to have large numbers of persons still owing allegiance to their former sovereigns even after they had become American citizens. In order to be consistent the American laws on expatriation also had to be liberal. Americans could shed their American nationality with little difficulty. This attitude was not always reciprocated as some states did not permit expatriation. To a limited degree this is still true today.

The Congress went beyond permitting voluntary expatriation and established a long list of factors which would result in the loss of American
nationality irrespective of the wishes of the individual concerned. Moreover a distinction was made between native born and naturalized citizens.
The latter could lose their American nationality by extensive residence
abroad.

Among the many ways in which nationality could be lost were voting
in a foreign election, serving in a foreign army unless compelled to do so,
and deserting from the American army. The law had some rather strange
results. After World War II a number of Italo-Americans went back to
Italy and voted in an Italian election to help turn back the Communist threat.
They were under the impression that they were acting as patriotic Americans doing their bit to support the free world. Instead they lost their
American citizenship. The same thing happened in Japan. Congress had
to legislate readmitting them to citizenship.

At the present time the situation has changed radically as the result
of several court decisions to the effect that it is unconstitutional to make
a distinction between naturalized and native-born citizens and that the withdrawal of nationality cannot be used as a form of punishment. Since, however, the composition of the Supreme Court is changing, it is possible
that the trend of decisions favoring the individual in matters of nationality
will be reversed. An indication of that trend is the action of the Supreme
Court in upholding that portion of the law which requires an American born
abroad of one alien parent to establish a residence in the United States on
reaching maturity in order to preserve his American nationality. The
case of Rogers v. Bellei decided April 5, 1971, makes a curious distinction between citizens born or naturalized in the United States and citizens
born abroad of an American parent or parents. It was a 5 to 4 decision
with the minority very critical of the majority opinion.

It is quite clear that under various national laws an individual can
have more than one nationality. I can envision a situation in which a per
son could have four nationalities although I have never heard of such a
case. But suppose countries A, B, and C have laws concerning the acquisition of nationality similar to those of the United States. Let us assume a female child is born in A, of a father possessing the nationality
of B and of a mother who is a national of C. On reaching maturity she
marries a national of State D under whose law a wife automatically ac-
quires the nationality of the husband. She has all four nationalities unless
she specifically renounces some of them.

Conversely it is equally possible for a person to lose the one nationality he possesses and not to acquire any other or to become stateless.
There have been many instances when refugees from a country lost that
country's nationality without acquiring any other. Hitler deprived the
Jews of German nationality and left thousands stateless. But it also can
occur through the routine application of laws. If, for example, a female
from the hypothetical State D married an American she might lose her

own nationality as a result of the marriage and yet not acquire American nationality.

As a consequence the world is full of dual nationals and stateless persons. In some cases double nationality might permit a person to take advantage of two nationalities and even to travel on two sets of passports. Generally speaking, however, particularly for men, double nationality can create problems. One of the worst is the possibility of having to do military service in both countries. Nations are inclined to punish persons who have failed to perform military service even after the age of service has passed.

I remember a rather uneasy moment I spent in Bilbao, Spain. I should explain that I was born in Spain while my father was with the American Legation. My passport merely showed my birth in Madrid. When I presented it on collecting my steamship ticket at the shipping agency on whose ship I was returning home, there was a long telephone conversation, only part of which I could hear. Whether rightly or wrongly, I jumped to the conclusion that the shipping agent was discussing my case with the police. Fortunately nothing happened.

To eliminate the necessity of service in two countries the United States has entered into agreements with a number of states, the one with Sweden being typical. It provides:

"Article 1. A person possessing the nationality of both the High Contracting Parties who habitually resides in the territory of one of them and who is in fact most closely connected with that Party shall be exempt from all military obligations in the territory of the other Party."

Another great inconvenience to double nationality is that neither of the states involved can protect their citizens against injustice in the other state. The theory is that a state can treat its nationals as it pleases and if they happen to be nationals of another state that is irrelevant. To use a concrete example, the United States cannot protect one of its citizens who suffers mistreatment in Italy if he happens to be an Italian national as well. The reverse is also true.

The rule mentioned above has suffered some modification in cases before arbitral tribunals established to pass upon individual claims. The emerging concept is that the claims tribunal will look at the effective or dominant nationality of the claimant. The most recent case was one that I presented as Agent of the United States to the Italian-United States Conciliation Commission. In that case the claimant was the American wife of an Italian diplomat. During the war they had been stationed in Tokyo and she had travelled on an Italian passport. (Travelling on an American passport in Japan would not have been very healthy.) The Commission taking these and other factors into consideration concluded that she was more Italian than American and denied her claim. If, however, her predominant ties had been to the United States the result would have been different.

Actually I had hoped to win the case on another theory. The Treaty of Peace with Italy on whose basis the claim was brought specified that claims could be brought by United Nations nationals. (In the Treaty of Peace the word United Nations was used to mean the signers of the United Nations Declaration made during the course of the war, so in effect "allied national" was meant.) I argued that the Treaty constituted a departure from international law and that Italy could not interpose the defense of Italian nationality. So strong, however, was the Commission's feeling on this subject that my argument, which I still believe has validity, got nowhere. In Joe Jacobs' classic phrase "We was robbed."

Problems of statelessness can be even more severe. The individual lacking a state does not have a state to protect him abroad. If he travels there is no state to give him a passport.

At least some of the difficulty was alleviated in the days of the League of Nations. Stateless persons were given a so-called Nansen passport that permitted travel. This practice, although continued by the United Nations, helps the stateless person but it does not solve his basic difficulties.

One of the problems related to nationality is proving it. When an American citizen goes abroad he usually presents a passport to the Immigration authorities on his return attesting his right to reenter. He does not need a passport to visit some countries, for example Canada and Mexico, so on his return proves his American citizenship by voter registration cards or other documents attesting to his American citizenship.

Arbitral tribunals are inclined to be more formal and to require more definitive proof than a passport. The reason is simple. If state A establishes a claim commission with State B entitling the citizens of that state to bring claims against state A, a citizen of state C can draw no advantage from the arrangement. If, however, a little judicious bribery can obtain him a passport from state B he could present a claim, assuming the passport were sufficient proof of nationality. Hence claims commissions have been inclined to insist that the facts creating the nationality, for example birth in the state bringing the claim, be established by adequate evidence such as a birth certificate. Not all commissions are that technical. In Italy the Italian government was willing to accept my statement as Agent of the United States that the claimant before the Italian-United States Conciliation Commission was an American citizen. Had the roles been reversed I doubt if I would have been that trusting.

Generally speaking a nation has full liberty to determine who are its nationals. Nevertheless it cannot unreasonably force its nationality on an alien. Thus efforts by some states to give their nationality to purchasers of land has given rise to protests. Likewise, in an international adjudication, a court does not have to accept a nationality that is based on a flimsy foundation. In the famous Nottebohm case, a German residing in Guatemala decided that it would be a good thing in view of the

imminence of World War II to acquire another nationality. His reasoning
was based on the entirely sound premise that Guatemala would declare war
on Germany, that as a German he would become an enemy alien and his
property would be sequestrated. Having a brother in Liechtenstein who
obviously had influence, he managed after a very short stay in Liechtenstein to acquire Liechtenstein citizenship. Everything happened as he had
envisaged except that the Guatemalans refused to consider him a bona fide
Liechtensteiner. Liechtenstein brought a case on his behalf before the
World Court which sustained Guatemala, establishing the principle that an
international court can look into the bona fides of nationality. This is a
step beyond requiring proof of nationality, for in that case there was no
doubt that nationality had been conferred.

Up until quite recently it was generally conceded that a state was the
final interpreter of its nationality laws. It could not claim a person to be
a national if the facts revealed that he did not qualify and under the Nottebohm case could not claim on behalf of a national whose nationality was obviously dubious. Now, however, there is some doubt whether a state is
the final interpreter of its own laws. The problem came up in the Flegenheimer case submitted to the Italian-United States Conciliation Commission. In that case the claimant, Mr. Flegenheimer, had been born on what
became territory of the German Empire following the unification of Germany. His father had been an American national by naturalization at the
time Albert was born. Albert stayed on in Germany until driven out by the
persecution of the Jews. He then went to Italy and in turn had to leave that
country. He finally made his way to the United States where he discovered
that he might be an American citizen. The question hinged on early American laws and on the so-called Bancroft treaties between the United States
and the German states. Suffice it to say that the Department of Justice
ruled that Albert was an American citizen and had been one since his birth.
When the case was presented to the Commission, the Italian Agent challenged
the American interpretation of American law. The Commission examined
the law and found in favor of Italy. This, in turn, was a step beyond the
Nottebohm case as the Commission took it upon itself to interpret American law.

In essence, therefore, nationality can be challenged in an international court either on the fact or the law and on its bona fides.

Chapter XIII
NATIONALITY OF VESSELS AND LEGAL ENTITIES

The possession of nationality is not restricted to individuals. Legal entities and vessels are likewise considered to have a nationality of their own. (I use the term "legal entity" in preference to "corporation" for the simple reason that under the civil law, in contrast to common law, partnerships as well as corporations have a legal entity and, therefore, nationality. As, however, the rules governing the nationality of a partnership are quite similar to those governing the nationality of a corporation, I shall henceforth, for the sake of simplicity, refer to corporations alone.)

The most common test of the nationality of a corporation is its place of incorporation, that is, where it is chartered. In a good many instances this test is used in treaties to determine nationality.

If the charter is granted by a unit of a federal state as, for example, Delaware in the United States, the nationality of the corporation is that of the federal state--in the case of Delaware, the United States. Unfortunately, the test is not always adequate. Under some laws it is very easy for foreigners to acquire all of the shares of a locally chartered corporation with the possible exception of a small number of qualifying shares. In such a case the corporation is a domestic one in name only. In essence it is an organization of aliens.

During World War I the British were faced with the problem of how to treat a British corporation that was almost, if not entirely, German owned. There was a strong incentive to consider it to be German to permit the vesting of its property, that is, the taking of its assets as alien property. A British court therefore permitted what is technically known as "piercing the corporate veil," or looking behind the facade of the charter, and determining the real parties in interest who, of course, were German. As a consequence the owners were unable to hide their identity behind a corporate fiction.

For somewhat the same reasons the Department of State will not prosecute a claim on behalf of a corporation unless there is some proof that it is substantially owned by American citizens. Otherwise the Department would be spending the taxpayer's money in prosecuting a claim for the benefit of aliens. Hence even under such treaties as the Treaty of Peace with Italy which defined the nationality of a corporation by reference to its place of incorporation, the Department of State demanded proof of the nationality of the stockholders before it permitted the filing of a claim on behalf of a corporation under that treaty.

92

From what has been said it would appear that if the place of incorporation is considered inadequate as a test, one can look at the nationality of the stockholders to determine the true nationality of a corporation. Unfortunately, in some cases, this criterion raises all sorts of practical difficulties. In certain international corporations the stock may be widely held by divergent national groups. If a corporation has its stock held by Swiss, Germans, French and Americans, in more or less equal proportions, how can one use the nationality of its stockholders to determine the nationality of that corporation? Furthermore, if this test were used, the nationality of a corporation might shift with the transfer of blocks of stock. The problems become even more difficult with corporations having bearer shares whose transfer is not registered on the books of the corporation. It may be next to impossible at any given time to determine who are the stockholders.

A recent case decided by the International Court of Justice, the Barcelona Traction case, is instructive. In that case the Belgian government tried to bring a claim for alleged losses sustained by the Barcelona Traction Company, a corporation organized in Canada, at the hands of the Spanish authorities. The Belgian government predicated its right to submit the claim on the ground that 88 per cent of the stockholders were Belgian nationals whose interests it was entitled to protect. The Court refused, however, to recognize the right of Belgium to bring the case on behalf of its nationals.

Because the two tests which have just been discussed have proved to be insufficient, still other criteria have been suggested. Thus it has been proposed that the principal place of business should be an important test of nationality. This is not always very realistic as a corporation can establish itself abroad for purpose of business convenience without acquiring the attributes of the country where it has its head office.

Another proposal is that the nationality of corporations be determined by the principal place of operation, that is, the place where the activity of a corporation largely takes place. If this test is applied strictly, this would mean that a corporation incorporated in Delaware with American stockholders and with its principal place of business in New York would be considered a Saudi Arabian corporation since its principal activity, that of extracting oil, takes place in Saudi Arabia. On the face of it, it is clear that this test can also be inadequate.

As a result of the inconsistencies and the lack of definitiveness of any one particular method of determining nationality, it has sometimes been suggested that all of the facts discussed above should be taken into consideration, and that each case should be judged on its own merits. There is much to be said for such a suggestion, even though its application can often present practical difficulties. One therefore has to conclude that there is no one certain and unchallenged method for determining the nationality of a corporation, although the place of incorporation is usually controlling. A great deal depends upon the terms of treaties governing corporations

having interests or doing business in more than one country. The problem
is particularly acute in Europe.

As stated in the beginning part of this chapter, vessels also have their
nationality depending upon their place of registry. All vessels fly the flag
of the state of their registry and adopt a port of that state as their home
port. The name of that port is always shown on the stern of the vessel immediately under the name of the vessel. Sometimes the reference to the
home port may seem somewhat strained if one takes into account that the
ship may never see that port. Swiss sea-going vessels, for example, are
hardly likely to be able to navigate the Rhine to reach the port of Basel.
Moreover it is very dubious whether some of the vessels registered under
the Liberian flag ever see Monrovia.

There are several states which have induced the registration of vessels under their flag by offering relatively favorable terms to a ship owner,
that is, they provide what are known as "flags of convenience." At one time
the favorite flags of convenience were Liberian, Panamanian, Honduran,
and Costa Rican. Now, according to information supplied to me by the
Maritime Administration, the Honduran and Costa Rican flags are no longer
in general use. On the other hand, the flags of Lebanon and Cyprus are
being used for the same purpose. A list of the merchant marines of today
shows that Liberia stands in first place in terms of both gross and dead
weight tonnage, with Panama also having a sizeable fleet.

The reasons for using a flag of convenience are many. Thus an American ship owner, to avoid high union wages, may have registered his ship
under a foreign flag. Moreover, the laws of the states permitting registration on such favorable terms may be fairly lenient with regard to standards on board ship. Nor can the tax angle be overlooked completely for
a Liberian or Panamanian tax on a ship may be far less than the corresponding tax under the laws of what would normally be the vessel's home
state.

As may be expected, there has been considerable discussion and a
certain amount of outrage concerning flags of convenience, and in the Geneva Convention on the High Seas, discussed more fully in the chapter on
the Law of the Sea, it was agreed that there should be some link between
the vessel and the state registering the vessel. The convention specifically
provided:

> "Each state shall fix the conditions for the grant of its na-
> tionality to ships, for the registration of ships in its terri-
> tory, and for the right to fly its flag. Ships have the na-
> tionality of the State whose flag they are entitled to fly.
> There must exist a genuine link between the State and the
> ship; in particular, the State must effectively exercise its
> jurisdiction and control in administrative, technical and
> social matters over ships flying its flag."

A comparison has even been made between the link of nationality that binds a state and an individual as discussed in the Nottebohm case and the link of nationality in the case of vessels.

Obviously the law of nationality of vessels is not always crystal clear which nevertheless does not derogate from the importance of determining that nationality. For one thing, as has been pointed out in an earlier chapter, a nation can exercise jurisdiction over crimes committed on board one of its ships. Yet when the link is dubious and the ship never goes to its home port, as has been previously indicated, how can this basic principle of law find practical application?

Chapter XIV
THE RESPONSIBILITY OF STATES

A state has the theoretical right to exclude foreigners, to prohibit them from acquiring property within its borders, and to forbid its own nationals from dealing with aliens. In practice such a retreat into seclusion would be unthinkable for any modern state. Not since Japan under the Tokugawa regime retreated into its cocoon well over three hundred years ago has an important nation tried to keep completely aloof from the world. Japan's isolation was destroyed in 1853 when Commodore Matthew Perry landed at the mouth of the Bay of Tokyo. Since then all but the most remote and inaccessible principalities or sheikdoms have taken part in the ebb and flow of international life. Nations presently vie to attract qualified emigrants, to lure tourists, and to entice foreign investors. Moreover, they are bound by innumerable treaties whose terms would be inconsistent with a policy of national withdrawal.

Once having permitted foreigners to enter its territory personally or through investments and acquisitions of property, a state has a certain obligation to protect them and their property from harm. That obligation can take the positive form of making certain that the alien does not suffer injustice at the hands of the government and its agencies, and the negative form of providing him with a reasonable degree of protection from the unlawful acts of private individuals. Moreover, if that protection fails, a state must endeavor to apprehend and punish the guilty parties.

Obviously, the duty to protect is not at all the same thing as an absolute guarantee against harm. No government, however well run, can prevent crime altogether, and it is not expected to provide a personal bodyguard to every tourist. The alien's own action may have a bearing on a state's responsibility. If the alien insists on going into the wilds and exploring areas known to be infested by cannibals, his widow's only satisfaction, if he is found by the cannibals, will be that he has reduced their protein deficiency.

The commission of a wrong against the foreigner or the failure to extend to him the protection to which he is entitled, entails an obligation to make compensation to the injured party or, if he is dead, to his estate. The state whose national was injured has a right to present a claim for the losses suffered. The theory of such a claim is that the state was indirectly injured in the person of its national. The eighteenth century Swiss jurist Vattel gave that theory currency saying:

"Whoever ill-treats a citizen indirectly injures the State which must protect that citizen. The sovereign of the injured citizen must avenge the deed and, if possible, force the aggressor to give full satisfaction or punish him, since otherwise the citizen will not obtain the chief end of civil society, which is protection."

In some cases a nation may truly be hurt by losing a national. If a great atomic scientist on a holiday abroad is killed through the failure of the state he is visiting to afford him protection, his own state may indeed suffer a loss. In other cases the theory is manifestly twaddle. There are unfortunately persons who, after a lifetime of service to their government, retire abroad on a substantial pension. They nevertheless criticize their country and government unmercifully. Can it truly be said that the nation to which they nominally belong suffers a loss if they pass from the scene?

Moreover, other than in rare instances, the government making the claim does it on behalf of the injured party and turns over to him any payment it may receive. One of the few cases to the contrary stemmed from the sinking of the Canadian rum runner I'm Alone in circumstances that made the American government liable. In that case the Canadian government collected both on behalf of the crew and of itself. That case, however, is an exception to prove the rule. Usually the government's only compensation is the knowledge that it has successfully protected its citizens.

It would be much more honest and straightforward to admit that the theory of having to compensate for internationally illegal acts is based on a fiction and that the real reason for insistence on retribution is that the fear of having to pay damages may be a deterrent to illegal conduct, or put inversely, a spur to living up to international obligations. Moreover the poor victim should be compensated and it seems only just that the delinquent government should bear the brunt.

So long as the practice is recognized as a fiction no harm is done. If Tunisia can, by resort to a fiction, decree that a man can have only one wife, why should not international law also rely on fiction to reach a desired end? After all fictions have been widely used to develop law.

Another example of a fiction is provided by the rule that the failure to apprehend and punish an offender against an alien gives him or, if he is dead, his successor, the right to demand damages. The argument is that the failure to punish causes grief and anguish, a highly dubious proposition in some cases.

The leading case on the subject is the Janes case. In that instance an American was murdered in cold blood by a Mexican. The Mexican authorities did virtually nothing to capture the murderer who rather leisurely escaped into the hills. The Mexican-American Claims Commission of 1923 to which the claim was brought adjudged that the grief and sorrow suffered by Mrs. Janes, by reason of the failure of the Mexican authorities to punish her husband's assailant, entitled her to a money reward.

There is no reason to doubt that Mrs. Janes really was distressed that the murderer remained unpunished. But suppose that in a similar case the Mexican Agent had been able to produce a letter from the widow to a friend saying, "I hear that my husband was killed in Mexico. I'd like to pin a medal on the man who did it. My husband was a skunk, leaving me to starve with five children while he went to Mexico with some blonde floozy he picked up at a bar."

Would such a letter have been given any weight? I doubt it very much. In one actual case the Mexican Government argued that an award should not be made to an incompetent who could not possibly have had the mental facilities to know that a crime had remained unpunished.

Here again we see the wholly legitimate concept of using a fiction to invoke a penalty against a government which has failed in its duty; the unrebuttable fiction being, of course, that in every case there is grief and sorrow.

The responsibility of states can be looked upon from the nature of the act supposedly making a nation liable. It can be a default in a contract obligation or a wrongful act or what in law is known as "tort." Responsibility can also be looked upon from the standpoint of the agency or individual whose act is the basis of complaint.

Taking the last sentence first, responsibility can be attributed to the acts of the executive, judicial or legislative branches of government. A legislature can capriciously abrogate a contract concession to the detriment of a foreigner, and a corrupt court can render a decision against a foreigner that is obviously partial and prejudiced. Usually, however, responsibility is engendered by the executive as that branch of the government normally executes the laws and is in greatest daily contact with the foreigner. It is also that branch of the government that provides protection to a foreigner.

It does not matter whether the branch of the government accused of wrongdoing is federal or state, national or provincial. A federal union may consider that there are sharp lines of demarcation between the central government and the authorities of the constituent states or provinces. In international law, however, all authorities whether federal or state, central or local, engage the responsibility of the state. Otherwise a state whose citizens have been offended would have little recourse since it can complain diplomatically only to the national authorities.

Nations, including at times the United States, have attempted to plead their lack of responsibility on the ground that local officials over whom they did not have constitutional control were the offenders. Such efforts have not been very successful.

On one famous occasion in the last century a mob broke into the jail at New Orleans and lynched some Italians suspected of connections with the Mafia while the police stood by and did little to prevent the killings. The United States tried to deny responsibility but finally paid compensation.

The duty to provide protection rises in proportion to the importance of the individual or property being protected. Thus a nation should exercise greater care in protecting an ambassador and an embassy than a private individual and a private dwelling. Even here, however, the obligation is not absolute for no system has been devised which is proof against a cunning fanatic or against a mob suddenly aroused. A state that failed to afford protection when it knew that an embassy would be attacked would be responsible, but not if it had no forewarning of the attack and there was no reason to suspect danger.

In recent years Ambassador Edwin O. Reischauer was wounded by a Japanese zealot. The Japanese government paid the bills for his hospitalization, but it was never suggested that Japan was internationally liable. In 1968 Ambassador John Gordon Mein was assassinated by guerillas in Guatemala. Again, since there was little the government in Guatemala could have done to prevent the crime, Guatemala was not considered to be internationally responsible.

A very real question arises with regard to the duty of a state to ransom a kidnapped diplomat by the release of political prisoners. Failure to do so resulted in the death of the German envoy to Guatemala. Was Guatemala internationally responsible? More recently an Israeli Consul in Turkey met his death at the hands of kidnappers.

The nature of the offense giving rise to responsibility can be infinite in its variety. It could be an instance where a policeman maltreated an alien, or an instance where an alien was unlawfully jailed or kept under conditions incompatible with normal standards of civilization, or it could be, as indicated in a prior paragraph, the result of a miscarriage of justice in a court.

Generally speaking, a nation is responsible for the acts of its officials. Nevertheless when the official is acting in a purely private capacity and not as a representative of the state, there can be a very real question as to the responsibility of the state. Thus if a policeman on his day off mistreats an alien against whom he has a personal grudge, it is very dubious whether the state should be responsible. In order to avoid responsibility, however, the state must provide a court or other forum in which the individual maltreated may seek a remedy for the injury suffered by him. Needless to say, it is sometimes very difficult to draw the exact line between action that gives rise to responsibility and action which may be highly detrimental to an individual but does not invoke the responsibility of the state.

In a previous paragraph I referred to the theory that a state should not subject a prisoner to treatment below a certain standard of civilization. Yet what is the standard and is it always uniform? In a country with a winter climate does not heat its jail cells in winter time, is that a cause for complaint when most houses are also unheated? How bad must the food be in a jail in order to give rise to a legitimate claim that the rights of an imprisoned alien have been violated?

I have also referred in the past to claims resulting from contract. One claim that was advanced very often in the past was predicated on the default of a nation or one of its political subdivisions on a bond issue. Since some states were, as a result of revolution, often going bankrupt, there were nearly always some such claims pending. Generally speaking, governments have been rather chary of encouraging such claims and particularly, taking up the cudgels in behalf of the claimant. Bonds of foreign countries are often bought at bargain rates more or less as a speculation. Moreover any person dealing with a foreign government should evaluate the risks before he invests his money.

There also have been a large number of claims based upon the breach of ordinary contracts as, for example, a contract to sell locomotives to a government or upon the arbitrary abrogation of a concession permitting the exploitation and exportation of minerals. Here again governments are somewhat reluctant to present the claims for the claimant should have known what he was doing and the risks that he was taking. Furthermore, most states allow themselves to be sued on the contract and the claimant must do what he can to seek redress in local courts or, in technical terms, to exhaust legal remedies, before he turns to his government for assistance.

It would nevertheless be a mistake to say that contract claims in the field of international law are a thing of the past. There are still undoubtedly instances when a valid claim may arise as a result of an alleged breach of contract between a government and an alien although they are not as numerous as claims based on wrongful acts.

The responsibility of a state normally arises out of actions taking place in its own territory. This is not necessarily so. An agency of a government operating abroad can cause injury as well as an agency operating at home. When an American airplane dropped unexploded atom bombs in Spanish territory there was little doubt that the American Government was responsible. On the basis of the same principle nations have been developing a system of international responsibility whereby damage resulting from objects in space dropping on populated centers would receive compensation.

Nations are understandably reluctant to accept responsibility in instances where they are not legally liable. Once in a while a so-called ex gratia cash payment is made to compensate an alien as a gesture of good will. Usually those are instances where a government is liable but will not admit it and the other government is willing to settle on the basis of compensation without forcing a decision on the legality of the demand. There is nevertheless at least one exception to this rule. The United States Armed Forces realized during the last war that it would be a matter of good public policy to pay for damages resulting from the action of American military in non-military operations. Hence a law was enacted permitting the armed forces to settle claims irrespective of the legal liability of the United States. In fact, a very large number of such claims have been paid under the provision of that Congressional legislation.

It would be too much to say that this action of the United States has crystallized into an international rule. Nevertheless it seems to me to be an important development in the field of international responsibility.

A difficult question arises at this point. Does a government that makes a voluntary payment have to make it to everyone in a similar situation? I had that problem facing me in Japan when the Commission on which I sat was faced with a demand for compensation on some Japanese government bonds. What had happened was that during the course of the two world wars the real value of the bonds had fallen drastically with the depreciation of the currencies in which they were payable. Wishing to maintain its foreign credit the Japanese government was willing to pay holders of bonds circulating abroad on a far more favorable basis than that used in paying persons holding the same bonds circulating in Japan. An American company that had posted some of the bonds as a deposit in Japan claimed discrimination. We decided that where the alleged discrimination had a basis, as in this case, there was no claim. I am sure, however, that if the discrimination had been arbitrary, say blue-eyed bond holders would be paid at a higher rate than brown-eyed bond holders, we would have had second thoughts.

In general, the field of responsibility of states is a very broad one and unanswered and sometimes unanswerable questions arise constantly. One of them concerns the right of a state to expropriate or confiscate, without adequate payment, the property of foreigners in pursuance of real or alleged social reforms as, for example, agrarian reform. Confiscating states have argued that private property must yield to social progress. A number of such confiscations have taken place in both the Communist world and the developing countries, and others are undoubtedly in the offing. The most that one can say with any definitiveness concerning the law on the subject is that the attitude of the United States is likely to be different from that of India or of a Communist regime.

Chapter XV

THE PROTECTION OF NATIONALS

The protection of nationals, as that term is habitually used, is the reverse side of the responsibility of states. It concerns the measures taken by a state to obtain fair treatment for its citizens in other lands and to see that they are compensated for such injuries as they may sustain at the hands of a foreign state for which the latter is responsible. The term can also have a broader connotation and include all measures taken by a government and its agencies to assist its nationals when they meet with difficulties abroad. Such difficulties may have nothing to do with the responsibility of states in the usual sense of the term. For example, when a destitute seaman has to be repatriated from abroad, there is no responsibility on the part of the state where he is stranded. When an American dies, the American Consul intervenes to make certain that the property of the deceased is safeguarded and that his body is shipped home if the family so desires. This is protection in the broad sense of the term.

First I will consider protection in the narrow or usual sense, that is, trying to make certain that an alien does not suffer an injury at the hands of a foreign state or that, if he does, the government of that state makes amends. In practice this means that diplomatic and consular officers must exercise preventive action to forestall the happening of events which would give rise to responsibility in addition to providing assistance in making claims for injustices that have taken place.

Thus it has long been an obligation of the American Consul to visit local jails to determine that the treatment of Americans is up to standard and that their rights are protected. Most consular conventions contain a provision with regard to the right of a consul to visit prisoners in jails. In the recent Consular Convention with Japan the pertinent article reads:

"(1) The appropriate authorities of the receiving state shall, at the request of any national of the sending state who is confined in prison awaiting trial or is otherwise detained in custody within his consular district, immediately inform a consular officer of the sending state. A consular officer shall be permitted to visit without delay, to converse privately with, and to arrange legal representation for any national of the sending state who is so confined or detained. Any communication from such a national to the consular officer shall be forwarded without undue delay by the authorities of the receiving state.

(2) Where a national of the sending state has been convicted and is serving a sentence of imprisonment, a consular officer in whose consular district the sentence is being served shall, upon notification to the appropriate authorities of the receiving state, have the right to visit him in prison. Any such visit shall be conducted in accordance with prison regulations, which shall permit reasonable access to and opportunity of conversing with such national. The consular officer shall also be allowed, subject to the prison regulations, to transmit communications between the prisoner and other persons."

A consular officer who takes his work seriously will cultivate a friendly rapport with the prosecutor's office and with the police so that he can have a good working relationship with those branches of the government and nip potential complaints in the bud.

This does not mean at all that a consular officer should intervene when there is good cause for the imprisonment or detention of one of his co-citizens. In some cases the last thing that an American Consul would want is to have all constraints lifted from an American citizen. Lest he seem hard-hearted, it may be well to mention the continuing problem of the FTJ's or seamen who fail to join their ships. What happens is that an American seaman, or for that matter any seaman, as this is not a fault restricted to Americans, comes ashore on a shore pass issued by the local immigration authorities, then proceeds to become rousingly drunk, and at the time of the sailing of the ship is safely ensconced in the arms of some local beauty. If the ship sails without him, quite possibly short-handed, the immigration authorities, knowing he has not joined his ship, start looking for him as an illegal entrant and, when he is found, the agent for the shipping company and the consul have to find means to repatriate him. If during the time he is awaiting repatriation he is free to roam around and visit additional bars, word gets around quite quickly in the merchant marine that such-and-such a port is a good port in which to miss ship. American consuls are, therefore, by no means discontent to have FTJ's held in detention so long, of course, as they are not maltreated. By the same token if a nation failed to control and punish drug addicts and vendors, it could become a Mecca for American drug users and vendors who would scarcely be welcomed by American Consular officers.

When an injury has occurred to an alien for which a state is responsible, a diplomatic protest can be made through official embassy channels to the Foreign Office. That protest can include a request for compensation or for remedial action. In some instances, although they may not be very numerous, the Foreign Office may recognize the justice of the complaint and heed the request. In other instances the case may have to be referred back to the Department of State for further consideration. The Department may decide to present a claim through diplomatic channels. On the other hand it may consider that the claim is insubstantial or that it would be a sheer waste of time, because of political considerations, to try to persuade the offending government to pay. In the latter case the claim will be hopefully filed in the Department's archives for future reference in case there is a general understanding later on between the two countries for a settlement of outstanding demands.

Such understandings do occur. They can take the form of a claims tribunal to hear the claim or, sometimes, a series of claims. We have, for example, had several arbitral tribunals with Mexico which did decide on a number of cases and made awards to substantial groups of claimants. The other possibility is to reach a lump sum settlement on all claims outstanding with a foreign government and then divide the proceeds from that settlement among the claimants. For that purpose the Congress has established the Foreign Claims Settlement Commission which has recently distributed funds derived from lump sum agreements with several of the Communist states.

The newest development in this picture is to have the Foreign Claims Settlement Commission decide on the merit of the claims in advance of their submission to a foreign government so as to guide the Department of State in ascertaining the amount that should be claimed. From my own viewpoint the method has advantages and disadvantages. It gives the Department a much clearer picture of how much should be demanded. In the past when it was largely a matter of guesswork and compromise, the amounts that were paid were often insufficient. On the other hand, I am afraid that the present system will give the claimant the idea that he will actually receive the amount the Foreign Claims Settlement Commission awarded.

The foreign government can assert that in the Foreign Claims Settlement Commission it never had an opportunity to be heard so that the merits of the claims were determined by a body essentially friendly to the claimant rather than in what is known as adversary proceedings. If the claimant then does not receive what he considers to be due him he will be quite disappointed. This is a method that is now being tried on a series of claims against Cuba. Time will tell how it works.

The lump sum settlement compromise has many advantages. It is quicker than the usual claims procedure, and the entire matter can be settled without the potential rancor of individual claims. It is a method the United States has used many times. Part of the purchase price of Louisiana was in effect a lump sum settlement, that is, the United States assumed the obligation to pay American claimants for losses suffered at the hands of the French during the early Napoleonic wars.

When a claim has to be presented individually to a government through diplomatic channels, the Department of State will look at it quite carefully and will not espouse it unless it is a manifestly good claim. Where the claim is presented to an established arbitral commission, the Department is likely to be far more lenient with the claimant on the theory that there is a body in existence whose specific task is to determine the validity of claims, and that a claimant should be entitled to his day in court before that body. This does not mean, of course, that a government is entitled to present to a claims commission spurious or tainted claims for it has the preliminary responsibility of winnowing out claims that for one reason or another are completely insubstantial. As I have just said, however, where there is some substance to a claim, even though the claim may be dubious from a legal standpoint, the American representative before the arbitral tribunal will be instructed to present the claim.

From a psychological standpoint there is also something to be said for this approach. If the United States presented only cases that were one hundred percent perfect, the Commissioners, including the American Commissioner, would necessarily have to rule in favor of the United States in all instances. This might give a totally erroneous impression as to the actual impartiality of the Commission. As a member of a Commission I welcomed an occasional bad case which permitted me to rule in favor of the opposing government. This does not mean that I would not have ruled in favor of the United States if I had been convinced of the justice of every claim. But I was just as glad that I did not have to do so.

The protection of nationals by the United States and the major powers of Europe during the nineteenth century and the beginning of the twentieth century was often accompanied by threats and, in some instances, the use of force. When a number of claims were being pressed against Venezuela by various foreign nationals at the turn of the century, Great Britain, Germany and Italy sent warships to blockade the Venezuelan coast and, on one or two occasions, to bombard Venezuelan territory.

A number of other instances could be cited of the landing of forces to collect debts or to enforce claims. Naturally, this was a situation that was not relished very greatly by the weaker states. For the major part those weaker states during the nineteenth century were the Latin American states since the other portions of the world were largely held under colonial domination. In many of the Latin American states perpetual revolution and weak and unstable governments led to confusion and further exacerbated the situation. In some instances the action of the more powerful states resulted, in some degree at least, in the establishment of a regime in favor of their citizens which was somewhat akin to extraterritoriality. During the long dictatorship of Porfirio Diaz in Mexico before and after the turn of the century, it was commonly acknowledged that the foreigner was in a favored position.

The Latin American states were in no position to meet force with force. Hence they tried to develop theories of international law which would diminish the right of a state to intervene on behalf of its nationals.

One of the most important of the theories designed to curb diplomatic interposition or the interjection of a state on behalf of its citizens, is that an alien cannot expect to receive better treatment than a national. If he runs afoul of the law and is put into jail where there are cockroaches five inches long, he has, according to this theory, no complaint if a native likewise has to contend with the same cockroaches.

The powers endeavoring to press the welfare of their citizens abroad did not agree, holding that there was a minimum standard of treatment established by international law. Unfortunately, it was sometimes very difficult to determine the precise limits of that minimum standard particularly as in some areas it is clear that physical facilities, from the very circumstances of the situation, cannot be, to put it mildly, very luxurious. Thus it is too much to expect that a small and isolated town in the highlands of Nicaragua would have the same amenities in its jail as a jail in a larger town.

Needless to say, the argument as to what is adequate treatment and whether or not a nation is bound to afford an alien better treatment than its own nationals results in endless disputes, many of them inconclusive.

In addition to relying on the concept of national treatment, Latin American nations enunciated various other doctrines designed to curb diplomatic protection. Thus an Argentine writer on international law, Luis Drago, argued that there should not be any intervention for the collection of public debts. That doctrine was accepted to the extent that at the Second Hague Convention in 1907 the nations agreed that the collection of contract debts by force, as had so often happened in the past, would be severely circumscribed.

Another Argentine writer, Carlos Calvo, went further than Drago and made the point that there should not be any diplomatic intervention for damages resulting from revolution and domestic uprisings. The Latin American nations then proceeded to take Calvo's theory, which had become known as the Calv Doctrine, and to apply it in concrete terms by requiring every alien making a contract with one of their governments to renounce diplomatic interposition in advance. The renunciatory provision became known as the Calvo clause. There is a considerable question whether an individual can bind his government not to intervene as there might be instances when the government, to maintain a principle, would want to interpose irrespective of the wishes of the individual.

There is also a question as to the effect of such a clause on the presentation of a claim to international tribunals. On this point there are widely diversified opinions among the arbitral tribunals considering the problem. The more recent cases seem to indicate that if there had been a real denial of justice and the resources of the local courts had been exhausted the clause would be inoperable. This does not mean that the issue is finally settled.

As the Latin American countries acquired additional experience they made a further modification in the Calvo clause stipulating that if diplomatic protection were requested, the contract or the concession, as the case may be, would be subject to cancellation.

It can be readily seen that such a clause might act as a serious limitation on the willingness of an alien to seek the protection of his government. Naturally, if the contract or concession has been cancelled as a whole the alien has nothing to lose by asking for interposition. Moreover the total cancellation of a contract or concession would presumably also result in the cancellation of the Calvo clause since it is part of the contract. There may be instances, however, where an alien holding a concession from a foreign government containing a Calvo clause suffers some injustice rather than risk the loss of a profitable concession. For example, a concessionaire may have a lucrative agricultural concession with the right to own land and buildings. In a period when the concession is bringing in considerable returns the government runs a road through the property and, in the process, condemns a building by eminent domain for which it pays an amount considered to be wholly insufficient by the concessionaire. From a practical standpoint would any lawyer advise his client to seek diplomatic protection when it might result in the loss of the entire concession?

Even though the Latin American states tried to develop interpretations of international law which would curtail the rights of powers seeking to protect their nationals, the Latin American lawyers were too steeped in the traditions of European law, which was part and parcel of their heritage, to consider that international law, or at least certain segments of it, might not apply to them. This has not been altogether true in some of the new states of Asia or Africa which believe that they have little or nothing to do with the development of international law which was based on the Judeo-Christian tradition and that, as a consequence, some portions of the law may not be applicable to them. In particular, they consider that part of international law which protects the sanctity of private property is not appropriate in instances where private property must be taken for social reforms. On this point the views of an Indian jurist writing in the American Journal of International Law are revealing.

> "This does not, however, mean that the "new" Asian-African countries are not prepared to accept the whole body of present international law. International law has in fact come to be accepted by these countries except where it is still found to support past colonial rights or is clearly inequitable by the present standards of civilization. [Underlining supplied.] ...The whole attitude of the "new" countries could be summarized in the liquidation of imperialism in its widest meaning, with all its political, military, economic and psychological implications. They want to change the status quo, and are striving to restructure their societies and the international society to reach a more equitable situation in which they can share the blessings of modern civilization on an equal footing. They want to modify some of the nineteenth-century conceptions of international law to bring them into conformity with the principles of the United Nations Charter."

It may thus be seen that the process of diplomatic protection is undergoing a continuing examination in the present day and that some of the concepts that have prevailed in the past will not necessarily govern in the future.

In the earlier part of this chapter I mention the fact that the term "protection" could be used in a general sense to encompass every type of aid and assistance given by a government to its citizens abroad. In practice the extent of such aid and assistance is considerable. An American consular officer, in addition to seeking justice for American citizens, has all sorts of other ties and obligations to such citizens. He must, as has been said, take part in preserving the estates of deceased Americans. He must make every effort to inform Americans at home concerned with the welfare and whereabouts of a member of their family supposedly in his consular jurisdiction, of the health and location of the missing relative. He must also endeavor to furnish as much assistance as possible to an American stricken with illness abroad, and he must try as far as possible to preserve harmony in the American community. The latter is not always easy.

I had one case when I was Consul General in Yokohama where an American who had successfully operated a bar decided to open another one. He called the new bar the V.F.W. at which point the local post of the Veterans of Foreign Wars was inclined to take summary and drastic action. The owner of the bar insisted that under Japanese law he had a perfect right to call the bar by whatever name he wanted--which was true, and that, in any event, V.F.W. meant "very fine women." The controversy was finally settled by the bar owner's promise to change the name and the understanding that he be allowed a certain amount of time to obtain a new sign which, as it turned out, was somewhat scurrilous. Its saving grace was that it did not offend the V.F.W.

One of the great problems that a consular officer faces in extending protection, in the broad sense of that term, is the problem of providing repatriation for destitute Americans. The consular officer and the Department of State are caught on the horns of a dilemma, for if they do everything possible to facilitate the return of Americans who become destitute abroad they issue an open invitation to irresponsible persons to come to Paris and other glamourous places expecting the consul and the government to repatriate them. On the other hand, it sometimes does happen that an American will fall ill abroad, through no fault of his own, and does need assistance. Moreover, the consular officer and the American community may be desirous of repatriating an American who has proven to be somewhat of a black sheep and who sheds little luster on the reputation of the United States.

The Department of State makes some limited loans for repatriation. They are, however, relatively difficult to obtain and, in any event, are for repatriation alone and do not cover such contingencies as an illness which may keep an American in a foreign country pending recovery. To take care of such situations the American consul usually has to rely on the good will and generosity of the American community. In Yokohama that community had a special fund raised which was jealously doled out in instances where no other funds were available and assistance to Americans was imperative.

Still another facet of protection is the limited insurance provided by the Federal government for American business investments in the less developed world. The insurance is not absolute but at least it does protect the business concern from some of the greater risks in investing in the developing world. It serves to encourage private investment and furthers the aid program through private enterprise.

It can be seen from the foregoing that protection has many aspects. It is probably one of the most important of the duties of a diplomatic or consular officer, and its wide implications should be generally understood.

Chapter XVI
HUMAN RIGHTS

The protection of nationals has long been recognized and has a solid foundation in international law. The protection of human rights, on the other hand--concerned with the human being as an individual and not as a national of one particular state--is of relatively recent origin.

One can point to the Magna Carta of 1215, the English Bill of Rights of 1689, to the American Constitution, and to the French Declaration of the Rights of Man, and to other documents, as proof to the contrary. They were, however, with the possible exception of the French Declaration, primarily intended to apply within a national state. The English Bill of Rights, for example, concerned England and England alone. Moreover, they did not always mean what they said. How can one reconcile the rhetorical statement in the American Declaration of Independence that all men are created equal and endowed with the inalienable right to liberty with the existence of slavery in a large number of the thirteen colonies? Furthermore, aristocratic and sometimes despotic domination by the governing group, economic misery, a lack of social consciousness on the part of the wealthy, unbelievably strict criminal laws and other factors made it impossible for the humble to obtain many of the rights that the average citizen now takes for granted.

Following the Protestant Reformation some efforts, it is true, were sometimes made by one state to protect coreligionists in another state. Moreover, some historians see the beginnings of a social consciousness in the 18th century. Largely, although not entirely, this was on the basis of Lady Bountiful helping the poor. Also the French philosophers pointed toward a better day. Some concepts such as Rousseau's belief in the noble savage were highly idealistic and out of touch with reality. The first real and practical stirrings of concern with human rights in general had to wait until the 19th century when there was the rise of humanitarianism noted in an earlier chapter.

The first significant humanitarian effort of the nineteenth century related to the suppression of slavery and the slave trade.The former was done on a national scale only, that is, England abolished slavery in its colonies in 1833 but did not concern itself with the existence of slavery in Brazil which ended only toward the end of the century. The suppression of the slave trade, on the other hand, had international implications. Efforts to eliminate it were originally handicapped by the unwillingness of the American government to permit British warships, which were the only warships capable of patrolling the African coast, from boarding American vessels. That unwillingness stemmed from the tragic experience of the United States with the British impressment of seamen from American vessels during the Napoleonic wars. The end result was to encourage every slaver to fly the American flag, and thus carry with impunity his suffering cargo of helpless Africans across the ocean.

During the same century, concern grew with the treatment of minorities and the abuse of the native populations in colonial areas. The pogroms of the Jews in Russia and Rumania, the crushing of the Hungarians following the 1848 revolt led by Kossuth, the Spanish treatment of the Cubans, the massacre of the Armenians in Turkey, and the cruelties inflicted on the black peoples of the Congo are examples of situations that roused world concern. Others could be provided, but the ones given will serve as illustrations.

The expressions of sympathy were sporadic and were often voiced by nations that were by no means guiltless themselves. It was a little anomalous for the United States to complain about Jewish pogroms and the repression of the Cubans by Spain while it permitted the systematic decimation of the Indian and kept the Negro in a state of enforced inferiority. Nor was it consistent for the Hungarians to suppress their own Slav minorities while protesting their own lack of freedom.

Relatively few positive measures were taken. Turkey was forced to agree to improved treatment of its minorities. As one author states:

> "...the Turkish atrocities in Armenia in 1894 aroused such international concern that finally the Turkish government was constrained to allow representatives of Britain, Russia and France to accompany a commission of enquiry into the massacres. As a result of this, certain administrative reforms were pressed on the Turks and were finally accepted (though they did not prevent even worse massacres the following year)."

The Congo atrocities also received attention, and a change was imposed on King Leopold of Belgium who at that time controlled the Congo.

The end of World War I saw the breakup of the Austro-Hungarian Empire and the general redrawing of frontiers in Europe. As a consequence, a large number of individuals found themselves belonging to minority groups. Efforts were made to extend protection to them by writing provisions in the Peace Treaties designed to safeguard minority rights.

Concern with human rights was not restricted to the safeguarding of minorities. A convention providing for the abolition of slavery, which still existed in parts of the world, was approved and measures were taken to alleviate the plight of the innumerable refugees who flooded Europe at the end of the war, including as has been mentioned earlier, the issue to them of a League of Nations travel document known as the Nansen passport. The International Labor Organization began sponsoring a series of conventions designed to improve the lot of the worker. Attention was focussed

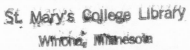

on the traffic in drugs and in women and children. Moreover, the creation of the mandate system provided at least some protection for the inhabitants of the mandated areas.

It would be a mistake to suppose that all of these efforts were ushering in a millenium for the poor and the oppressed. Even massacres were not eliminated. In Turkey the record was soiled by the continuance of the same bloody killings that had prevailed in the past. A witty and cynical Italian diplomat serving at the League of Nations quotes a parody of a resolution proposed by a colleague reading:

> "Article 1. No massacre of Armenians shall take place without the Council of the League being notified <u>one month</u> in advance.
>
> Article 2. If the massacre should include women and children, the notification to the Council of the League shall be given <u>two months</u> in advance.
>
> Article 3. Any massacre of Armenians which takes place without these formalities being observed shall be considered as null and void (nul et non avenu)."

Moreover, in the same part of the world the exchange of Greek-Bulgarian and Turkish-Greek populations appeared to be the only method of preventing them from flying at each other's throats. Even though the end result may have been desirable the exchange of populations, with all the tragedies that necessarily accompany uprootings and transplantations, is a drastic method whereby to provide for the rights of man.

During World War II human rights, or at least certain aspects of them, were mentioned in the Atlantic Charter and the United Nations Declaration. At the same time the war witnessed some of the most brutal atrocities perpetuated in human history. What is more, accusations have been made that those who might have done something to mitigate the horrors did relatively little to help. Pope Pius has been accused of indifference to the fate of the Jews in Rolf Hochhuth's <u>The Deputy</u>, and President Roosevelt has come under strong criticism for failing to help the Jews sufficiently in a recent book entitled <u>While Six Million Died</u>.

The Nazi atrocities did create a sense of revulsion which led to the establishment of the Nuremberg Trials to pass upon Nazi war crimes. While there was little sympathy for the Nazis, many were concerned at a court condemning the accused on the basis of laws that were not in being at the time of the commission of the crimes. There is some question whether this was actually necessary to effect punishment as the military occupation courts could, generally speaking, have applied the existing laws of war and the German criminal laws to effect the same result. The latter laws had never been repealed by the Third Reich. What had permitted the Nazis to proceed with impunity was that they were immune from prosecution. If that immunity had been removed they could have been punished for many of the horrifying acts of which they were guilty without invoking a law that necessarily was applied on an ex post facto basis. It is a little-known fact that the Department of State did urge such an approach but found scant sympathy in the Pentagon. To my knowledge this divergence in views has never received any publicity. I happen to know about it because I prepared a memorandum on the subject for Judge Hackworth, the Legal Adviser of the Department, and accompanied him to a meeting where we ineffectually tried to present our point of view. Later on, to provide a law for the future to cover similar brutalities, the United Nations sponsored the Genocide Convention to which the United States is not yet a party.

At the present time the brutalities in Viet Nam and, more particularly, the case of Lieutenant Calley, have revived the entire question of war crimes and the applicability of the Nuremberg laws to the present situation. As a result, the Nuremberg decisions have been re-examined minutely and it has been brought out that among the principal defendants only Rudolf Hess, still languishing in Spandau, was convicted solely on the basis of a crime against peace. The rest were convicted for offenses against the laws of war and crimes against humanity, primary emphasis being on the former.

Concern with war crimes and genocide did not mean that the preservation of human rights generally was overlooked. A number of human rights provisions were included in the Charter of the United Nations. The United Nations as a whole, the General Assembly, the Economic and Social Council and the Trusteeship Council were all charged in one form or another with the study and promotion of human rights. Furthermore, the first Peace Treaties that were signed after World War II--those with Italy and the Axis satellite powers--contained a provision concerning human rights that in the Rumanian Treaty read:

> "Roumania shall take all measures necessary to secure to all persons under Roumanian jurisdiction, without distinction as to race, sex, language or religion, the enjoyment of human rights and of the fundamental freedoms, including freedom of expression, of press and publication, of religious worship, of political opinion and of public meeting.

> Roumania further undertakes that the laws in force in Roumania shall not, either in their content or in their application, discriminate or entail any discrimination between persons of Roumanian nationality on the ground of their race, sex, language or religion, whether in reference to their persons, property business, professional or financial interests, status, political or civil rights or any other matter."

Other peace treaties had a more or less corresponding provision.

In view of what has happened beyond the Iron Curtain the provision just quoted has proved to be illusory. It proved impossible of enforcement, for when Rumania, Hungary and Bulgaria were charged with violations, they refused to appoint a commissioner to sit on a commission envisaged by the terms of each treaty to settle disputes arising out of the treaty. The International Court of Justice added to the irony by holding in an advisory opinion that there was no way in which the problem could be resolved.

Shortly after the United Nations was established the Assembly approved the Universal Declaration on Human Rights. This was in no sense a treaty. Essentially it was a voicing of aspirations. It has nevertheless been widely accepted as a standard to which agreements on civil rights should conform. In one American case a lower court invoked the declaration as interpretative of the Charter, even if it was not a treaty itself.

Since adopting the Universal Declaration, the United Nations has sponsored a whole series of conventions based on various aspects of human rights. The International Labor Organization has likewise continued in the task of suggesting agreements in the labor field. As of now it has prepared more than one hundred conventions on a variety of subjects related to labor conditions, including those concerning women and children and compulsory servitude. UNESCO has also suggested a convention on education.

The General Assembly has likewise sponsored a number of agreements of which the most important are the International Covenant on Economic, Social and Cultural Rights and the International Covenant on Civil and Political Rights. To some extent the former is confined to a statement of economic hopes, as it is obvious that some of its provisions are unenforceable. How, for example, does one enforce Article XII, Paragraph I: "The States Parties to the present Covenant recognize the right of everyone to the enjoyment of the highest attainable standard of physical and mental health."?

Theoretically, the two covenants are supposed to cover two different fields. There is, however, some overlap. Such overlap is particularly marked in the provisions concerning trade unions. I am reproducing both articles side by side so the overlap can be seen. They read:

Economic	Political
Article 8--1	Article 22--1
"The State Parties to the present Covenant undertake to ensure: (a) The right of everyone to form trade unions and join the trade union of his choice subject only to the rules of the	"Everyone shall have the right to freedom of association with others, including the right to form and join trade unions for the protection of his interests."

organization concerned, for the
promotion and protection of his
economic and social interests.
No restrictions may be placed
on the exercise of this right
other than those prescribed by
law and which are necessary in
a democratic society in the interest of national security or
public order or for the protection of the rights and freedom
of others."

The United States has been quite derelict in signing and ratifying the various conventions. Writing in Foreign Affairs in 1967 one author said:

"...While the United Nations has been struggling to establish global norms of conduct, the United States has been
the chief laggard in translating them into international law.
At the present time the U.S. Senate has yet to ratify a single human rights treaty.

By next year the United Nations and its specialized agencies will have completed about a dozen conventions on human rights including one banning religious intolerance
(scheduled for adoption in the 1967 session of the Assembly)
and the twin covenants on civil and political rights and on
economic, social and cultural rights. Thereafter the focus
of the effort will shift to methods and machinery for effectively implementing the measures."

A couple of years later the situation had not changed appreciably. Chief Justice Warren commented on it in these words:

"How far then have we come in developing this international law of human rights? Over 20 major human rights
conventions have been adopted by the United Nations, the
International Labor Organization, and UNESCO (United Nations Educational, Scientific and Cultural Organization).
A few of them are in force among the parties which have
acceded to them. Unfortunately, the United States is a party to only two of them, and this status has been reached only
in the last year. We are still not a party to such major conventions as the Convention on the Abolition of Forced Labor, the Convention on the Political Rights of Women, the
Convention on the Prevention and Punishment of the Crime

of Genocide, and the Convention on the Elimination of All
Forms of Racial Discrimination. Nor have we as yet even
signed, no less ratified, the two Conventions on Civil and
Political Rights and Economic, Social and Cultural Rights,
which grow directly out of the Universal Declaration."

Part of the American problem arises from Federal-State relationships and the reluctance of the Federal Government to invade a sphere
normally reserved to the states. The problem is much more political than
legal for it would seem fairly clear that the United States would not be
barred by the American Constitution from entering into a human rights
treaty.

In order to understand the legalities of the situation it is necessary
to describe the treaty-making powers. Such a discussion should normally
fall in the material on treaties. Since, however, that material comes
later and it is imperative to appreciate the constitutional scope and effect
of treaties to comprehend the human rights issues in the United States, a
departure will have to be made from logical sequence to permit mention
at this time of the effects of treaties on Federal-State relationships.

The Constitution provides that the President "shall have power by
and with the advice and consent of the Senate to make treaties, provided
two-thirds of the Senators present concur." It goes on to say "This Constitution, and the laws of the United States, which shall be made in pursuance thereof; and all treaties made, or which shall be made, under the
authority of the United States, shall be the supreme law of the land..."
From this phrase one might gather the impression that a statute and a
treaty stand on equal terms. The Supreme Court in the famous case of
Missouri v. Holland held otherwise ruling that a treaty can sometimes
treat matters not subject to Federal legislation. Specifically the court
held that the Federal Government could provide for the protection of mi-
gratory birds by a treaty with Canada, whereas it could not provide such
protection by legislation without infringing upon the reserved powers of
the States.

The same principle was obviously relied upon when the United States
entered into a convention on road traffic. Potentially that treaty could give
the Federal Government authority to demand that the States observe certain rules concerning road conditions that are normally within the police
power of a state. Article XVII, Section 5, prohibiting boards and notices
that might be confused with road signs, is an illustration.

Following the same principle it would seem fairly easy to defend the
constitutionality of the Human Rights covenants in general. Unfortunately
the problem is far more political than legal. Naturally, a good many of
the rights guaranteed by the Human Rights covenants are the same as those
the citizen enjoys under the American Federal and State Constitutions.
There are, however, two essential facts to be considered. In the first
place, their provisions go further in certain respects than some of the

existing laws. In other words, they give an individual a right he may not possess under existing American practice. Article 14, Section 6 of the Covenant on Civil and Political Rights can serve as an example. It reads:

> "When a person has by a final decision been convicted of a criminal offence and when subsequently his conviction has been reversed or he has been pardoned on the ground that a new or newly discovered fact shows conclusively that there has been a miscarriage of justice, the person who has suffered punishment as a result of such conviction shall be compensated according to law, unless it is proved that the non-disclosure of the unknown fact in time is wholly or partly attributable to him."

In the second place, an individual's reliance on a Federal treaty for the protection of his rights enables him to invoke the jurisdiction of the Federal courts, a fact which may, in some instances, be of utmost importance. It can be anticipated that there will be objections on both scores from states already concerned with the scope of Federal power. Hence the human rights covenants are likely to have a difficult time in the Senate.

While the United Nations has been concerned with civil rights on a global basis, efforts have also been made to promote civil rights on a regional basis. The most successful by far have been those of the European community whose Human Rights Commission has been functioning with vigor for many years. Moreover, the Court on Human Rights to which the Commission may refer cases has rendered a landmark decision in the Lawless case. Lawless was an Irish insurrectionary who was placed in preventive detention by the Irish Government. After being released he alleged that his rights had been infringed. The Court of Human Rights ruled that his imprisonment under the circumstances was justified. It could, however, have ruled the other way thus setting the precedent of an international court ruling in favor of an individual citizen against his own government.

The United Nations Human Rights Covenants are not backed by the same enforcing authority. States can submit themselves to complaints from other states and can even go so far as to agree to respond to complaints from individuals. There is, nevertheless, no obligation on the part of a state to abide by the findings of the bodies hearing the complaints.

When the situation is looked at in its entirety there is undoubtedly some progress being made in the implementation of human rights. But it is a pitifully slow process travelling on a road full of pitfalls and detours.

Chapter XVII
PEACEFUL SETTLEMENT OF DISPUTES

The dream of nations reaching understanding in the face of conflicting claims without the use of force has long dominated the thinking of those concerned with the promotion of peace. Naturally the simplest method of settling disputes is by direct negotiation. This is very often done, probably more often than the general public realizes, since it is not the settled controversies but rather the unsettled ones which bring attention.

In some instances a settlement by negotiation is hindered by the unwillingness of each of the disputing parties to take the first step. When that happens an offer of good offices by a third power, by an international organization or by the Pope may serve to bring them together. They can appear to be acting out of respect and deference to the mediator rather than to be yielding to the demands of the opposite side. Since nations as well as individuals have to "save face" this may be important. A third party can either restrict its activity to bringing the contesting nations together for the purposes of negotiation or can try to mediate the dispute, that is, to suggest a compromise solution.

Sometimes it is very difficult to determine just where good offices stop and mediation begins, and it is probably not too profitable to try to draw a fine line of distinction between the two approaches. History records a number of instances of good offices or mediation where disputes have been settled through the intervention of a third party. One of the most celebrated was the action of President Theodore Roosevelt in inviting Japan and Russia to meet in the little town of Portsmouth, New Hampshire, to negotiate the Treaty of Peace that ended the Russo-Japanese War.

During the administration of Woodrow Wilson when the United States became embroiled with Mexico and there was no easy solution to be seen Argentina, Brazil and Chile, known as the ABC Powers, offered their services to help the United States and Mexico resolve their differences. With their help the crisis passed.

More recently the Soviet Union supported by the United States was successful in bringing Pakistan and India together and reducing the tensions over Kashmir.

Unfortunately the efforts of the major powers and of the United Nations to mediate the disputes between Israel and the Arab states are meeting with far less success.

Another method of helping to solve disagreements is to establish a commission of inquiry to determine the facts surrounding the dispute in the expectation that an impartial report will lead to settlement.

This did indeed happen at the beginning of the century during the Russo-Japanese War. The Russian fleet sailed from the Baltic on the way to meet its fate at the Battle of Tsushima. As it passed over Dogger Bank the Russian commander thought he saw Japanese destroyers looming in the mist and shadow and opened fire. It turned out that the "destroyers" were really peaceful British fishing boats. There was a strong outcry in Britain with much talk of war. Instead the facts were investigated by a commission of inquiry which determined that the boats were fishing vessels, but implied that the Russian commander had not acted in disregard of humanity. The Russian Government then paid an award to the English Government and hostilities were averted.

In some instances a commission, known as a conciliation commission, can be established to suggest ways and means of arriving at a solution and offering recommendations on the proper action to take without the states who are involved being bound to accept the recommendations of the commission.

When William Jennings Bryan was Secretary of State, the United States entered into a whole series of conciliation agreements with other nations. Unfortunately they have been very little used.

Much more recently the United States and Italy entered into an agreement to have a commission to pass upon the meaning of certain language in the Air Transport Agreement between Italy and the United States. The commission was called an arbitration commission but since the acceptance of its recommendations was not mandatory, it functioned much more as a conciliation commission having power of recommendation only. As it turned out the recommendations of the majority of the commission were not accepted by Italy.

In addition to resorting to the various procedures that have just been mentioned two states in disagreement can agree to submit the dispute to arbitration. The arbitral commission is supposed to give an award based upon the applicable law and that award is binding on the parties unless, of course, the commission exceeds its own authority.

An argument has been made that arbitral commissions endeavor to conciliate disputes rather than restricting themselves to passing upon the legal issues involved. There is no doubt that in some instances some arbitral commissions have tried to find the easy way out by compromise. This is not, however, the true role of an arbitral commission which should act as an ad hoc judicial body for the determination of the points at issue.

I think the belief that arbitral commissions go beyond the limits of the law in trying to conciliate disputes is based upon a misunderstanding as to the function of an arbitral commission during the initial stages of the case. In that period an arbitral commission, being small and relatively elastic, can suggest ways and means whereby the litigation can be reduced and a settlement reached.

I know this is true in the case of the Commission on which I sat in Japan. In that instance we had been considering for some time a tangled series of legal issues in a series of claims involving interests in Japanese corporations and had come to the conclusion that because of the vagueness of the applicable legislation we had to interpret, it would be very difficult to effect a proper decision. Also since the claims related to war damages and to destruction of properties during the war we were rather appalled at the prospect of having to evaluate the damages on the basis of incomplete records and faulty memories. Hence the Japanese member of the Commission and I, at that point, tried to determine whether the parties could not reach an agreement to avoid endless litigation and the great expense to both the claimants and the Japanese Government.

Our efforts which were approved by the third member were successful so that, based upon the agreement of the parties and our own concept of how some of the issues should be resolved, we were able to render a decision confirming the understanding and awarding almost twenty million dollars which put an end to the litigation.

A commission can also be elastic in the preliminary disposal of issues and generally taking the lead to insure the success of an arbitration. In the famous Alabama claims the United States brought a claim against Great Britain for permitting the construction in the United Kingdom of several Confederate raiders, including the Alabama which produced immense havoc on the Union merchant fleet. The British agreed to arbitrate the dispute. At the last moment the United States made a claim on Great Britain for the entire cost of the last two years of the Civil War on the grounds that the raiders had prolonged the war for that period of time. The British were outraged and the situation became very tense. Fortunately, the Commission under the inspiration of the American member, Charles Francis Adams, interposed before the question had really been put to it and ruled that the disposition of such a claim was beyond the scope of the Commission.

Hence it is true that in the very early stages a commission may try to smooth the path of the arbitration and endeavor to eliminate claims that appear ready for settlement by mutual agreement to a considerably greater extent than a large-sized court. If, however, a settlement is not in the offing an arbitral commission conscious of its responsibilities proceeds to the stage of deciding the case on the basis of its legal merits.

I do not believe that arbitral commissions in this respect are too different from domestic courts for any judge, solicitous of the interests of justice, will probably do anything he can to encourage a quick settlement in the preliminary stages, even though he will be prepared to render a legal judgment if the parties cannot reach agreement.

Arbitration had its great vogue during the nineteenth century starting with the Jay Treaty of 1794 between the United States and Great Britain which resolved at least some of the problems that had arisen in the early relationships of the two countries. Thereafter the United States arbitrated a number of disputes with various powers, most of them concerning boundaries and claims. In 1899 when enthusiasm for arbitration was probably at its zenith, the major powers of the world adopted the First Hague Convention on arbitration which established the Permanent Court of Arbitration. Actually this name was somewhat of a misnomer since the "court" was not really a court. Instead the convention provided that each of the signatory states would nominate four jurists who collectively would constitute a panel, from which judges for arbitral tribunals could be selected. Each tribunal was a separate one and there was no guarantee, in fact little probability, that the same panelists would serve on two successive commissions.

The 1907 Hague Conference likewise produced a convention on the Permanent Court of Arbitration. Essentially it was confirmation of the earlier one.

History records that the "court" was used on a number of occasions to resolve some rather important disputes. In addition the nations of the world, including the United States, also created arbitral commissions or tribunals outside of the framework of The Hague system to pass on a variety of cases.

All of the arbitral bodies, no matter how brilliant and learned their members, suffered from a lack of continuity.

An arbitral commission could look at past precedents but, since it was a new body, there was no assurance that it would follow them. Hence there was a great desire on the part of international jurists to create a permanent court that would sit as one body through the years developing a jurisprudence, providing cohesion, and being ready at any time to hear a dispute instead of having to be constituted specially for the occasion. It is interesting that the American delegation at The First Hague Conference was instructed to suggest the creation of an international court in the true sense of that term.

That desire was finally fulfilled with the establishment of the Permanent Court of International Justice immediately after World War I. The court as eventually constituted by the time it ended its existence consisted of fifteen judges elected for a nine year term. Moreover, if a party to the dispute did not have one of its nationals on the court it could designate an ad hoc judge so that, theoretically at least, the court in certain instances might number seventeen.

During the intra-war years between World War I and World War II, the Permanent Court of International Justice heard a number of important cases which constituted valuable precedents in international law. In addition to hearing cases it also rendered advisory opinions to the League of Nations on points of law that concerned that institution.

At the same time a number of arbitrations took place. In the case of the United States the use of arbitration was natural since it was not a member of the court. Other nations also resorted to arbitration as in some instances an arbitral commission, with its small size and elasticity, was better adapted to resolving a dispute or a series of disputes than the fifteen judge world court.

The United States never joined the Permanent Court of International Justice. To a large part this failure to join was attributable to the isolationist feeling that prevailed in the United States in the post World War I period. There was, in particular, objection on the part of the United States to a court rendering an advisory opinion under the belief that somehow or other that might affect the interests of the United States without its consent. The reluctance to accept the advisory function of the court was, moreover, stimulated by the dislike of advisory opinions held by the American jurist Judge John Bassett Moore, who was then serving on the Court.

At the end of World War II the United States adopted a wholly different position towards international organizations and was the leader in the establishment of the United Nations and of several other organizations, such as The Food and Agriculture Organization, that now function as specialized agencies of the United Nations.

By the same token the United States renewed the interest it had manifested at the turn of the century in promoting a genuine court and worked actively to constitute a new court--The International Court of Justice. The statute of the new court is very similar to the statute of the old court so that in many respects, although not all, the new court is a continuation of the old one. Since the coming into being of the new court it has not been used very widely despite the fact that every member of the United Nations is automatically a member of the court.

From its inception the court has rendered thirty-one decisions and thirteen advisory opinions. The number of decisions is deceptive as in several instances the court made more than one decision on the same subject matter either because its initial decision was a preliminary one or the decision required further interpretation. Moreover, a number of decisions never concerned the merits of the disputes, being decided on jurisdictional grounds.

During the same period, arbitration was likewise somewhat in the doldrums. The two largest arbitrations with which the United States was concerned arose from treaties of peace. Both the Italian and Japanese Governments under their respective treaties of peace obligated themselves to compensate allied nationals for war losses sustained in Italy and Japan respectively. Obviously this was a disguised form of reparations for ordinarily there is no indemnification for war losses. In both cases the apparent feeling was that Italy and Japan should pay for the damages sustained by American interests, even though those damages may have resulted from Allied bombing, since both were deemed to have started the war.

The Italian-United States Conciliation Commission, an inappropriate name since it had the power to decide rather than just conciliate, before which I was the first Agent, dragged on for many years. In the process it did, nevertheless, render a number of decisions which constitute important landmarks in international law. Probably the one that is referred to most is the Strunsky Mergé case concerning double nationality which is dealt with in the chapter on nationality.

In addition to these arbitrations the United States also entered into an arbitration agreement with France to interpret the air transport serfice agreement. More recently the United States ended an arbitration with Canada based on claims resulting from the overflow of a dam, incredibly enough called "Gut Dam."

If the United States has not been very fervent in the use of arbitration, neither has it been active in the presentation of cases to the International Court of Justice. In fact, every case which was presented to the court by the United States involved damages caused to airplanes by the Soviet bloc. It was a foregone conclusion that the Communist nations would never accept the jurisdiction of the court, so it is legitimate to surmise that to a considerable degree the cases that were submitted by the United States were presented largely for propaganda purposes.

The reasons that the United States has made rather infrequent use of the World Court or of arbitral processes in the years following the war are extremely difficult to determine. It would seem that the failure to use the judicial process is attributable in part to the Connally Amendment (which will be discussed in the next paragraph), to the tensions of the cold war which have rendered difficult any agreement for a peaceful settlement and to the unfamiliarity of so many of the new nations of today with international arbitral or judicial processes. Moreover, in some areas, as in Japan, litigation is not the favored method of settling disputes. In Japan differences are usually resolved by arriving at a consensus, a domestic practice that probably carries over into the international field. As one author said:

> "In Western society, it is taken for granted that in principle there exist tensions between legal rules and the social world, and that the latter is evaluated and controlled by the former. The most striking, or exaggerated, expression of this idea is "Fiat iustitia pereat mundus." Japan, however, does not have the idea of this determinate dualism. What has existed in Japan is not a tension between these two antitheses, but a continuum from one to the other, or, rather, a compromise between these two antitheses. As Northrop points out, what the people of the West approve as 'sticking up for one's rights' would be regarded in Japan as 'trouble making,' and lawsuits which the people of the West would approve as 'law enforcement' would be viewed by the Japanese as unjustified resort to political power, which would not help to settle disputes."

As will be recalled, Article 36 of the Statute of the International Court of Justice provides that the parties to the statute may recognize the compulsory jurisdiction of the court with respect to all other states accepting the same obligation. The United States did accept the compulsory jurisdiction of the court. In doing so, it stipulated that the jurisdiction of the court did not apply to:

> "b. disputes with regard to matters which are essentially within the domestic jurisdiction of the United States of America <u>as determined by the United States of America</u>." (Underlining supplied.)

This amendment is known as the Connally Amendment after Senator Connally of Texas.

Since the Court operates more or less on the principle of reciprocity, this means that any state sued by the United States can also raise the same defense, that is, that the dispute relates to a matter which is essentially within its domestic jurisdiction and that it has the ultimate say in the matter. As a consequence, the jurisdiction of the court in cases involving the United States is limited. Moreover, a good many other states have attached their own limitations to the acceptance of jurisdiction. In effect, the court, to a very large extent, can function only if the parties to a dispute are in agreement that the dispute should be submitted to the court.

Whether this relative lack of use of arbitral tribunals or the International Court of Justice by the world as a whole or by the United States in particular will continue is difficult to prophesy. The Connally Amendment remains in full force and vigor. Nevertheless, the United States has entered into a whole series of treaties and agreements which include a clause obligating the United States to submit a dispute under the treaty or agreement to the International Court of Justice or to arbitration. In some cases the parties agree that the precise method of settling a dispute, that is, whether by arbitration or by adjudication, will be left for later determination. Such clauses are known as "compromissary clauses." To the extent that these agreements are subsequent in point of time to the Connally Amendment, they serve to supersede it within the limited field to which they apply. As agreements containing "compromissary clauses" multiply, there will be a network of clauses giving jurisdiction to an international judicial body. This is bound to erode the Connally Amendment. Hence the future of arbitration and adjudication in the years to come is not necessarily bleak. Adjudication and arbitration may again become important weapons in the diplomatic repertoire of the United States.

Quite possibly arbitration will become dominant. There was, as has been mentioned, a wide interest in developing an international court. A certain amount of disillusionment has now set in. It has been argued that the International Court of Justice is too large, too costly, and too clumsy for the average small dispute. In fairness to the Court, however, it should be pointed out that the inordinate length of the memorials and oral argument is attributable to the zeal of counsel and not to anything insisted upon by the court. Moreover, no use whatsoever has been made of the Chambers envisaged by the Court under Articles 26-30 of the statute which would be much smaller than the Court as a whole. Another element of discontent with the Court was provided by the decision of the Court in the South West Africa case. In a preliminary decision on the right of Ethiopia and Liberia to institute a suit against the Republic of South Africa, the Court held in a narrow 8-7 decision that the suit was properly brought and the Court had jurisdiction. Four years later, after protracted hearings and the submission of a great deal of evidence, the majority lost one vote as the result of fortuitous circumstances. The right of Ethiopia and Liberia to bring the suit was considered once more. This time the vote was 7-7 which gave the presiding judge the casting vote which was cast against the Liberian and Ethiopian position. The American Judge Philip Jessup did not hesitate to criticize the opinion, saying that he considered the judgment "completely unfounded in law."

The Court has also been criticized for the length of time it took to decide the Barcelona Traction Company case. Notwithstanding the faults found with the Court, the Department of State has suggested that the Ecuadorian tuna boat controversy mentioned in the next chapter should be referred to the Court. Whether Ecuador will agree is highly dubious. Moreover, Senator Jacob Javits has indicated that an effort will be made to have the Connally Amendment changed.

While the number of cases adjudicated in recent years has been minor, arbitration has settled boundary disputes between Chile and Argentina, and Pakistan and India. It also settled a controversy between France and Spain with regard to use of the waters of Lake Lanoux. In such cases arbitration has shown its merits.

Before concluding the discussion on intergovernmental arbitration and adjudication, mention should be made of the many suggestions offered over the course of the years to permit an individual to appear in his own right before an international tribunal to press a claim. Some suggestions have envisaged a whole system of international courts on a regional basis with a possible appeal to one central court.

In a few instances individuals have already been given access to international courts. They were permitted to appear before the short-lived Central American Court of Justice that functioned at the beginning of this century. Individuals also could resort to the Mixed Arbitral Tribunals established after World War I to pass on a host of problems arising out of the postwar settlements.

Generally speaking, however, nations have been reluctant to permit individuals to use an international court. In part the reason may be that individuals are usually not considered to be subjects of international law. One suspects that the real reasons are far more pragmatic as states are seldom influenced by pure theory.

A state may not want to permit a claim to be brought by one of its citizens because in a period of delicate relations between two countries a vigorously pressed claim might upset a precarious balance. Moreover, the claim, if vindicated, may establish a theory highly disadvantageous to the claimant's nation as a whole even though the individual claimant might benefit. Likewise he might have a perfectly good argument which he might lose because of his own and his lawyer's unfamiliarity with international law. My own experience derived from many years with claims commissions is that there is a vast number of improperly prepared cases that invite defeat for lack of adequate presentation. Hence a state may be chary of permitting a citizen to bring a case even when it supports the principles he is advocating.

In some instances, moreover, a state may have a direct interest which it would not want jeopardized by an improperly presented case. Under the American income tax legislation a corporation pays in the neighborhood of fifty percent tax. If it sustains a loss abroad it can deduct the amount as a business loss. On the other hand, if it recoups the loss by obtaining an international award for the damages sustained, the tax must be paid. On a sizeable award that amount is not negligible.

Finally a system of international court hearings and appeals pyramided presumably on top of litigation in domestic courts practically insures that it will be only the wealthy who can benefit. One remembers the saying of a noted British jurist that the English courts, like the Ritz Hotel, are open to all. It is not too much to expect a government to protect its citizens and to bear the costs of prosecuting their claims. This has always been the traditional duty of a government and there are compelling reasons against change.

A chapter on the peaceful settlement of disputes would not be complete without a mention of a relatively newly arisen method lying somewhere in between intergovernmental arbitrations and the determination of grievances through the normal processes of the civil courts. In fact I think it could almost be considered a separate field although it borrows from the established practice of intergovernmental arbitration and of international commercial arbitration between private parties. I allude to the settlement through arbitration between a government and a foreign corporation or individuals arising usually, if not invariably, out of a contract between the two. In such an arbitration the state whose nationality the corporation or individual possesses is not involved.

This practice which provides considerable elasticity and avoids the appearance of one state suing another has had quite wide ramifications in Europe and bids fair to increase. In the United States the ability of the government to enter into arbitration agreements of this type is circumscribed by a ruling of the Comptroller General of the United States that a government department cannot enter into an arbitration agreement unless authorized by law, an authorization which is usually lacking.

When I was serving as Legal Adviser of the American Embassy in Rome I did sit on an arbitration panel to resolve a dispute between the American Battle Monuments Commission and an Italian contractor. The facts were that the contractor was building a reservoir for the Commission to store water for irrigating the grass at the cemetery for the American dead who fell at Anzio and Nettuno. After the reservoir was completed, but before it was delivered and filled with water, an unexpected flash flood swirled around and under the reservoir lifting the concrete structure like a boat. When the water receded the structure fell back but cracked in a number of places. From an engineering standpoint the whole job had to be done over. Who should bear the expense, the Monuments Commission or the contractor? The contract provided for an arbitration panel. The panel found that there was fault on both sides and so it decreed a compromise. The solution was fully reported to the General Accounting Office headed by the Comptroller General, which raised no objection, probably because a very unusual situation was presented.

It is a pity the American laws on arbitration are too restricted to permit more arbitrations between government agencies and foreign contractors as the process is elastic, inexpensive, and builds faith in the arbitral processes--a faith that can be carried over into more formal fields.

Chapter XVIII
INTERNATIONAL AGREEMENTS--
NATURE, PURPOSE AND NEGOTIATION

International agreements, as has been pointed out in an earlier chapter, take many names. In this chapter, to avoid confusion, they will be called by the generic word "agreements" unless the context otherwise requires. They can be multilateral, involving several states, or bilateral, involving two states only.

The term "international agreement" is usually reserved for accords having more than temporary significance. Nations are constantly developing operating procedures of mutual interest or disposing of routine cases by common consent. To take an extreme example, a state is usually asked to give custom clearances to an arriving diplomat. The consent to give such clearance is, in one sense, an agreement. Yet to include every such minor meeting of minds among the international agreements to which each state is considered to be a party in the usual sense of the term would swell the list to inordinate proportions.

A provision of the United States Code directs the publication of

> "....all treaties to which the United States is a party that
> have been proclaimed during each calendar year, and all
> international agreements other than treaties to which the
> United States is a party that have been signed, proclaimed,
> or with reference to which any other final formality has
> been executed, during each calendar year."

Obviously, before an international agreement is published, a determination must be made that it is more than a routine accord and deserves publication in accordance with the code provisions just quoted. I can testify from personal experience that it is not always an easy matter to decide which agreements merit publication.

Furthermore, Article 102 of the Charter of the United Nations provides for the registration of every treaty and every international agreement with the Secretariat. Moreover, Article 83 of the International Civil Aviation Convention of 1944 requires registration with the International Civil Aviation Organization of agreements relating to aviation.

The intriguing question arises whether an agreement which is not published domestically or registered with the Secretariat is an "international convention" within the meaning of Article 38 of the Statute of the International Court of Justice. The parties might not be able to invoke it before the court in view of the second paragraph of Article 102 of the Charter which precludes the invocation of unregistered treaties. But is it still a convention? I believe it is.

Agreements pass through several stages before coming into being. The first is negotiation which, when multilateral treaties are being considered, is usually done at a conference called for the purpose. The second is signature, an event that is sometimes accompanied by considerable solemnity. The third is the exchange of ratifications between the parties to a bilateral agreement and the deposit of ratifications in one central place in the case of multilateral agreements. It would obviously be impractical for many nations to exchange ratifications, so one government or international organization agrees to receive the ratifications and to record them. Quite often agreements come into force on signature, ratification not deemed being necessary.

The steps just mentioned do not include those that must be taken under the law of each signatory party preliminary to ratification, such as obtaining the "advice and consent" of the United States Senate with regard to treaties signed on behalf of the United States.

International agreements are entered into for a variety of purposes. It would be impossible even to enumerate all those purposes, but it may be helpful to list by way of illustration some of the principal ones. They are:

1. to settle an existing problem, such as a border dispute;

2. to provide for the arbitration or adjudication of a controversy;

3. to establish a framework of relations in a particular field as may be done by a Treaty of Friendship, Commerce and Navigation intended to regulate the reciprocal obligations of two nations in the realm of trade and commerce;

4. to provide technical guidance for the solution of such continuing problems as the allocation of radio frequencies;

5. to codify international law as exemplified by the Vienna Conventions on diplomatic and consular privileges referred to in an earlier chapter;

6. to demonstrate solidarity and support for a principle; and

7. to arrive at fiscal and trade arrangements.

An international agreement can consist of one document standing alone or several documents taken together. The latter occurs whenever an understanding is reached through the medium of an exchange of notes. In some instances, moreover, a protocol is added which is not part of the agreement proper. Sometimes it is an addendum which may or may not be accepted by the nations signing the basic text. Thus the Convention on Diplomatic Privileges and Immunities was accompanied by an optional protocol according to which the signatory nations could bind themselves to arbitrate disputes arising out of the convention.

A nation may also add an interpretation to the agreement at the time of signature or at the time of ratification. The purpose is to give that nation's viewpoint as to the proper interpretation of an otherwise supposedly obscure clause. Theoretically, an observation does not change an agreement in any respect since it is merely an interpretation. This is not always so, for an interpretation or observation given unilaterally by one nation can change the meaning of an agreement as it is understood by all the other parties to that agreement.

A reservation, on the other hand, is an outright modification of an agreement as it applies to the state making the reservation. A state can accept a treaty but refuse to abide by some one provision or insist that enforcement of some other provision be subject to certain limitations.

The practice of including reservations at the time of signature or ratification has grown. The reason is not hard to find. In the days when every clause of an agreement adopted at an international conference had to be approved by every participating state pursuant to the rule of unanimity, a state could be certain that the final version of the treaty to which it was asked to subscribe did not contain any clauses that met with its disapproval. Nowadays the unanimity rule has been broken and many provisions are adopted by a majority at a conference which may fall far short of unanimity. The Soviet Bloc has found at various conferences that it did not always have enough votes to prevent the adoption of clauses it did not favor.

At the same time that a nation disapproves of a particular provision it may consider that the agreement as a whole is beneficial and wants to sign and ratify it. In order to have the best of all possible worlds, it attaches a reservation which takes it out from the scope of the articles which it considers most objectionable.

The question immediately arises as to the effect of a reservation on other states. Can one consider that a nation that has signed an agreement which it will enter into only subject to a serious reservation, really consented to that agreement? Naturally, if a state questions all its co-signatories and there are no objections, there is no problem. If a state merely deposits its instrument of ratification with a reservation, what is the effect of that reservation on states that have signed and will ratify in the immediate future, or on states that will accede in the course of time?

The question aroused a great deal of discussion and considerable uncertainty. Not long ago, however, there was a conference at Vienna to draft a law on treaties. That conference gave birth in May of 1969 to the Vienna Convention on the Law of Treaties which will be discussed in considerable detail in the next chapter.

On the question of reservations, the conference adopted an ingenious solution which avoided some of the arguments of the past. In general, reservations are permitted if not specifically prohibited by the agreement. Another state may object to a reservation and make known its intention not to regard the agreement as entering into force between itself and the reserving state or, in the alternative, merely object, in which event that part of the agreement to which the reservation applies will be modified to the extent of the reservation in the application of the treaty between the two states. To take a simple if hypothetical example, if an agreement provides for mutual defense and includes a provision permitting one state to bring atomic weapons into the territory of another state, a reservation might be voiced with regard to such a provision leaving the rest of the agreement intact. Other states would, among themselves, maintain the treaty in its original terms.

There is an obvious affinity between contract law and treaty law, and the early writers on international law drew on the existing rules of contract law to develop precepts applicable to the law of international agreements. Nevertheless, as will be seen, there are wide differences between a contract and a treaty, and it is dangerous to seek parallels without seriously questioning whether the parallels really apply.

In drafting a contract the invariable rule is that the contract be as clearly worded as possible. There are, of course, disputes with regard to contracts, for no one can foresee all future contingencies, and inadvertent errors do creep in.

Customarily, international agreements will also be drafted to show the clear intention of the parties. In fact, any discussion on the drafting of treaties will normally emphasize the desirability of clarity and precision which is usually achieved. Nevertheless, there are instances where ambiguity or failure to deal actively with a particular problem related to the agreement and known to exist may be highly necessary or, at least, desirable. Opinions can vary on the importance of deliberate lack of precision in treaties and the weight that should be given to them in any discussion of treaty interpretation. At the risk of emphasizing the subject unduly, I will cite several instances of such ambiguity to illustrate the problem which may loom large in a particular incident.

At the end of the War of 1812 the American commissioners were anxious to have the treaty of peace provide against impressment of sailors and to regulate some of the other outstanding differences between the United States and the United Kingdom. The British commissioners likewise had optimistic ideas as to what they could force the United States to include in the treaty. As it turned out, neither side was able to prevail. Both sides did, however, want peace so that the discussions ended with a short treaty that concluded hostilities and provided for some relatively minor problems. The major issues were left outstanding to be settled at a later date or to die a natural death in the course of the years. The lesson to be drawn is that when there is a major objective to be attained some of the minor objectives can be permitted, if necessary, to remain unsettled.

In another celebrated instance involving the United States and the United Kingdom it was clearly advisable to stop the rivalry between the two states in the building of an interoceanic canal. The United States was also hopeful of persuading the United Kingdom to give up some of its possessions in Central America. When it became obviously impossible to achieve the latter objective, the parties became deliberately cloudy in the drafting of the treaty. A well-known American diplomatic historian described the situation in these words:

> "After prolonged diplomatic fencing, the famous Clayton-Bulwer Treaty was signed on April 19, 1850. By its terms both parties agreed to co-operate in facilitating the construction of an Isthmian canal; both bound themselves never to fortify or exercise exclusive control over it. As regards clashing territorial ambitions in Central America, the pact was less clear. London was dead set against relinquishing the Mosquito Coast, and had no intention whatever of abandoning British Honduras. Secretary Clayton knew all this, yet he could not make specific concessions on these points for fear of arousing a partisan clamor from the Britain-haters in America. Both negotiators therefore deliberately consented to the use of ambiguous language to conceal their official differences; otherwise, a treaty probably could not have been concluded." (Underlining supplied.)

In both instances vital political issues were involved. Other instances can be adduced when ambiguity has been consciously introduced into essentially technical agreements. Even arrangements sponsored by the theoretically nonpolitical Universal Postal Union are not always as clear as might be desired. In a study of the Union published by the Carnegie Foundation as part of The International Conciliation Pamphlet series, the writer, M.A. K. Menon, says:

> "Unanimity or consensus is sought on all issues with which the Union deals, but if a decision or the resolution of a problem cannot be reached by common agreement, the issue is settled by either a two-thirds or majority vote. Nor are the congresses above the art of compromise. Less than the desired legislation, e.g., in airmail rates, postal rates, and transit charges, is frequently accepted and a contentious issue phrased with deliberate vagueness or strong qualifications, when the lack of consensus cannot be overcome at a particular congress." (Underlining supplied.)

Still another example is provided by the terminology of the Vienna Convention on Diplomatic Privileges and Immunities. In an analysis of that Convention a British lawyer has said:

"Besides the functions of a solely diplomatic character which it may perform, a permanent mission may also carry out consular activities. The question, which is dealt with obliquely in Article 3, caused considerable debate at the Conference itself since a number of states, in particular the Soviet Union, wished the Convention to provide that diplomatic missions might automatically perform consular tasks, whilst others, whose main spokesman was the Spanish delegate, wanted to give the receiving State the power to say yes or no. The <u>wording selected is deliberately non-committal</u>: the conduct of consular functions by diplomatic missions is not prohibited by the Convention, but neither is it expressly authorized; the end result is that the receiving State may continue to demand, if it wishes to do so, that its consent be obtained before such functions are conducted, but the sending State has some basis on which to rely in arguing that consular activities form part of the accepted range of functions of a permanent mission." (Underlining supplied.)

I must confess that I have quite consciously recommended the same practice myself. After I arrived in Libya as Counsellor of Legation, one of the major tasks that the Legation faced was the negotiation of base rights agreements for the use of Wheelus Field near Tripoli. At that time the base was of immense strategic importance to the United States, and our entire efforts were concentrated in preserving the rights of the United States for the use of Wheelus Field. Everything else was subsidiary.

The Legation staff, including the clerical staff, used the commissary at Wheelus Field which, for all intents and purposes, meant that they had access to duty-free imports. Naturally it would have been convenient to have included in the agreement a flat statement permitting all of the Legation personnel to continue to use the commissary. From a drafting standpoint nothing could have been easier. I knew only too well the Italian position with regard to the extension of customs privileges to the clerical staff and was very much afraid that since Libya had been an Italian colony it would adopt the same viewpoint. Even if the Libyan negotiators had been willing to accept a clear-cut obligation to allow everyone in the Legation commissary privileges, we were none too sure that such a privilege might not be seized upon by the opposition during the debates in parliament to muddy the entire issue. And this at all costs we did not want. Hence the provision concerning the commissary and the rights of the Legation staff to use the commissary was purposely made rather ambiguous. Long after I signed the agreement on behalf of the United States in the fall of 1954, the question did come up and the Libyans did make an objection to the use of the commissary by Embassy (it was by then an Embassy) personnel. That objection, however, was negotiated on a separate basis while the

United States kept on enjoying the use of the field. Possibly if we had used precise language in 1954 there would not have been any problem. Looking back on the situation I have no regrets whatsoever that we resorted to ambiguity. The stakes were just too high to take the chance of a minor issue flaring up and jeopardizing the basic objective.

Naturally, ambiguities do not help the interpretation of treaties. An understanding of why the ambiguities occurred may nevertheless assist in arriving at the basic meaning of agreements which is why I have spent so much time giving actual examples.

Ambiguities also occur sometimes in treaties with the U.S.S.R., particularly multilateral treaties, since it is sometimes preferable to let an unclear passage or relatively minor drafting error in an article previously agreed upon, pass uncorrected, even when detected, rather than running the risk of reopening the whole article and jeopardizing the negotiations.

Another factor that distinguishes an international agreement from a domestic contract is that the international agreement may have to be phrased in several languages. Ideally there should be perfect concordance between the languages, but this is not always achieved. From a practical standpoint negotiations are usually conducted in the main in one language with only the definitive texts being prepared in both languages. At the end the latter work may be done hastily and errors creep in.

At this point for a better understanding of treaty procedure it might be well to describe the actual process involved in the negotiations of an international agreement although admittedly that process varies widely depending on the circumstances. Moreover, the negotiations of a multilateral treaty which is most likely to be considered at an international conference will not follow the same steps as are involved in the drafting of a bilateral treaty. The latter process is much easier to understand so it may be well to concentrate on that process in the hope of providing some concept of the role of a negotiator and the methods that are followed.

The first point for a nation to determine is the desirability of reaching an agreement with another nation on some particular subject. If a positive decision is reached and an agreement is considered desirable, an agreement is usually prepared in draft form to reflect the position of the government proposing the pact. If it is an American-sponsored accord, the Department of State would advance it after consultation with other governmental agencies that are involved, as for example the Department of Defense. If the agreement were important enough, the President would also be consulted at least as to the general objectives. The next decision is whether to have the negotiations in Washington or the capital of the other state. In some instances the latter may be preferable, particularly if the principal officials to be persuaded are living in the foreign capital. Obviously one can deal with the Ambassador in Washington, but that means he has to relay Washington's position to his home government which he may or may not do in adequate fashion.

Assuming that the negotiations are initiated in a foreign capital, the draft of the treaty would be presented to the Foreign Office by the American diplomatic mission. If the agreement does not voice too many technical points the American Embassy staff may be charged with the duty of negotiation. If it is a technical treaty, as for example a Treaty on the Avoidance of Double Taxation, experts are usually sent from Washington to assist in the negotiation.

The foreign government may, of course, accept the treaty in toto. More likely, however, it will submit its own version or at least challenge some of the proposed American clauses. At this point the American negotiators must endeavor to resolve the differences. The accusation has been made that ambassadors and those under them are only puppets dangling at the end of a telephone wire and have no real initiative in negotiations. This is not quite true as a negotiator still has a large role to perform. He may be able to persuade a foreign government that its fears are unfounded and that an American clause should be accepted as proposed. On the other hand, he may realize that the foreign government does have a valid objection which was overlooked in the drafting of the agreement in Washington and that change must be made. His task at this point is to explain to Washington the objections of the foreign government and possibly to suggest alternate language that would resolve the differences and still protect the interests of the United States. Article by article, and sometimes clause by clause, the various provisions receive approval for inclusion in the final text. Nevertheless, the Department reserves the right to review the agreement as a whole and to make certain that the wording is consistent.

If the Department approves the English text, the next task is that of harmonizing that text with the text in the language of the other state. That text likewise has to be approved by the Department. When all is ready and the Department's approval has been forthcoming, the texts must be prepared for signature.

Where the texts are in languages using the Latin alphabet such as English and French they can be placed side by side in parallel columns. This does not work if the text is in a language such as Arabic which reads in a direction contrary to a Latin alphabet version. In such a case, placing the two languages in a parallel column is, of course, impossible, for the beginning of the English text would be opposite the ending of the Arabic text, and vice versa. In such a case the only thing to do is to have the two texts meet in the middle.

The right of a plenipotentiary to negotiate and sign and seal an agreement (he uses his own personal seal) is usually evidenced by a document known as a "full power." In the past, considerable emphasis was given to full powers. In more recent years there has been a gradual relaxation of the strict rules governing the necessity for the submission of a full power.

When I signed the base rights agreement for Wheelus Field with Libya on behalf of the United States in my capacity as chargé d'affaires, I was authorized to do so by a telegram from the Secretary of State. While it is true that the agreement was considered as an executive agreement by the United States, the Libyan government submitted it to their parliament for ratification and considered it to be a formal document, the equivalent to what under American Constitutional law would be considered a treaty.

In the Vienna Convention on Treaties mentioned previously, one article sets forth what seems to be a sensible procedure, providing:

"A person is considered as representing a State for the purpose of adopting or authenticating the text of a treaty or for the purpose of expressing the consent of the State to be bound by a treaty if:

(a) he produces appropriate full powers; or

(b) it appears from the practice of the States concerned or from other circumstances that their intention was to consider that person as representing the State for such purposes and to dispense with full powers.

In virtue of their functions and without having to produce full powers, the following are considered as representing their State:

(a) Heads of State, Heads of Government and Ministers for Foreign Affairs, for the purpose of performing all acts relating to the conclusion of a treaty;

(b) heads of diplomatic missions, for the purpose of adopting the text of a treaty between the accrediting State and the State to which they are accredited;

(c) representatives accredited by States to an international conference or to an international organization or one of its organs, for the purpose of adopting the text of a treaty in that conference, organization or organ."

Following the signature of an international agreement by the United States the text may have to be submitted to the Senate for its advice and consent under the constitutional language previously quoted.

As has already been mentioned, the fact that an agreement is not called a treaty does not mean that the President is exonerated from the duty of submitting it to the Senate.

In the years that have elapsed since the Constitution was adopted, there have been many arguments, some of them quite acrimonious, as to when an international agreement constitutes a treaty within the meaning of the Constitution. If it is not a "treaty" it is called an "executive agreement" although that term is somewhat misleading as some so-called executive agreements are based upon authorizations made in prior treaties or legislation or are given subsequent Congressional approval.

Just for example, the Treaty of Peace with Japan authorized the establishment of a commission to determine war claims, and that commission was established pursuant to a multilateral agreement which was never submitted to the Senate. Likewise the various reciprocal trade agreements were entered into pursuant to specific authority given by the Congress.

Sometimes an agreement, instead of being submitted to the Senate for its advice and consent to ratification, is approved by the House and the Senate in a joint resolution having the force of law. In fact there have been instances where the executive obtained such consent of Congress where he had been unable to obtain it previously through the usual treaty method. This was the case in the annexation of both Texas and Hawaii. To call agreements approved by joint resolution "executive agreements" is stretching the language.

There are, however, a large number of true executive agreements, that is, agreements entered into on the basis of a president's constitutional power, without prior congressional authorization or approval. Some of them, such as the destroyer-bases agreements entered into during the last war when the United States exchanged fifty over-aged destroyers for bases in British possessions, are quite important.

It is sometimes very difficult to determine when an agreement should be considered as a "treaty" or as an "executive agreement." Generally speaking, an agreement must be considered as a treaty subject to Senate approval if the agreement is of a considerable importance, involves the expenditure of funds that have not been appropriated or is contrary to existing federal or state law. Each of these points deserve a word:

1. The very importance of the subject matter may require Senate consultation. It would be unthinkable, for example, to settle an important boundary dispute by an executive agreement.

2. The implementation of the agreement will require the expenditure of funds. Under the rules of the House of Representatives, an appropriation for funds can only be made when the appropriation supposed to finance the activity has previously been authorized by existing law. It has been held that a treaty but not an executive agreement will serve as an authorization. An item in an appropriation bill to provide for an activity not previously authorized can be stricken on a point of order. It is possible under certain circumstances to restore that item, but it is not good practice to rely on that possibility.

3. The agreement modifies an existing statute. Under the Constitution as interpreted by the Supreme Court a statute and a treaty have equal force and the latter in point of time will prevail in case of conflict. Hence a treaty can amend a statute. It is more than dubious whether an executive agreement could also amend a statute. Furthermore, while it is clear that a treaty supersedes a state law, it is not so clear that an executive agreement would reach the same result.

In the entire history of the United States there has never been an instance when a treaty has been held unconstitutional. On the other hand, the exact limits of the treaty-making power have never been ascertained. That feature of the law has already been discussed in the chapter on human rights so a reconsideration of the subject would be repetitious . Suffice it to say that treaties sometimes can achieve an end that legislation cannot reach .

In the next chapter the application and interpretation of international agreements will be considered .

CHAPTER XIX
TREATIES--
INTERPRETATION AND APPLICATION

The signing and, if necessary, the ratification of an international agreement does not mean that it can be applied automatically or that arguments as to its scope and interpretation will never arise. The very first matter to determine is when the agreement comes into force--at the time of signature; upon exchange of ratifications; on the deposit of the requisite number of ratifications in the case of a multilateral treaty; on a specified date; on the occurrence of a particular event; or on still some other basis. The problem is usually settled by the terms of the agreement itself. When, however, those terms are not clear or unforeseen contingencies take place, there is room for dispute. For example, if a treaty provides that it shall enter into force when ten signatories deposit their ratifications and if four ratify with reservations which are acceptable only to some of the signatories, has the treaty come into force?

A sharp distinction must be made between the entering into force of a binding agreement and its immediate application. Thus The Hague and Geneva Conventions on the conduct of war were obviously not applicable so long as peace lasted. They came into practical operation only at the start of military operations.

By the same token, it is not always clear when an agreement ends. Naturally if the duration is definitely specified or the accord terminates on the happening of an easily identified event, it is not difficult to ascertain the final date. Moreover, if both parties agree to terminate an agreement, it is manifest that it is ended. If, on the other hand, one side breaches one or more of the provisions of an agreement but does not repudiate the agreement as a whole, does it still continue in force? An American court has held that in such an instance so long as the rest of its provisions are still valid, it is up to the other side to determine whether the entire agreement should be set aside. In that particular case Italy had refused the extradition of one of its nationals notwithstanding the terms of an extradition convention between the United States and Italy which provided for such extradition.

What if one of the provisions is obviously not acceptable to contemporary morals? A good illustration is afforded by the Treaty of Utrecht of 1713 between Spain and Great Britain whereby Spain ceded Gibraltar to England. England obligated itself not to permit Jews or Moors to reside in Gibraltar. That treaty has been attacked by Spain on the ground that Gibraltar was wrested by force from Spain and was maintained as part of Britain's colonial Empire which should now be liquidated, a position in which Spain has had the support of the United Nations General Assembly. Spain, however, has not argued, even during the heat of the controversy, that the treaty has been broken because a few Moors or Jews might have been living in Gibraltar.

Somewhat related to the effect on an agreement of an evolution in morals is the broader question of the effect of a change of circumstances. Obviously if the change involves the disappearance of a state by merger with another state, the agreements binding the vanished state will also disappear. It is, however, arguable whether the state that has absorbed the former state is not subject to at least some of the obligations of the agreements in question as, for example, a servitude created by a prior treaty. If Panama were to rejoin Colombia (an event that is not likely to happen but provides nevertheless a good hypothetical illustration of the point under discussion) it would seem that American canal rights on the Isthmus would continue in effect.

A much more difficult problem is posed by a mere alteration in conditions not foreseen when the agreement was originally drafted. Theoretically, if a change is such as to make the accord completely irrelevant it should fall by the wayside. The international lawyers have a term for the implied condition that an agreement will remain in force only so long as the circumstances envisaged at the time the treaty was negotiated continue in effect. That term is known as rebus sic stantibus which literally means "things being as they are." The difficulty with enforcing this concept is that it is almost impossible to judge when circumstances have changed sufficiently to invalidate a treaty. Life seldom stands still and new situations arise all the time. If changes in circumstances were normally considered sufficient to release a nation from its obligations, there are few treaties that could stand the test of time. Moreover, who does the judging? Hence the concept of rebus sic stantibus, although sometimes argued, is seldom invoked.

War can also have an effect on treaties. As has already been said, agreements such as The Hague and Geneva Conventions on the conduct of war become operative only on the outbreak of war. Up to that time they remain dormant. On the other hand, war can terminate a treaty. When Italy, a member of the Triple Alliance went to war in World War I against her erstwhile partners, Germany and Austria-Hungary, there was, to say the least, little left of the Triple Alliance.

Some other agreements, on the other hand, are merely suspended during a war and are given full application just as soon as hostilities end.

Still other agreements continue unaffected by war. Thus the New York Court of Appeals in an opinion by Judge Cardozo held that a treaty guaranteeing the inheritance of property to the nationals of the contracting parties, in that case the United States and Austria-Hungary, remained in effect during the war entitling an Austro-Hungarian national to inherit property in New York.

It can be seen that the picture is somewhat confusing. Further confusion (as if any more were needed) is added by the difficulty of determining when a war is a war and by the fact that agreements often have separable provisions some of which are affected by the outbreak of war and some of which remain in force. In other words, a part of the treaty may fail, while another part continues in being.

At the end of World War II the Treaty of Peace with Italy provided that:

" Each Allied or Associated Power will notify Italy within a period of six months from the coming into force of the present Treaty, which of its pre-war bilateral treaties with Italy it desires to keep in force or revive. Any provisions not in conformity with the present Treaty shall, however, be deleted from the above-mentioned treaties.

The American notification merely listed the bilateral treaties it wanted to keep in force or revive without trying to separate the two groups. Theoretically, the failure to distinguish between the two groups might have created difficulties. Obviously, rights can arise under a treaty that is in force. If, however, the treaty is suspended, the question is more dubious. Hence, the status of the treaty in time of war might have become important. Fortunately, at least as far as I know, the question never arose.

Many questions can arise while an agreement is in effect as to the proper interpretation of its terms. Obviously the applicable principles bear considerable analogy to the law of domestic contracts and to the rules governing statutory interpretations. It would be unsafe, nevertheless, to rely too much on these analogies for a variety of reasons including the existence of particular rules of international law which may be at variance with contract law; the deliberate ambiguity sometimes found in the terms of a treaty; the multilateral nature of so many agreements, and the difficulty of reconciling languages. The latter factor is usually not present in domestic contracts although, as has been said, some commercial accords between nationals of two or more countries might be written in more than one language.

There are, in addition, particular problems in international life that do not have any exact counterpart in domestic practice, as for example the most favored nation clause. The meaning and scope of that clause can be best explained by way of example. Let us assume that A and B have a treaty on tax privileges and concessions which contains a most favored nation clause. Later A negotiates a similar treaty with C, but the concessions given to C are wider than those previously given to B. C becomes the most favored nation, that is, the nation enjoying the most favorable treatment. However, by virtue of the most favored nation clause, B can claim the same concessions. The Treaty with Israel on Friendship, Commerce and Navigation, which contains several most favored nation clauses relating to various provisions, contains this definition:

" The term 'most-favored-nation treatment' means treatment accorded within the territories of a Party upon terms no less favorable than the treatment accorded therein, in like situations, to

> nationals, companies, products, vessels or other objects,
> as the case may be, of any third country."

There has been considerable discussion whether the concessions granted under the most favored nation clause have to be granted automatically or only upon a showing of reciprocity.

In commercial treaties as well as most other treaties the rule has been adopted that the concession will be made without proof that the other state has made a similar concession to the United States. The reason is that it is often almost impossible to equate concessions, taking into consideration the diversity of the various methods followed in establishing commercial and other privileges. The most favored nation clause in consular conventions will not, however, operate unless there is a showing of reciprocity. Probably the most important issue in which this principle is likely to arise in the future is in connection with the American Consular Convention with the Soviet Union as that consular convention has the unusual provision that consular officers shall enjoy diplomatic privileges and immunities. Before another state can claim that privilege for its consular officers in the United States on the basis of the most favored nation clause in an earlier consular convention, it must show that it has granted diplomatic privileges and immunities or is willing to grant them to American consular officers in that state.

From what has been said it is clear that the interpretation of an agreement can be a difficult matter and that all sorts of pitfalls are present. Generally speaking, the basic rule has been to determine the intent of the parties.

All sorts of methods have been used to fathom what the parties really meant. One is to consult the preparatory works including the preliminary drafts, the minutes of the conference or conferences, contemporary statements and so on. Another is to look at the application of an agreement when it first came into force for presumably the meaning given an agreement at that time reflected the intent of the framers.

As has been previously pointed out, agreements are often drawn in two or more languages with the texts equally authentic. Nevertheless, it is a rare case when all of the languages defined as "authentic" were used to an equal extent in the preparation of the final version, because, from a practical standpoint, the negotiators usually concentrate upon one language to prepare the terms of the accord. Hence, in the case of divergent texts the intent may be reflected more accurately in the language used for working purposes than in the other "authentic" languages. In other words, if I may coin a phrase, one language may be more authentic than the other.

Moreover, a treaty will be interpreted in the case of ambiguity against the state that sponsored it and presumably prepared the original draft on the perfectly valid theory that it has the onus of making its meaning clear. This is particularly true in the case of punitive provisions such as may be found in a treaty of peace. Other rules of interpretation exist, but the ones mentioned illustrate the extent of the problem and the diversity of the methods used.

As might have been expected the complexity of the subject gave rise to considerable disagreement on the governing rules to follow in arriving at the proper interpretation of a treaty. This uncertainty coupled with the desirability of clarifying other questions concerning treaty interpretation, rendered the time ripe for codification. Hence, the International Law Commission prepared a draft which served as the basis for the Vienna Convention on the Law of Treaties which was opened for signature on May 23, 1969, following a conference in the Austrian capital. That agreement, which has already been mentioned in a previous chapter, constitutes the latest effort in the codification of basic international law taking its place with the Law of the Sea Conventions and the Conventions on Diplomatic and Consular Privileges and Immunities. The Convention covers eighty-five articles. Although some of these articles have already been quoted or referred to, there are a sufficient number remaining to make it impossible to analyze each one thoroughly. It is nevertheless worthwhile to look at some of the more important ones.

Article 4 of the Vienna Convention provides that:

> "Without prejudice to the application of any rules set forth in the present Convention to which treaties would be subject under international law independently of the Convention, the Convention applies only to treaties which are concluded by States after the entry into force of the present Convention with regard to such States."

(A "treaty" is defined as an international agreement, irrespective of its particular designation.) Theoretically, therefore, the interpretation of treaties existing before the coming into force of the Vienna Convention is governed by previously established rules, confused as they may be. It is highly unlikely, however, that the provisions of the Vienna Convention, where pertinent, will not be used to interpret most, if not all, treaties as a persuasive statement of the law, if not as a binding treaty commitment.

While there is certainly room for argument, the most important articles of the convention are, in my opinion, the ones that lay down the rules for interpretation. They are Articles 31, 32, and 33 which are so fundamental as to be worth quoting in extenso. They read:

Article 31

General rule of interpretation

1 A treaty shall be interpreted in good faith in accordance with the ordinary meaning to be given

to the terms of the treaty in their context and in the light of its object and purpose.

2. The context for the purpose of the interpretation of a treaty shall comprise, in addition to the text, including its preamble and annexes:

    (a) any agreement relating to the treaty which was made between all the parties in connexion with the conclusion of the treaty;

    (b) any instrument which was made by one or more parties in connexion with the conclusion of the treaty and accepted by the other parties as an instrument related to the treaty.

3. There shall be taken into account, together with the context:

    (a) any subsequent agreement between the parties regarding the interpretation of the treaty or the application of its provisions;

    (b) any subsequent practice in the application of the treaty which establishes the agreement of the parties regarding its interpretation;

    (c) any relevant rules of international law applicable in the relations between the parties.

4. A special meaning shall be given to a term if it is established that the parties so intended.

Article 32

Supplementary means of interpretation

Recourse may be had to supplementary means of interpretation, including the preparatory work of the treaty and the circumstances of its conclusion, in order to confirm the meaning resulting from the application of Article 31, or to determine the meaning when the interpretation according to Article 31:

    (a) leaves the meaning ambiguous or obscure; or

    (b) leads to a result which is manifestly absurd or unreasonable.

Article 33

Interpretation of treaties authenticated in
two or more languages

1. When a treaty has been authenticated in two or more languages, the text is equally authoritative in each language, unless the treaty provides or the parties agree that, in case of divergence, a particular text shall prevail.

2. A version of the treaty in a language other than one of those in which the text was authenticated shall be considered an authentic text only if the treaty so provides or the parties so agree.

3. The terms of the treaty are presumed to have the same meaning in each authentic text.

4. Except where a particular text prevails in accordance with paragraph 1, when a comparison of the authentic texts discloses a difference of meaning which the application of Articles 31 and 32 does not remove, the meaning which best reconciles the texts, having regard to the object and purpose of the treaty, shall be adopted.

The Convention touches on a host of other problems including, among other topics, the obligations and rights of third states, the amendment of treaties, the circumstances determining the invalidity of treaties, the termination of treaties and the consequences of coercion.

On the very difficult questions of state succession and effect of war, the negotiators obviously considered agreement hopeless. They therefore inserted a provision which in effect said that those two questions were hot potatoes they did not want to handle. The language of the treaty, which naturally is phrased in more diplomatic terms, is that:

"The provisions of the present Convention shall not prejudge any question that may arise in regard to a treaty from a succession of States or from the international responsibility of a State or from the outbreak of hostilities between States."

It is clear that while the Vienna Convention represents a long step forward in the law of treaties, it by no means settles all problems. Some will still have to be decided upon the basis of existing practice, and perhaps some others will require completely new approaches.

Before leaving the Convention it is worth mentioning that it contains a specific provision that a party may not invoke the provisions of its internal law as justification for its failure to perform a treaty.

This paragraph raises inferentially the question of the relation of an agreement to the internal law of a nation. According to some jurisdictions, it is considered to be an essential and integral part of the domestic law as of the time it enters into force. The English practice seems to be that generally speaking a treaty enters into domestic law only when legislation placing the treaty into force is enacted. Treaties enter into force without implementing legislation only in limited circumstances. That position is summarized succinctly by a British jurist in these terms:

> "
> It has become established that:--
> a) Treaties which:--(1) affect the private rights of British subjects, or (2) involve any modification of the common or Statute law by virtue of their provisions or otherwise, or (3) require the vesting of additional powers in the Crown, or (4) impose additional financial obligations, direct or contingent, upon the Government of Great Britain, must receive parliamentary assent through an enabling Act of Parliament, and, if necessary, any legislation to effect the requisite changes in the law must be passed."

The American position is somewhat different. Generally speaking, a treaty is the law of the land and, as has been pointed out in earlier chapters, can effect certain results unattainable by legislation. To a lesser extent, this is also true of an executive agreement. Nevertheless, there are treaties which must have legislation to implement them. The outstanding example, of course, is a treaty calling for the expenditure of funds. Since both Houses of Congress must agree to such an expenditure it is obvious that the treaty cannot become fully effective until the necessary amount is appropriated by law. In the long history of American diplomacy there is no record of funds to implement a treaty ever having been denied. There have, however, been disagreements and debates on the subject. As has already been indicated under American law a statute that is inconsistent with a treaty supersedes the treaty domestically even though the international obligations continue.

The role of a treaty in domestic law brings to mind the argument that has taken place between the so-called monist and dualist theorists. In essence, the monists maintain that international law and national law compose one concept of law, whereas the dualists assert that they are separate and apart from each other. In the realm of treaties the corresponding argument would hinge on the role of a treaty in domestic law.

I do not think that the argument, from a practical standpoint, is particularly important. I believe that Professor Bishop disposes of it in his 1965 lectures at The Hague Academy when he said, speaking of the monist and dualist theories, "I am not sure whether either contributes much to a clear understanding of international legal phenomena."

In my own experience in various capacities I cannot recall one instance where the theories made any difference in the resolution of a practical problem. They are mentioned at this point only because they are given currency in a number of texts.

In any event whatever concept is adopted, treaty interpretation is likely to be important for a long time from both an international and a domestic standpoint.

CHAPTER XX
THE LAW OF THE SEA

From time immemorial the sea, covering two thirds of the globe, has been the source of food and the great highway of the world. History has recorded fierce struggles for the mastery of the seas or at the very least for the freedom to use them unimpeded. Typical of the latter were the American protests against British impressment during the Napoleonic Wars, the campaigns against the Barbary pirates of North Africa to eliminate their depredations and the efforts of the neutral trading nations in the League of Armed Neutrality to limit the rights of belligerents to interfere with ocean commerce. There were also numerous disputes over fishing and similar rights.

Historically speaking however, the oceans were so illimitable, their resources so vast and man's imprint on them so puny, that many of today's problems concerning the seas simply did not exist. The seas did of course receive some attention from jurists and some basic concepts were laid down fairly early. Thus the theory that the sea is legally divided into four parts, each with its different regime, is not a novel one. Those four parts are (1) internal waters consisting of bays and harbors and other incursions of the sea into the land over which a nation exercises the same control as over its land areas; (2) territorial waters which differ from internal waters by being subject to the rights of friendly foreign vessels to navigate them for peaceful and legitimate purposes--the so-called right of innocent passage; (3) the contiguous zones; and (4) the open seas.

Territorial waters and contiguous zones warrant special comment. A state felt the need to control the seas adjacent to its coast for obvious reasons. At the time the concept of the territorial sea took form an easy way to determine the width of the adjoining sea which a nation could and should control was the range of cannon shot. In the old Latin phrase "Imperium terrae finiri ubi finitur armorum potestas" (The domain of the land ceases where ends the power of arms). Since cannon at that time had a range of about three nautical miles that was the extent of the marginal or territorial seas. Nowadays, of course, with long range guns and missiles capable of traveling thousands of miles, this system of measuring the territorial sea is patently absurd. Unfortunately, no other adequate criterion has been substituted so that the extent of the territorial seas claimed by various coastal countries varies immensely. Claims range from three miles to two hundred miles.

The contiguous zone begins where the territorial sea ends. It is a zone over which the coastal state does not have quite the same measure of control as over the territorial sea but over which it nevertheless does exercise some authority. Thus to facilitate enforcement of customs laws the United States, very early in its history, prohibited certain activities twelve miles from shore.

Quite recently, the United States following the lead of other nations, established a fishing conservation zone. The pertinent portions of the Act of October 14, 1966 creating that zone read:

> ". . . there is established a fisheries zone contiguous to the territorial seas of the United States. The United States will exercise the same exclusive rights in respect to fisheries in the zone as it has in its territorial sea, subject to the continuation of traditional fishing by foreign states within this zone as may be recognized by the United States.
>
> The fisheries zone has as its inner boundary the outer limits of the territorial sea and as its seaward boundary a line drawn so that each point on the line is nine nautical miles from the nearest point in the inner boundary."

Other efforts have also been made to limit foreign activities close to shore. Later on in the chapter the problem of the contiguous zone will be explored more fully.

As the decades succeeded one another, more and more problems concerning the sea began to demand the attention of, and cause concern to, the lawyer, the scientist and the politician. Moreover, it does not require Jeanne Dixon to prophesy that many more lie in the not too distant future.

The problems are many and any attempt to list all of them is doomed to failure. Nevertheless, it may be worth listing at least some of them and giving an indication of the attention they have drawn or may reasonably be expected to draw in the future. No attempt is made to arrange them according to their importance, since relative importance is always debatable. The problems relate to:

1. The preservation and development of the riches of the sea and the allocation of fishing and kindred rights.

2. The advancement of humanitarianism at sea.

3. The promotion of safety of life at sea.

4. The prevention of pollution.

5. The guarantee of free navigation.

6. The exploitation of the ocean-bed.

7. The use of the sea to affect climate.

8. The use of the sea for desalination plants.

The effort to bring the foregoing problems under control is a gradual process as new questions come to the fore or old questions grow in importance. In some instances the necessity for legal action was realized in the last century. In others the legal framework--even now by no means complete--was developed in this century. Contributing to the growth of the law cf the sea were international agreements, both multilateral and bilateral, domestic proclamations and edicts, court decisions and the acceptance of maritime customs regulating conduct at sea.

Prior to 1958 the International Law Commission prepared the draft of four conventions which were rather grandiloquently called the "Law of the Sea." They were submitted for consideration to a conference held in Geneva in 1958 from which emerged the four conventions based on the drafts submitted.

Actually there is a great deal more to the Law of the Sea than these four conventions, important as they undoubtedly are in codifying the ocean law. Moreover, in some fields, as has been indicated, the law may be just developing, while in others, potential problems are still far away from legal consideration, presently existing largely in the form of scientific speculation. Thus there has not as yet been any serious effort to cover those relating to the legal phases of the last two problems listed previously, that is, climate and desalination. In fact, scientific progress in these two fields is still not very far advanced. It is interesting, nevertheless, that John Gunther recorded in <u>Inside Russia today</u> that a Russian scientist suggested a joint Russo-American effort to dam the Bering straits to keep the icy waters of the Arctic Sea out of the northern Pacific and thus create a milder climate in Alaska and Eastern Siberia.

Another reported Russian venture that may affect climate is a plan to direct the waters of three large Siberian rivers from the Arctic Sea to interior lakes. If this is done, the salinity of the Arctic water will increase, the water will freeze less easily, and climate may be affected with possible world wide repercussions.

From time to time one also reads Jules Verne type speculations on diverting the Gulf Stream. So far none of this has come to pass but if science does progress to the point of diverting currents and actual attempts are made to do so, the present legal difficulties concerning the sea will be like ant hills compared to Mt. Everest. Imagine Europe without the Gulf Stream!

Desalination may also present legal problems for the future. So far it is limited in practical operations to a few plants such as the one at Guantanamo Bay or in Kuwait to produce water for domestic purposes as well as to distillation plants on board ships. But what will happen if there is a breakthrough in the cost of desalination and immense quantities of water are taken from the sea for irrigation purposes? What will that do to the ecology of the region and what legal issues will arise?

It is interesting that the United States and the Soviet Union have cooperated for the mutual development of desalination plants. Presumably this cooperation is primarily technical in nature and does not allude to the ecological question just mentioned.

The exploitation of the ocean bed, that is, the bed of the high seas, is receiving increasing attention but as yet no solution has been evolved to resolve the legal problems looming on the horizon. The only concrete measure taken so far is the negative one of prohibiting the emplacement of weapons of mass destruction on the seabed. President Nixon referred to U.S.-U.S.S.R. proposed treaty neutralizing the seabed in his Report to the Congress of February 25, 1971 saying:

> "This Administration took the initiative to negotiate a treaty banning weapons of mass destruction from the seabeds. The United Nations overwhelmingly approved the treaty this fall, and I will soon submit it to the Senate."

The seabed weapons treaty, whatever its merits, does not provide a solution for the orderly development of the seabed for peaceful purposes. One possibility is to consider the ocean bed subject to exploitation by whatever nation or group has the industrial and technical potential to effect such exploitation. This means that when such exploitation becomes feasible there will be a rush among the nations to place major portions of the ocean bed under their respective control. In a sense it will be somewhat like the efforts of the colonial powers in the last century to colonize Africa and to parcel it out among themselves.

Still another possibility is to divide the ocean floor among the nations bordering on the ocean. There is little likelihood that this solution will ever be adopted since states like the United States would control to the middle of the Atlantic and Pacific leaving little, if any, control to states having limited coastlines and, naturally, none at all, to inland states.

The whole subject is receiving increasing attention among writers, scientists and lawyers and in the halls of the United Nations as the wealth lying at the bottom of the ocean, including mineral nodules, is beginning to be appraised. At the 22nd General Assembly in 1967 Malta suggested a resolution whose purpose was summarized in the International Conciliation resume of the "Issues Before the 23rd General Assembly" in these terms:

> " It was Malta that drew the attention of last year's Assembly to this impending colonial competition-- 'a virtually inevitable consequence of the present situation.' The sea-bed, argued its representative, is the legacy of all mankind, and involves the acceptance by the international community of entirely new legal principles that go beyond the traditional ones of the oceans as res communis or res nullius. He went on to propose that the United Nations establish machinery to ensure that the ocean floor beyond the present limits of national jurisdiction be reserved exclusively for peaceful purposes, and to regulate the activities of all states in order to allocate the financial benefits from exploitations of the sea-bed primarily to the developing countries."

Since then the quest for a solution has stimulated continuing attention, but as yet an acceptable plan has not been evolved. To avoid any mis-understanding it should be emphasized that what has been said does not re-late to the continental shelf which is the extension under the water of the continental limits of a country into the relatively shallow sea before there is a drop into the abyss of the sea. The continental shelf will be dealt with much more fully later in this chapter in discussing the Law of the Sea Con-vention on that subject.

In summary, legal action with respect to the last three problems pre-viously listed still lies around the corner. This is not true with regard to the first five problems although the degree of action taken varies widely with the problem.

In addition to approving the Law of the Sea Conventions of 1958, the United States and a number of other maritime nations have entered into a series of bilateral arrangements and a number of multilateral agreements designed to regulate and protect interests at sea, many of which predate 1958 by many years. Furthermore, the United States has submitted a num-ber of questions, particularly with regard to fishing rights and conserva-tion, to arbitration. One important arbitration was the North Atlantic Fish-eries Arbitration of 1910 which ended a series of longstanding fisheries dis-putes between the United States and Canada and formed the basis for a sub-sequent agreement on the subject. The other arbitration which stands out in American diplomatic history is the Bering Sea Arbitration concerning the conservation of the fur seals on the Pribilof Islands.

Here elements of humanitarianism enter in for the indiscriminate slaughter of the helpless seals had induced a sickening revulsion among many persons. The United States lost the arbitration but was able to reach an agreement with the offending parties that mitigated most of the evils.

Something of the same fervor may be observed nowadays as the re-sult of the campaign of Paris Match and other magazines to save the baby seals being slaughtered on Canadian shores.

Other instances of nations being impelled to regulate activities at sea from humanitarian motives readily come to mind. One of the most im-portant was the determined efforts to stamp out the infamous oceanic slave trade. For the same reasons the coolie trade from China likewise caused indignation and led to its eventual extinction.

Concern has also been expressed with the methods used for hunting sea-going mammals which are wanted for their meat, their furs, and their oil (the oil in the head and jaw of porpoises is particularly valued for lu-bricating watches). The slaughter of the seals has already been mentioned. Efforts have also been made to preserve the whale and to provide that the kill will be made in as painless a way as possible.

Conservation has not been restricted to the whale and the seal. The United States has entered into bilateral agreements with the Soviet Union, Japan, Canada and Mexico concerning fishing rights and the conservation of sockeye salmon, halibut, the king crab, and other species of marine life. Also as will be seen more fully later, one of the four 1958 conventions on the Law of the Sea concerns conservation. New legal difficulties may be created as aquaculture develops with the breeding of fish in enclosed stocks, particularly if the enclosures constitute navigational hazards.

The promotion of safety of life at sea has been primarily a matter of multilateral action. The convention for the unification of certain rules with respect to assistance and salvage at sea was signed at Brussels on September 23, 1910. Ironically the Titanic went down with the ship's band playing Nearer My God to Thee and carrying 1,513 persons to their death on April 15, 1912, less than two years after.

The Titanic disaster did give rise to the North Atlantic ice patrol which is now financed by nearly twenty states. Yogoslavia, interestingly enough, is the only Communist state contributing.

Other measures designed to promote safety at sea were agreements on load lines (the line on the hull which disappears in the water if the vessel is overloaded) and on safety standards at sea which regulate the construction of vessels, the holding of life-boat drills, and so forth. Probably no foreign flag ships meet the strict American specifications for safety but there is at least a minimum international standard to which all maritime nations must conform.

Pollution is now becoming a major concern of ocean law. The seas are being contaminated by industrial wastes and by the dumping of radioactive elements into the water. Moreover, there has always been dumping of garbage from shore and from ships at sea.

Probably the major problem is oil pollution. Some of it comes from the normal operation of ships and the dumping of wastes. Much of the tar that litters the beaches is attributable to that source. Even more serious is the spilling of huge cargoes of fuel such as followed the Torrey Canyon disaster when a very large loaded oil tanker ran aground on a rock near the French and British coasts. Causing equal concern are oil explorations that get out of control such as the one off the coast of Santa Barbara, California. An agreement to control at least some facets of the problem was signed in London on May 12, 1954. Moreover, an international convention relating to intervention on the high seas in cases of oil pollution casualities and an international convention on civil liability for oil pollution damage were approved in Brussels in November of 1969. It is dubious, however, whether the existing international agreements are a panacea for all of the ills of pollution. Thus the convention applicable to oil pollution casualties only affects a situation "following upon a maritime casualty" by which time it may be too late to prevent pollution.

The guarantee of free navigation becomes important primarily in time of war when neutral nations are harassed by stringent rules on contraband and by blockades. Otherwise questions concerning navigation relate primarily to the use of the territorial sea which will be discussed in the analysis of the Law of the Sea Conventions.

The Law of the Sea Conventions, because of their importance, deserve separate consideration. They are: The Territorial Sea and the Con-

tiguous Zone, the High Seas, Fishing and Conservation of the Living Resources of the High Seas, and the Continental Shelf.

It might be expected that the convention on the territorial sea would
define the width of that sea. As has been previously stated, the three nautical miles width has been subjected to increasing challenge.

An effort was made, which proved to be unavailing, to define the territorial sea at a Codification Conference at The Hague held in 1930. The
next real effort was made in Geneva in 1958. The United States, seeing
that it was a hopeless battle to try to keep the three mile limit, was willing
to agree to a six mile limit plus a contiguous zone of an additional six miles
within which measures could be taken for the conservation of fishing
rights.

The American delegate to the Conference, Mr. Arthur Dean, summarized the objections of the United States to the extension of the territorial sea
in an article he wrote after the conference in the October 1958 issue of The
American Journal of International Law. Among those objections were the
increase in the striking power of enemy submarines who could seek shelter
in a wide territorial sea, and the doubt that commercial airlines could over-
fly the territorial sea without the consent of the State to which the seas belonged. There were several other reasons as well, but the two cited serve
to illustrate at least some of the motives for the reluctance of the United
States to enlarge the territorial sea. Despite a strong endeavor, the American efforts to have the nations agree on a narrow territorial sea proved
unavailing.

An additional effort was made in 1960 to define the territorial sea at
another conference in Geneva, but once more it was unsuccessful. As a
consequence, at the present time the legal extent of the marginal sea is
difficult to determine with any precision. The United States has apparently
accepted a twelve mile limit if a treaty can be negotiated and will provide
for freedom of navigation through and over international straits.

At the same time more and more nations are claiming and enforcing
a marginal sea 200 nautical miles in width. In 1970 Argentina, Brazil, Chile,
Ecuador, El Salvador, Nicaragua, Panama, Peru and Uraguay declared at
Montevideo that

> "...the
> signatory States have, by reason of conditions peculiar to them
> extended their sovereignty or exclusive rights of jurisdiction
> over the maritime area adjacent to their coasts, its soil and
> its subsoil to a distance of 200 nautical miles from the baseline
> of the territorial sea."

The 200 mile limit has rather understandably given rise to controversy. American fishing vessels have on a number of occasions been seized
and fined by Peru and Eduador for fishing within the prohibited zone. Hopefully the extent of the territorial sea will be decided at a Law of the Sea

Conference to be held in 1973. In view of the difficulties of reaching agreement in the past, the possibility of arriving at a solution in 1973 does not appear very bright.

While the convention on the territorial sea does not specify its outer limits, there are rather elaborate provisions in the first law of the sea convention concerning the land points from which measurements should begin in determining the territorial sea. Currently those measurements have only a marginal importance since the outer limits are unsettled. It does little good to determine whether the measurement should start from A or B points on the shore when X, the outer limit, is unknown. If, however, there is ever agreement on the width of the territorial sea the provision to determine where the measurements should begin may be significant.

In particular there are two important questions to consider. First of all, when the nation has a rather rugged coastline studded with islands and bays, should the outer limits of the territorial sea, whatever they may be, be measured from a straight line running from headland to headland and island to island, or should it follow the sinuosities of the coast?

The second problem is whether the measurements should commence from high tide or low tide or from a point in between. In most cases the tides are not sufficiently high to make much difference. In some instances, however, wide stretches of the sea bottom become dry land at low tide. One of the best known of those locations is the beach at San Malo made famous by the cathedral of Mont St. Michel. The Convention resolved the problems in these terms:

"Article 3
Except where otherwise provided in these Articles, the normal baseline for measuring the breadth of the territorial sea is the low-water line along the coast as marked on large-scale charts officially recognized by the coastal State.

Article 4
1. In localities where the coastline is deeply indented and cut into, or if there is a fringe of island along the coast in its immediate vicinity, the method of straight baselines joining appropriate points may be employed in drawing the baseline from which the breadth of the territorial sea is measured."

While, from an international law standpoint, the provisions may make little difference so long as the outer limits are not defined, they may make some difference if a nation has by domestic legislation defined the width of the marginal sea around its coast. At least the legislation should coincide with the starting point as defined by the convention.

If ultimately a twelve mile territorial sea is adopted, some of the principal straits of the world such as the English Channel, Gibraltar and Singapore would be wholly within national territory so that passage through territorial seas is unavoidable. Moreover, in still other instances, ships sometimes hug the coast for navigational reasons. Thus ships moving southward along the Florida coast come quite close to the shore to prevent sailing against the Gulf Stream. They have the right of innocent passage which is guaranteed in Article 15 of the Convention in this manner:

" 1. The coastal State must not hamper innocent passage through the territorial sea.

2. The coastal State is required to give appropriate publicity to any dangers to navigation, of which it has knowledge, within its territorial sea."

Naturally, the right of innocent passage cannot be abused. Thus if a fishing trawler tries to obtain a catch while passing through the territorial seas, the coastal State would not be under any obligation to consider the vessel in innocent passage even though it had been constantly in motion.

As has already been indicated, the United States, in addition to claiming a territorial sea, has for a long time claimed the right, and conceded to other nations a similar right, to exercise limited authority in a contiguous zone for the purpose of enforcing customs regulations and providing for conservation measures.

The key provisions on the contiguous zone are contained in Article 24 of the convention and read:

" 1. In a zone of the high seas contiguous to its territorial sea, the coastal State may exercise the control necessary to:

(a) Prevent infringement of its customs, fiscal,immigration or sanitary regulations within its territory or territorial sea;

(b) Punish infringement of the above regulations committed within its territory or territorial sea.

2. The contiguous zone may not extend beyond twelve miles from the baseline from which the breadth of the territorial sea is measured."

American policy has not always been entirely uniform with regard to the contiguous zone. During prohibition days, for example, the United States attempted to control liquor smuggling in any area within one hour of sailing distance of the coast measured by the speed of the rum runner or the motor boats that attended it, which, of course, made for a highly variable contiguous zone. More recently, as shown by the Act of October 14, 1966 previously quoted, the United States has also provided for conservation measures in the contiguous zone.

The United States also, with the help of the Latin American nations, tried to prevent a substantial portion of the Western Atlantic from being used for any naval hostilities during World War II, but the prohibition was not particularly successful. The citizens of Montevideo gathered on the shore to watch the battle between the Graf Spee and the British cruisers which was only prevented by the scuttling of the Graf Spee at the hands of the German crew.

The second of the conventions agreed upon in Geneva is the one on the high seas which reiterates the principle that the high seas are open to all nations. In addition, that convention contains a number of other provisions which unfortunately cannot be taken up in detail for lack of space. Two or three do warrant comment. One of them has already been mentioned in connection with the discussion of the nationality of ships in an earlier chapter. Another constitutes a definition of piracy as an act of depredation committed for private ends.

In addition there are several articles devoted to hot pursuit which is always an interesting topic. Hot pursuit into the high seas occurs when an infraction of the coastal state's laws or regulations has taken place in the territorial sea or the contiguous zone, and the offender flees into the high sea pursued by the authorities of the coastal State. Probably the most celebrated instance of hot pursuit involved a Canadian rum runner I'm Alone. In this case a United States Coast Guard cutter had intercepted the rum runner intent on delivering its cargo in the United States. It could not, however, effect its capture before the little ship had fled to sea. The Coast Guard cutter followed in pursuit and, when it found that its guns had jammed, requested another Coast Guard cutter to take up the chase in its place. The rum runner was finally overtaken over two hundred miles from shore and was captured with shots from the Coast Guard vessel.

The legality of the American action was submitted to arbitration but the decision hinged on the appropriateness of the amount of force used by the Coast Guard cutter rather than on its right to maintain hot pursuit under the circumstances of the case. Both the American and Canadian jurists who constituted the Commission, found that excessive force had been used and made an award in favor of Canada and its seamen, one of whom was a French national. The legality of extending the hot pursuit over two hundred miles and of having one vessel take over from another, which in a sense broke the continuity of the operation, was never decided. In the convention on the high seas the question is also left somewhat in abeyance, as the pursuit can be continued only if it has not been interrupted, leaving unanswered whether the substitution of one pursuing vessel by another constitutes interruption. The convention does, however, authorize a combined airplane and ship pursuit.

The third of the conventions on the law of the sea relates to the fishing and conservation of the living resources of the high seas. That convention establishes rather elaborate procedures for resolving rights on fishery disputes which have been touched upon previously. As has been said, some of the procedures seem to have quite a bit in common with what might be contemplated if the case were to be decided on an ex aequo et bono basis.

Finally, the fourth convention on the law of the sea concerns the concerns the continental shelf. The theory of the continental shelf is essentially predicated on the geologic fact that along many coasts the land mass projects itself into the sea until it finally drops off into the depth of the ocean. Generally speaking, the water over the continental shelf is not particularly deep so that the resources of the continental shelf are subject to exploitation with present technical means. The theory has had a relatively recent origin in international law since technology was not capable of undertaking any serious exploitation of even the shallow bottom of the sea until the present century. When, however, it became clear that it was possible to exploit the continental shelf and its mineral and other resources, nations became interested in making certain that such exploitation would be reserved to the coastal state.

Although the concept of the continental shelf and its relation to the coastal states had been developing for some years before 1945, President Truman gave it a great impetus by making a proclamation claiming the right for the United States to exploit the continental shelf and its resources. There was surprisingly little opposition to that proclamation. In fact, most coastal States seemed to agree wholeheartedly that President Truman's proclamation was a sound measure. Hence when the time came to codify the law of the sea, or at least certain branches of it, one of the conventions dealt with the continental shelf. Probably the most important article of that convention is Article 1 which defines the continental shelf. It reads:

> "Article 1. For the purpose of these Articles, the term 'continental shelf' is used as referring (a) to the seabed and subsoil of the submarine areas adjacent to the coast but outside the area of the territorial sea, to a depth of 200 metres or, beyond that limit, to where the depth of the superjacent waters admits of the exploitation of the natural resources of the said areas; (b) to the seabed and subsoil of similar submarine areas adjacent to the coasts of islands."

Regrettably, the definition is not as clear as it might be since there can be considerable argument as to what constitutes the exploitation of the natural resources of the seabed at a depth in excess of 200 metres sufficient to establish that particular seabed as constituting part of the continental shelf. Another argument concerning the continental shelf arises when several States border on the sea and each claim a portion of the seabed as theirs. That question was submitted to the International Court of Justice by the nations surrounding the North Sea. While the International Court of Justice provided general guidelines of the subject, it referred the question back to the several states for settlement among themselves in accordance with such guidelines.

A legitimate question can be raised as to what constitutes the resources of the continental shelf that are subject to exploitation. An attempt to answer that question is made in paragraph 4 of Article 2 of the continental shelf convention in these words:

"The natural resources referred to in these Articles consist of the mineral and other non-living resources of the seabed and subsoil together with living organisms belonging to sedentary species, that is to say, organisms which, at the harvestable stage, either are immobile on or under the seabed or are unable to move except in constant physical contact with the seabed or the subsoil."

While the language on the surface appears to be rather clear, the application of it to certain species may not be so simple. One normally thinks of shellfish as lying on the bottom of the ocean. Yet anyone who has viewed Jacques Cousteau's moving pictures of underwater life will have been struck by the way certain claims manage to be quite mobile by opening and shutting their shells. Generally speaking, however, it does seem clear that the language which has just been quoted gives a coastal State a right to exploit the mineral resources of the continental shelf and the sedentary species living in the sea bottom.

The Law of the Sea Conventions are an important step forward in codifying the applicable rules. Nevertheless, even with respect to the subjects they cover, old questions such as the extent of the territorial sea are left unsolved and new problems have been created. The scientists, for example, feel that the Law of the Sea Conventions render oceanographic research much more difficult than in the past.

In essence, the legal problems of the sea are still very much with us. It is safe to say they will increase in importance as time goes on. Moreover, a whole new field may be opened up with the proposed draft treaty banning emplacement of nuclear weapons on the seabed agreed to by the United States and the U.S.S.R.

Chapter XXI

THE LAW OF OUTER SPACE

The law of outer space is at the moment very much the young brother of the law of the sea. Possibly, it will ultimately grow in complexity and depth and eventually overshadow in importance the law of the sea. But not yet.

At the present time everyone is interested in outer space. The glamour of the moon explorations and the infinite possibilities for the future have caught the attention of governments and international organizations as well as of the statesman and the common man. In 1968 the United Nations held a conference on the exploration and peaceful uses of outer space. Moreover, a General Assembly Committee on the Peaceful Uses of Outer Space gives continuing attention to the subject.

Some of the problems that may be foreseen have already been subjected to treaty stipulations. Others, including the determination of where outer space begins, are still being debated. All sorts of tests have been suggested to determine where outer space begins. One suggested criterion is the limit of atmospheric lift which is calculated to be fifty-two miles above the earth. Much lower and much higher limits have also been mentioned. An intriguing question is whether, if a limit is ever decided upon, it will be measured from sea level or follow the rise and fall of the land just the way the territorial sea follows the projection of the shore. Fifty miles above the top of Mt. Everest is not the same thing as fifty miles above New York City.

The most important multilateral treaty--in fact, the basic charter of the international law of space--is the Treaty on Principles Governing the Activities of States in the Exploration and Use of Outer Space, Including the Moon and Other Celestial Bodies. After some introductory recitals the treaty provides that the exploration of outer space will be done for the benefit of all countries, and that bodies in outer space would not be subject to appropriation, a provision reminiscent of the Antarctic Treaty. Next, the treaty stipulates that exploration shall be carried on in accordance with international law. Moreover, it prohibits the installation of nuclear weapons in outer space, either on man-made satellites or on celestial bodies, and provides that the latter shall be used "exclusively for peaceful purposes."

Another article concerns itself with mutual assistance to astronauts both in space and on their return to earth. Thus if a Soviet astronaut landed in Great Britain, the British authorities would be obligated to give him all the assistance possible.

The treaty then takes up the question of international responsibility and the control of objects launched into space. These articles do not refer to a hypothetical state of facts that may never occur, for on June 5, 1969 wreckage from a Soviet space vehicle badly damaged a small Japanese freighter and injured five crew members. With all the debris there is in the air, there is no reason to suppose that such accidents will not occur in the future. One can only hope that a spent satellite does not crash in Times Square at the noon hour or on New Year's Eve.

When objects from outer space are returned to earth the nations participating in the treaty have an obligation to return such objects to the original owner. On May 7, 1969 the United States returned to the Soviet Union a metal sphere dropped from a Soviet space vehicle which eventually washed ashore in Alaska.

After disposing of the problem of responsibility and the ownership and control of objects launched into outer space, the treaty admonishes states from contaminating the earth with extra terrestrial matter. The quarantines imposed on the returning astronauts are an indication of the seriousness with which the United States believes in its obligations under that clause.

The treaty ends with a series of articles providing for the exchange of information, the observation of flights, and the mutual visitation of installations.

Evidently it was considered that the provisions in the basic treaty were not sufficiently detailed with regard to the rescue of astronauts. Hence another treaty on that specific subject was opened for signature on April 22, 1968 which spells out the obligations of the parties in considerable detail. Even this treaty has been criticized as inadequate.

Undoubtedly as time progresses additional multilateral agreements will regulate the conduct of nations in space. One factor seems clear, the disinclination of nations to start an arms race in space. Section 102 (2) of the National Aeronautics and Space Act of 1958 specifically provides:

"The Congress hereby declares that it is the policy of the United States that activities in space should be devoted to peaceful purposes for the benefit of all mankind."

In addition to the general multilateral treaties on space, the United States has entered into three multilateral agreements - to which over eighty states are parties - concerning communications satellites. Furthermore, a series of bilateral agreements and arrangements with a number of countries relating to joint experiments in outer space on ultraviolet, earth mapping, and earth resource surveys, ionospheric research, communication satellites, tracking stations and related activities have been negotiated by the United States. There are some four hundred such arrangements. Some of them are obviously considered too transitory or too technical to warrant being included in the treaties and other international acts series.

The United States even has a space treaty with an international organization--the European Space Research Organization. Undoubtedly as time goes by and science ranges further and further, such agreements will continue to multiply. In general, space law is still in its swaddling clothes.

Chapter XXII
CONCLUSION

In the preceding chapters I have endeavored to outline the current problems of international law and to indicate the direction in which that law is going. It is impossible to be completely tidy as international law spills over into the intricacies of international organizations, international commercial law, admiralty law, private international law, and other technical fields. Moreover, it can only be understood in the framework of the political world of today and in relation to the ever-increasing economic and social problems that test the ingenuity of statesmen. I have tried, however, within the limited bounds of this volume to provide in general terms the basic elements of the international law of peace and to relate those elements to the context of other sciences and of the world at large, often using my own experience as a point of departure. The reader can tell better than I whether I have succeeded.

As can be readily seen, I am fully aware of the fact that international law has many problems to solve and great difficulties to overcome. Nevertheless I continue to be a firm believer in the salutary benefits of that law and its potential in the international life of today. As I see it our task is not to bewail the undoubted weaknesses of international law but to clarify its discrepancies, fill its gaps, and seek its acceptance and implementation. In a sense I see the quest for international law as part of a wider search for morality and law. In the words of that old Latin saying," Sol justitiae illustra nos."

CHAPTER NOTES

EXPLANATORY COMMENTS
ON THE NOTES

The notes are keyed to the text by page and catchword, which avoids the annoyance of numerical reference in the text. The system was borrowed from the books of Mrs. Lester (Barbara) Tuchman, who has graciously consented to my copying her ingenious method.

As a general rule, well known historical events or tendencies are not documented in the interest of saving space. However, where an event is relatively little known or where the substantiating material is of particular human interest, an exception is made.

To support particular facts, encyclopedias and standard reference books are widely used, as they are available in most libraries and are thus within easy reach of the reader who wants to verify a statement. Moreover, I have found that some encyclopedia articles are the best short synopses of particular topics and are written by outstanding authorities such as Quincy Wright or Leo Gross.

I cite very few articles from legal periodicals. This is not because they are unimportant. Neither am I unaware of their existence, although not having lived as long as Methuselah I have not had the time to read them all. I omit them only because access to them can be obtained rather readily through the sources cited in the bibliography. Books, such as those by Bishop and Rhyne, contain extensive annotations to periodical literature. To the maximum extent possible, I have tried to cite material that is not usually referred to in the standard international law texts. It would have been nice to include full citations to every relevant article and text, but then this book would have extended into several volumes.

The system adopted is not perfect, but I am consoled by the West African proverb that "even the best firewood has some ants on it."

INTRODUCTION

NOTES:

Page

1   PRIVATE INTERNATIONAL LAW: Bishop, International Law, 1971. pp. 4 and 5; Beale, Conflict of Laws, 1935, p. 8.

2   EXTRADITION: It is interesting that when Schwarzenberger refers to extradition in his Manual of International Law, 1960, p. 108, he includes that reference under a heading entitled "International Criminal Law." Admittedly the question is essentially one of semantics.

2   AUSTIN: There is a good thumbnail sketch of Austin in Whitaker, Politics and Power, 1964, p. 35.

2   KENNAN: Realities of American Foreign Policy, 1966, p. 38.

2   VON BETHMANN HOLLWEG: The History of Twelve Days, by J.W. Headlam, 1915, p. 388, quotes British Ambassador Sir Edward Goschen to Sir Edward Grey.

3   HITLER: A popular biography, Himmler, by Willi Frischauer, 1962, p. 97 et seq., indicates the lengths to which Hitler went.

3   KENNAN: Realities of American Foreign Policy, 1966, p. 39.

3   WELL KNOWN INTERNATIONAL JURIST: Leo Gross, Book Review in the October 1969 issue of 63 A.J.I.L. 839.

4   FICTION: One of the best, if not the best,summations of fictions is to be found in Roscoe Pound, Jurisprudence, 1959, Vol. III, pp. 448 et seq. There is also the classic treatment of this subject in Ancient Law by Sir Henry Maine, 1888, pp. 20 et seq.

The Tunisian law on marriage was furnished to me through the courtesy of the Tunisian Ambassador to Washington. His letter to me and its enclosure follow:

"Following your letter of January 16, 1969, in which you asked if we could provide you with a citation on the Tunisian Law prohibiting multiple marriages, please find enclosed a translation of this law, taken from the Code du Statut Personnel, published by Mr. Mohamed Tahar Es-Snoussi, in Tunis. The law is part of the Decree of August 13, 1956, Book I: 'On Marriage,' in the section on 'Impediments to Marriage,' Article 18, page 18.

"I have furthermore enclosed photocopies of the french text which was translated for you."

(signed) Rachid Driss
Ambassador

"Article 18.

Polygamy is forbidden. (1)

The polygamist will incur a sentence of imprisonment for a year and a fine of 240.00 franss or either one of these penalties.

(1) In prohibiting multiple marriages, this article is based on the fact, well proven for centuries, that the polygamist can never treat equally all of his wives.

Furthermore, God has said: 'And you could not be equitable in your behavior towards the women (the wives) even if you tried.'"

CHAPTER I
The Development of International Law

TEXTS:

A. Nussbaum, A Concise History of the Law of Nations, 1947.

A. Hershey, The Essentials of International Public Law and Organization, 1927.

C. Phillipson, The International Law and Custom of Ancient Greece and
Rome, 2 Vols., 1911.

J.H.W. Verzijl, International Law in Historical Perspective, 1970.

J.B. Scott, editor, The Classics of International Law. This is a series
of reproductions and translations of the works of the early founders
of International Law, including of course Grotius. Printed and
reprinted in various years.

H.G. Jacobini, A Study of the Philosophy of International Law as seen
in Works of Latin American Writers, 1954.

Mohammad Talaat Al Ghunaimi, The Muslim Conception of International Law and the Western Approach, 1968.

S. Prakash Sinha, New Nations and the Law of Nations, 1967.

J.J.G. Syatauw, Some Newly Established Asian States and the Development of International Law, 1961.

NOTES:

Page

7   STOIC PHILOSOPHY: The discussion of the interrelationship of jus
     civile, jus gentium, and jus naturale has, for obvious reasons, been
     simplified. A more thorough study would indicate that the jurists do
     not always agree. W.W. Buckland in his Textbook of Roman Law from
     Augustus to Justinian, 1932, points out on page 53 that not all Roman
     jurists saw the problem with the same eyes: "For Gaius jus gentium
     and jus naturale are the same thing; the law which nature has instilled
     into all nations. But the other jurists who mention the matter, who are
     later, commonly distinguish, pointing out that slavery is juris gentium
     contrary to jus naturale. Ulpian goes further and identifies jus natur-
     ale with instinct, and Justinian adopts the views of Gaius and Ulpian as
     if they were the same. Accordingly, it has been maintained that, for
     the age of Hadrian and before, there was no difference, but that in the
     late classical age the two ideas began to be distinguished, and the
     distinction became a standing part of medieval political thought."

7   MATTINGLY: Renaissance Diplomacy, 1955, p. 24.

8   LAW OF THE SEA: The Medieval sea law is referred to in Chapters
     3 and following of The Law of the Sea, 1950, by William McFee.

8   ROLES OF OLERON: The Laws of Oleron, or the judgments of the
     sea, A.D. 1375, from Black Book of the Admiralty - reprinted 1871 by
     Louis F. Middlebrook, Mystic, Conn., 1935, pp. 171-182.

9   LUIGI GONZAGA: Mattingly, Renaissance Diplomacy, 1955, p. 71.

9   EXTRATERRITORIALITY: The origin of capitulations is given quite
     succinctly and accurately in an article on that subject in the Encyclo-
     pedia Britannica. A longer explanation is to be found in P.M. Brown,
     Foreigners in Turkey, 1914. To a minor degree, the problem is touched
     upon by Majid Khadduri in his introduction to The Islamic Law of Na-
     tions, 1966.

9   FIRST CONSULAR CONVENTION: This Convention of November 14,
     1788, is found in Vol. 2, Treaties and Other International Acts of the
     United States of America, edited by Hunter Miller, 1931, p. 228. Ar-
     ticle 12 on page 239 is the pertinent article.

9   OMAR: This quotation and mention of the precedent instituted by Omar
     are found on page 103 of E. Foda, The Projected Arab Court of Justice,
     1957.

10   RED CHINA: A useful summary of early relations with the Far East
     is Chapter 21 of Thomas Bailey's A Diplomatic History of the Ameri-
     can People, 1969, pp. 299 et seq. The chapter is entitled, "The Dawn
     of Asiatic Interests."

11   THE ORIENT: The lusty story of Hong Kong in its early days is told
     by James Clavell in Tai-Pan, 1966, as well as in many other works of
     fiction.

11   POSTAL SYSTEM: The development of the Postal System is described
     in an International Conciliation pamphlet No. 552, March 1965, on the
     Universal Postal Union by M.A.R. Menon.

11   HUMANITARIANISM: It is unnecessary to document in detail the con-
     ditions prevailing at the beginning of the 19th Century and the gradual
     rise of humanitarianism. Most of the facts recited are well known, not
     only through historical texts but through the novels of Dickens. The
     Hornblower saga, which vividly portrays the British Navy, was spun
     into several volumes by C.C. Forrester.

12   RED CROSS: One of the early points in the turning of the tide grew

out of Jean Henri Dunant's description of the aftermath of the Battle of Solferino. A Memory of Solferino led to the establishment of the Red Cross. (Among many editions is one published by the American National Red Cross in 1939.)

CHAPTER II
The Sources of International Law

TEXTS:

> C. Parry, The Sources and Evidences of International Law, 1965.
> Cheng Bin, General Principles of Law as Applied by International Courts and Tribunals, 1953.
> G. Schwarzenberger, International Law as Applied by International Courts and Tribunals, Vol. I (3rd Edition) 1957; Vol. II 1968.

NOTES:

Page

14   SOURCES: The sources of International Law are dealt with quite fully by Michael Virally in an essay by that name forming pp. 116 et seq. in the Manual of Public International Law, 1968, edited by Max Sørensen.

14   STATUTE OF THE COURT: The official American text of the statute is given in 59 STAT 1055, 1945.

15   PLETHORA OF TERMS: It is interesting that Leo Gross, writing for the Encyclopedia Americana, 1970, Vol. 27, p. 51, somewhat cynically says: "Among the 38 or more terms generally and often inconsistently employed by states are convention, charter, covenant, protocol, final act, declaration, agreement, pact, statute, exchange of notes, modus vivendi, concordat, agreed minutes, joint declaration, and memorandum of agreement."

15   IN THE UNITED STATES: E.J. Byrd, Jr. in his Treaties and Executive Agreements in the United States, 1960, says on page 2: "...there appears not to be a modern text on American government which professes to reveal the limitations on the treaty power or which will state an overall rule on the difference between treaties and executive agreements as to the extremities of subject matter with which they can deal."

16   CUSTOM CONSISTING OF: The case usually cited to illustrate the development of custom is the Paquete Habana, The Lola, 175 US 677 (1900).

16   THE GENERAL PRINCIPLES OF LAW: C.W. Jenks in his The Prospects of International Adjudication, 1964, has an extensive chapter on general principles beginning on page 266. He cites many examples and inclines to the belief that the use of general principles by the International Court of Justice has been "wide and varied." Jenks, however, refers

on page 290 to "a distinction between recourse to national legislative practice or municipal decisions to establish a general principle of law and reference to national legislation or municipal decisions as evidence of customary international law . . ."

All I can say is that the two times I wanted to use general principles (in election of remedies and as a guideline to the probative value of evidence) I felt thwarted.

17   UNITED STATES JAPANESE PROPERTY COMMISSION: The Anglo-Japanese Property Commission case on the value of precedents may be found in Decision on Cases AJ-17, 18, 19 and 20 on the respective claims of Mrs. M. Struthers, Brigadier J.O.E. Vandeleur, Executors of the Estate of John Duncan Fraser and the Union Insurance Society of Canton, Japanese Annual of International Law, No. 6, 1962, p. 151 at 153. I am, of course, particularly impressed with the soundness of the reasoning of the Anglo-Japanese Commission, since the decision they approved was one that I had written for our Commission.

18   DAMAGES IN INTERNATIONAL LAW: Marjorie Whiteman, Damages in International Law, 1937.

20   EX AEQUO ET BONO: Jenks, cited above, also has a long chapter on equity and its relation to the principles of ex aequo et bono, Chapter 7, pp. 316 et seq. Jackson Ralston in his The Law and Procedure of International Tribunals, 1926, gives examples from an earlier period.

21   AGREEMENT: 3 UST 4054, 1955.

CHAPTER III
The Contribution of International Organizations
to International Law

TEXTS:

R. Higgins, The Development of International Law through the Political Organs of the United Nations, 1963.

H.W. Briggs, The International Law Commission, 1965.

W.L. Tung, International Organization under the United Nations System, 1969.

NOTES:

Page

22   GREAT DESIGN: The Great Design of Henry IV, from the Memoirs of the Duke of Sully, with introduction by Edwin D. Mead, 1909.

22   OTHERS VOICING SUGGESTIONS: William Ladd, An Essay on a Congress of Nations, 1916. Introduction pp. xi et seq.

22   JAY TREATY: John Bassett Moore, The Principles of American Diplomacy, 1918, pp. 306 et seq. discusses that treaty and the arbitrations that followed.

22   HOLY ALLIANCE: One of the most readily available sources for the Holy Alliance is the article in the 11th (1911) Edition of the Encyclopedia Britannica, Vol. XIII, p. 621. This article reproduces the short text in full. It is also reproduced in the Quest for a Principle - see Quadruple Alliance below.

23   TREATY OF CHAUMONT: The Cambridge Modern History, 1906, Vol. IX, p. 666, says: "Thus, while the Holy Alliance was distinctly regarded by the statesmanship of Europe as a declaration of principle leading to no direct results, the agreement between the Four Powers based upon the Treaty of Chaumont meant not only the renewal of an offensive and defensive Quadruple Alliance of the utmost moment, but also the actual beginning of the congressional epoch of European politics."

23   QUADRUPLE ALLIANCE: Mendenhall, Henning and Foord, The Quest for a Principle of Authority in Europe 1715 - Present, 1957, Article VI, p. 100.

23 UNIVERSAL POSTAL UNION: A history of the Union is given by M.A.K. Menon, Universal Postal Union, in the International Conciliation pamphlet No. 552, March 1965.

23 CAPE SPARTEL: Malloy, Treaties, Agreements, etc., 1910, Vol. I, p. 1217.

23 NATO, CENTO: The texts of their constitutional documents are found in Amos J. Peaslee, International Governmental Organizations, 1961, 2 Vols.

23 TABULATION: Yearbook of International Organizations, 1968, p. 13. See pp. 44, 49, and 432 for other references.

24 STAVROPOULOS: "The United Nations and the Development of International Law 1945-1970," United Nations Monthly Chronicle, June 1970, Vol. VII, pp. 79 et seq.

25 24TH GENERAL ASSEMBLY: Resolutions Adopted by the General Assembly during its Twenty-fourth Session, Official Records: Twenty-fourth Session Supplement No. 30 (A/7630).

26 ANTARCTICA: Analysed in Chapter V, Territory.

26 WHO CONSTITUTION: Bevans, Treaties and Other International Agreements, 1970, Vol. 4, p. 125.

26 SUCH REGULATIONS: "International Health Regulations - Adopted by the Twenty-second World Health Assembly at Boston July 25, 1969," Treaties and Other International Acts Series 7026.

26 INTERNATIONAL LAW COMMISSION: The Work of the International Law Commission, United Nations Publication 67 V. 4., June 1967.

27 SPECIAL MISSIONS: Resolution No. 2530, adopted 8 December 1969. Resolutions Adopted by the General Assembly during its Twenty-fourth Session, p. 99.

27 STATELESS PERSONS: The text is given on pp. 135 et seq. of the Work of the International Law Commission and is commented upon in that same work, pp. 28 et seq., cited supra.

27 EUROPEAN COURT OF HUMAN RIGHTS: The Court is the subject of Articles 38-56 of the Convention for the Protection of Human Rights and Fundamental Freedoms. It is conveniently reproduced in Ruth C. Lawson's International Regional Organizations, Constitutional Foundations, 1962, pp. 41 et seq.

27 COURT OF JUSTICE: A good thumbnail sketch can be found in Michael Palmer, John Lambert, and others, A Handbook of European Organizations, 1968, pp. 187 et seq.

CHAPTER IV
Members of the International Community

NOTES:

Page

29   NAURU: The status of Nauru is given in a nutshell form in The Far
      East and Australia, published by Europa Publications Limited, 1971,
      p. 1170. It is a very interesting example of the international commun-
      ity, being one of the wealthiest per capita areas in the world (96 Read-
      ers Digest 211, January 1970). It does have a Minister of Foreign Af-
      fairs, who apparently combines those functions with those of Minister
      for Island Development and Industry. The incumbent is also the Presi-
      dent. Nauru has a representative in Australia and in the United King-
      dom and has a special membership in the Commonwealth - which, how-
      ever, does not permit it to participate in meetings of the Common-
      wealth Heads of Government. It is probably those factors that led Facts
      on File (1968/48/A3) to say, at the time Nauru achieved independence,
      that "Nauru would be completely independent, responsible for its own
      defense and foreign relations." I think this is a slight exaggeration as
      its small size, lack of a military establishment, and limited participa-
      tion in international organizations - including the Commonwealth -
      are obviously making it necessary for Nauru to lean on Australia.

      Speaking of Western Samoa and Nauru, Von Glahn in his Law Among
      Nations, 1970, says on page 77: "Western Samoa elected not to join
      the organization but created an arrangement under which the former
      colonial power, New Zealand, will represent Samoan interests in the
      United Nations, leaving Western Samoa free to join specialized agen-
      cies of the UN whenever such may appear desirable."

29   LIECHTENSTEIN: The refusal to admit Liechtenstein to the League
      of Nations is recorded in the League of Nations, Records of the First
      Assembly: Plenary Meetings, 1920, pp. 652, 667. Although not a
      member of the United Nations, Liechtenstein is a member of the In-
      ternational Court of Justice and has participated in litigation before that
      body.

30   VOTING SYSTEM: The question of voting in international organiza-
      tions has given rise to an extensive literature. A good short summary
      may be found in Philip Jacob and Alexine Atherton, The Dynamics of
      International Organization, 1965, pp. 26-28.

30   PROTECTORATES, COLONIES: A quick and simple method of ascer-
      taining the status of existing protectorates, colonies, etc. is to consult

that part of the World Almanac which gives thumbnail descriptions of foreign countries. A statement concerning each dependent area follows the summary concerning the mother country.

At present, excluding the United States, the nations still holding overseas possessions are Great Britain, France, Portugal, Spain and the Netherlands. Greenland, though originally a Danish possession, is now an integral part of Denmark.

30 MANDATE SYSTEM: The origin of the mandate system is described in the opening chapter of Aaron M. Margalith, The International Mandates, 1930. With the gradual disappearance of the trusteeships, the remaining trusteeship problems have been considered by the United Nations in conjunction with colonial and neo-colonial issues. Thus, although the Trusteeship Council continues, the Committee of 24 (now reduced to 21) can examine information on the Trust Territories.

30 REPUBLIC OF SOUTH AFRICA: The progress of the long and tangled question of Namibia (the African name for South West Africa), including the successive cases before the International Court of Justice, can be traced through the International Conciliation Series (of the Carnegie Endowment for International Peace) devoted to the issues before the then-pending General Assembly. The most recent advisory opinion of the Court, which reaches back and refers to prior opinions, is printed in International Legal Materials, July 1971, p. 677. A popular account of the situation is found in Newsweek of July 5, 1971, p. 43.

31 STATES OF A FEDERAL UNION: Article I, Section 10. There is a short notation on the question of Treaties and Alliances in The Constitution of the United States of America, Analysis and Interpretation, prepared by the Legislative Reference Service, Library of Congress, 1964, p. 374. Friedmann, Lissitzyn and Pugh cite a number of precedents relating to the right of component states of federal unions to enter into agreements, Cases and Materials on International Law, 1969, p. 308.

31 QUEBEC-LOUISIANA AGREEMENT: A reference to the Quebec-Louisiana agreement is made in the April 1970 issue of 64 A.J.I.L. 380 by Raymond S. Rodgers. At the time the agreement was under consideration in September 1969, the discussion received considerable attention in the Montreal French language press: See an article in La Presse, Montreal, Mercredi, 10 Septembre 1969, p. 2, headlined "Le Secrétariat d'Etat empêche la signature d'un accord Louisiane-Québec."

31 BELLIGERENTS AND INSURGENTS: The law on belligerents and insurgents reflects a well-established practice. See citations under

Chapter VI, Recognition.

31 INTERNATIONAL ORGANIZATIONS: Friedmann, Lissitzyn and Pugh devote pages 202-213 of their book (cited supra) to the legal status of international organizations, quoting the major part of the Folke-Bernadotte case.

32 INDIVIDUAL HAS A PERSONALITY: The status of individuals in international law has been hotly discussed in many publications. Charles Fenwick, specifically referred to in the text, speaks of the individual on page 147 et seq. of his International Law, 1965. The remark that the argument is a highly theoretical one occurs on page 150.

CHAPTER V
Territory

TEXTS:

R. Jennings, The Acquisition of Territory in International Law, 1963.

NOTES:

Page

33 TRUDEAU: Federalism and the French Canadians, 1968, p. 153.

33 CHILE AND ARGENTINA: The decision is reported in 61 A.J.I.L. 1071, 1967.

33 RANN OF KUTCH: J. Gillis Wetter, The Rann of Kutch Arbitration, 65 A.J.I.L. 346, 1971.

34 BELGIUM AND HOLLAND: Case Concerning Sovereignty over Certain Frontier Lands (Belgium/Netherlands), I.C.J. Reports, 1959, p. 209, summarized in 53 A.J.I.L. 937, 1959.

34 ENGLAND AND FRANCE: The Minquiers and Ecrehos Case, I.C.J. Reports, 1953, p. 47.

34 WILLIAM TEMPLE FRANKLIN: Samuel Flagg Bemis, John Quincy Adams and the Foundations of American Foreign Policy, 1949, p. 19.

34 NORTHEAST BOUNDARIES: Robert H. Ferrell, American Diplomacy, A History, 1969, pp. 226 et seq.

34 MIDDLE OF THE STREAM: The problem of riparian boundaries also arises in the relations of the states of the American Union, and the Supreme Court has applied international law in the settlement of such problems. Arkansas v Tennessee, 246 US 158 (1918).

34 USSURI RIVER: I discussed the problem in a book review I wrote on War Between Russia and China by Harrison Salisbury. This review appeared in California Western International Law Journal, Vol. I, No. 1, 1970, pp. 168 et seq.

35 COLONIAL EXPANSION: Colonial expansion reached its zenith at the end of the 19th century. The method used by Russia to wrest territory from China is graphically described by Emil Lengyel in his book, Si-

beria, 1943, pp. 108 et seq.

35 THIRTY YEARS WAR: The pitiful state of Europe and particularly of Germany following the Thirty Years War is described in Vol. IV, pp. 417 et seq. of the Cambridge Modern History, 1911.

36 RUSSIAN MINISTER: An interesting account is given by Frank A Golder, "The Purchase of Alaska," in Vol. 25, The American Historical Review, 1920, pp. 411 et seq.

36 LOUISIANA PURCHASE: The bathroom episode is related in an elementary but quite amusing book by Robert Tallant entitled, The Louisiana Purchase, 1952, pp. 120 et seq.

36 SECTOR PRINCIPLE: In a January 28, 1970 letter to me, Robert D. Hodgson, The Geographer, Office of Strategic and Functional Research stated: "The U.S. has never accepted the sector principle nor has it made a claim nor have we ever been able to find sector claims by Denmark, Iceland or Norway."

37 ANTARCTICA: The treaty is given in 12 UST 794, 1959.

37 DISCOVERY AND SETTLEMENT: The discovery and settlement of territory, as well as other means of acquiring territory, are usually dealt with in some length in most books on International Law, with the citation of copious authority. Bishop, International Law, 1971, devotes Chapter 5 of his book (pp. 398 et seq.) to the subject; and W.L.Tung, International Law in an Organizing World, 1968, speaks of the subject, pp. 160 et seq. Since most, if not all of the examples cited in the next two pages are also mentioned in these two texts, not to mention Jennings, Acquisition of Territory in International Law, 1963, the specific examples adduced on the next two pages will not be supported by footnotes.

39 TREATY OF PEACE: 3 UST 3169, 1955.

39 RETURN OF OKINAWA: The Department of State Bulletin of July 12, 1971, contains the text of the agreement, Vol. 65, No. 1672, pp. 35 et seq.

39 LIMITATIONS ON THE USE OF: Helen D. Reid, International Servitudes in Law and Practice, 1932.

40 FRANCE DIRECTED WATER: Lake Lanoux arbitration, 3 Whiteman's Digest 1966.

40 POLLUTION: The leading case on pollution is the decision in the Trail Smelter Arbitration between the United States and Canada, 3 U.N. Rep. Intl. Arb. Awards 1905, 1949.

40 NEUTRALITY LAWS: 22 USC 441.

40 WORLD HEALTH ORGANIZATION: TIAS 7026, Article 31, p. 12.

CHAPTER VI
Recognition

TEXTS:

Ti-Chiang Chen, The International Law of Recognition, 1951.
H. Lauterpacht, Recognition in International Law, 1947.

NOTES:

Page

41   REVOLTED SPANISH COLONIES: The study on John Quincy Adams by
Dexter Perkins in The American Secretaries of State and their Diplomacy, 1958, edited by Samuel F. Bemis, relates fully the Florida negotiations and early U.S. relations with Latin America, Vol. IV, pp.
7 et seq.

41   RECOGNIZED THE CONFEDERACY: F.L. Owsley and Harriet C.
Owsley, King Cotton Diplomacy, 1959, p. 84 and p. 453.

42   ESTRADA DOCTRINE: Charles G. Fenwick, International Law, 1965,
p. 196.

42   PUNGENT COMMENT: T. Baty, "Abuse of Terms: 'Recognition':
'War'", 30 A.J.I.L. 377-378, 1936. Quoted by Marjorie Whiteman in
Vol. 2, pp. 3 and 4 of her Digest. Incidentally, over 750 pages in that
volume of the Digest are directed to the problems of recognition.

The Department of State has attempted to summarize the underlying
principles concerning recognition in GIST, No. 20, of February 1970.
(GIST is a series of leaflets on varying subjects intended to constitute
"a quick reference aid on U.S. foreign relations.") GIST says we are
moving in the direction of the Estrada Doctrine. Moreover, the same
leaflet says: "Since 1965 the U.S. has attempted to avoid formal statements of recognition in cases of coups d'etat and other revolutionary
changes of government."

The United States Senate has tried to remove some of the confusion in
a Senate Resolution of September 25, 1969, reading: "Resolved, That
it is the sense of the Senate that when the United States recognizes a
foreign government and exchanges diplomatic representatives with it,
this does not of itself imply that the United States approves of the form,
ideology, or policy of that foreign government." Congressional Record, Vol. 115, p. 27718.

43   CUBA: The United States severed relations on January 4, 1961. GIST, No. 22, March 1970.

43   TWO GOVERNMENTS IN SPAIN: The case of the Government of the Republic of Spain v. S.S. Arantzazu Mendi and others, Great Britain, House of Lords, February 23, 1939, 55, The Times Law Reports 454, is revealing.

43   ONE WRITER ON RECOGNITION: Ti-Chiang Chen, The International Law of Recognition, 1951, p. 289.

44   AS A BELLIGERENT: Since belligerency and insurgency are old concepts, some of the older writers may be better than some of the newer ones in defining these terms. See, for example, W.E. Hall, International Law, Eighth Edition, edited by A.P. Higgins, 1924, where belligerency is defined on page 36 and insurgency on page 46.

44   CAN RECOGNITION BE EFFECTED: The American Law Institute, Restatement of the Law, Foreign Relations Law of the United States, 1965, devotes a whole chapter to "Methods of Effecting Recognition," pp. 328 et seq.

44   CONSUL GENERAL IN MOSCOW: A colorful description of the problems faced by my father is contained in Peter Lisagor and Margüerite Higgins, Overtime in Heaven, 1964, pp. 63 et seq.

44   COMMUNIST CHINA: On October 25, 1971, the General Assembly voted to seat the representatives of Peking in the Assembly by a vote of 76 in favor, 35 opposed, and 17 abstaining (New York Times, October 26, 1971, p. 1, column 6).

44   MONROE DOCTRINE: A Compilation of the Messages and Papers of the Presidents, Vol. II, 1897, p. 787.

45   WOODROW WILSON: J. Fred Rippy, The United States and Mexico, 1931, pp. 349 et seq.

45   TOBAR DOCTRINE: Fenwick, cited supra, p. 193. Fenwick, who has devoted a great deal of attention to Latin American affairs, is a particularly good interpreter of the slippery concepts of recognition in Latin America.

46   UNITED STATES HAS NOT RECOGNIZED: Fact Book of the Countries of the World, Background Notes, Reprinted from Materials Published by the U.S. Department of State, 1970, p. 457.

47 BELIZE: David Vela in <u>Nuestro Belice</u>, published in Guatemala in 1939, starts his book by saying: "Nuestro pueblo sabe por tradición, aparte de haberlo oído desde niño en la escuela, que Belice es parte integrante del territorio de Guatemala . . ."

CHAPTER VII
The Representation of States

TEXTS:

E.M. Satow, A Guide to Diplomatic Practice, 1917.

C.W. Thayer, Diplomat, 1959.

S. Simpson, Anatomy of the State Department, 1967.

A. Lall, Modern International Negotiation; Principles and Practice, 1966.

F.C. Iklé, How Nations Negotiate, 1964.

W. Strang and others, The Foreign Office, 1955.

NOTES:

Page

48   DEPARTMENT OF STATE: William Barnes and John Morgan, The Foreign Service of the United States, 1961, pp. 37 et seq.

48   WHITE HOUSE STAFF: An article by Charles Yost in the October 1971 issue of Foreign Affairs, Vol. 50, p. 59, "The Instruments of American Foreign Policy," stresses the growing imbalance between the National Security Council and the Department of State.

49   CIA: There have been many books written on the CIA. A critical one, which has to be taken with a grain of salt but which is often referred to, is Andrew Tully, CIA The Inside Story, 1962. On the other hand, see Allen Dulles, The Craft of Intelligence, 1965.

49   PRESIDENT KENNEDY: The letter is reproduced in Department of State Foreign Affairs Manual, Vol. 2, Section 030. The Nixon letter is given in Department of State News Letter, December 1969, p. 7.

50   CHIEFS OF MISSION: For an account of the status of early chiefs of mission, see Barnes, cited above, pp. 41 et seq.

50   CHARGÉ D'AFFAIRES: Permanent chargés d'affaires were also sometimes referred to as chargés d'affairs en pied. See footnote on page 20 of B. Sen, A Diplomat's Handbook of International Law and Practice, 1965. On page 19 et seq., Sen discusses the inflation in diplomatic titles.

51   MOST OFFICERS WILL BE FOREIGN SERVICE OFFICERS: Moreover the latest plan is to decrease the number of Foreign Service Staff Of-

ficers and to make them instead Foreign Affairs Specialists holding unlimited appointments as Reserve Officers. This new innovation is part of the constant shifting of Department of State personnel policies, which swing like a pendulum from one side to the other. I am not sure doctors recognize "pendulumitis" as a disease. If they do, I think one can safely say that the Department is afflicted. The new policy is explained in Department of State Newsletter, March 1971, p. 12.

51   THEIR OWN FOREIGN SERVICE PERSONNEL SYSTEM: The systems are found in 22 USC 1221 et seq. (U.S.I.A.), 7 USC 1761 et seq. (Agriculture), and 22 USC 2385 (AID).

CHAPTERS VIII, IX, & X
Privileges and Immunities

TEXTS:

C.W. Jenks, International Immunities, 1961.
C.E. Wilson, Diplomatic Privileges and Immunities, 1967.
R.A. Falk, The Aftermath of Sabbatino, 1965. (Usually acts of state are not considered as coming under the heading of privileges. Since, however, I have included the subject in Chapter IX, I am including this reference. At the end of page 224, there are a number of references to literature on the Act of State doctrine.)
J.M. Sweeney, The International Law of Sovereign Immunity, 1963.

NOTES:

Page

58   CONVENTIONS: Philippe Cahier and Luke T. Lee, Vienna Conventions on Diplomatic and Consular Relations, International Conciliation pamphlet No. 571, January 1969, gives a good general view of those conventions.

58   SIR WILLIAM BLACKSTONE: Commentaries on the Laws of England, edited by William Carey Jones, 1916, Vol. I, pp. 377 et seq.

60   THE ITALIAN STAND: The Italian theory is well explained by Angelo Piero Sereni in his The Italian Conception of International Law, 1943. See in particular pages 327-328. While this book is now almost thirty years old, I do not believe that the concepts have changed, at least to any material degree.

60   DEFRAUD THE SOVIET UNION: Russian Socialist Federated Republic v. Cibrario, 235 N.Y. 255, 139 N.E. 259 (1923).

61   RECOGNIZED GOVERNMENT: The right of a foreign government to sue was established at an early date. Some of the old precepts are collected in Moore's Digest, 1906, Vol. II, p. 85. This does not mean that the privilege of a foreign state to sue can override the Constitution. Monaco tried to sue Mississippi on defaulted bonds but was unable to do so, as suits against a state of the union without its consent are barred by the Eleventh Amendment - Monaco v. Mississippi 292 US 313 (1934).

61   AMERICAN VESSEL: The Schooner Exchange v. McFaddon, 7 Cranch 116 (U.S. 1812).

61 TOOK THE LEAD: Letter of Secretary Lansing of November 8, 1918,
    to the Attorney General and reply of the latter, Hackworth's Digest,
    1941, Vol. II, p. 429.

62 JACK TATE: The letter is quoted by William Bishop in his International
    Law, 1971, p. 670.

62 BELGIAN COURT: S.A. de Chemins de fer Liegeois-Luxembourgeois
    v. Etat Neerlandais, quoted by Bishop in his Second Edition of Inter-
    national Law, 1962, p. 562. (It is not quoted in the 1971 Edition.)

62 FOREIGN GOVERNMENT PROPERTY: A case in point is Ocean Trans-
    port Co. v Government of Republic of Ivory Coast, 269 F Supp. 703
    (1967), summarized in 62 A.J.I.L. 197, 1968.

63 LAW IS NOT QUITE SO CLEAR: The leading case on the subject is
    National City Bank of New York v Republic of China et al, 348 US 356
    (1955). In a footnote to his dissenting opinion, Mr. Justice Reed said:
    "...there is no tenable distinction between the setoff of an unrelated
    claim, a proceeding for a judgment over a counter claim, and a direct
    suit against a foreign sovereign..." (p. 369).

63 COURT OF APPEALS: Salimoff & Co. v Standard Oil Co. of New York,
    262 N.Y. 220, 186 N.E. 679 (1933).

63 BRITISH COURTS: A.M. Luther v James Sagor and Co. (1921) 1 K.B.
    456 (1920).

63 POSTAL MONEY ORDERS: Hopkins case, Opinions of Commissioners,
    General Claims Commission, United States and Mexico (1927) pp. 42
    et seq.

64 SABBATINO: Banco Nacional de Cuba v Sabbatino, Receiver, et al, 376
    US 398 (1964). The Sabbatino case has generated a vast literature in-
    cluding a book by Eugene F. Mooney, Foreign Seizures: Sabbatino and
    the Act of State Doctrine, 1967. It appears from Banco Nacional de
    Cuba v the First National City Bank of New York - decided by the United
    States Court of Appeals for the Second Circuit (the decision is given in
    10 International Legal Materials 536, 1971) - that the leeway given by the
    Hickenlooper Amendment will be used very cautiously.

64 OUTSIDE OF THE JURISDICTION: Moscow Fire Ins. Co. v Bank of New
    York & Trust Co., 280 N.Y. 286, 20 N.E. 2d 758 (1939).

65 CONFUSING ELEMENT: United States v Pink, 315 US 203 (1942) The
    Supreme Court discusses the Moscow case at some length.

65 CASES SUPPORTING THE DECREES: The somewhat tortuous series of decisions on Jewish confiscations is analyzed in Banco Nacional de Cuba v The First National City Bank of New York, cited supra.

65 INVIOLABILITY APPLIES: On page 44 of his little book on Modern Diplomatic Law, 1968, Michael Hardy points out that the Vienna Convention on Diplomatic Relations permitted no exception to the inviolability of a diplomatic mission. Also see Philippe Cahier and Luke T. Lee, Vienna Conventions on Diplomatic and Consular Relations, 1969, p. 20. Nevertheless, I find it difficult to believe that if a fire broke out in the middle of the night in an Embassy Chancery, the firemen would stand idly watching the fire burn, while they discussed fine points of diplomatic immunity. In a famous case involving consular premises, police and spectators rushed to the courtyard of the Soviet Consulate General in New York, when a woman, Mrs. Kasenkina, who was being detained, jumped out of the window. Bishop has a comment on the case on pages 721 et seq. of his International Law, 1971.

The Kasenkina case recalls the famous incident involving Sun Yat-sen when he was imprisoned in the Chinese (Manchu) Legation in London at the end of the last century. The Embassy was warned that "serious steps on behalf of Her Majesty's Government" were justified in view of the Chinese violation of diplomatic privilege. Harold Z. Schiffrin, Sun Yat-sen and the Origins of the Chinese Revolution, 1968, p. 123. The British also threatened to ask for the recall of the Minister. There is no evidence as to what the British would have done if they had begun to suspect that Sun Yat-sen would be killed in the Legation building. In view, however, of the finding of violation of diplomatic privilege, it is hard to suppose that the British would have stood idly by. Eventually Sun Yat-sen was released, so the crisis passed.

If a similar crisis were to arise today, the Vienna Convention (in my opinion, at least) is not likely to stand in the way. It will always be possible for the host country to say, as did the British government, that diplomatic privileges had been violated, relieving the local authorities from restraints.

66 DISTRICT OF COLUMBIA: Title 47 District of Columbia Code, Section 801A (c) (Taxation); Section 803 (Assessments for Improvements).

67 VIENNA CONVENTIONS: The Convention on Consular Relations is given in 21 UST 77 (1970). The Convention on Diplomatic Relations was signed on April 18, 1961, and was approved by the Senate by a vote of 85-0 on September 14, 1965. It has yet, however, to come into force for the United States. I believe the reason for the delay is that the Department of State wishes to conform the domestic legislation to the pro-

visions of the Convention. Hence I suppose that it can be considered that the United States is virtually a party. The text of the Convention, along with supporting documents, may be found in 111 Congressional Record, Part 18, pp. 23773 et seq., 1965.

67 A FEW AGREEMENTS: Michael Hardy, Modern Diplomatic Law, 1968, p. 5.

67 LAW ENACTED IN 1790: The Act of April 30, 1790, I STAT 117, now appearing in part as 22 USC 252 et seq.

68 THE VIENNA CONVENTION: As has been stated, the Convention is reproduced in the Congressional Record. It is also reproduced in 55 A.J.I.L. 1062 et seq., 1961.

69 FAMILIES OF DIPLOMATS: The rights of members of the family and of administrative and technical personnel are given in Article 37.

70 SERVICE STAFF: Covered by Article 37, as well.

70 ARRESTED COOK: Paragraph 4 of Article 37 relates to private servants. It reads: "Private servants of members of the mission shall, if they are not nationals of or permanently resident in the receiving State, be exempt from dues and taxes on the emoluments they receive by reason of their employment. In other respects, they may enjoy privileges and immunities only to the extent admitted by the receiving State. However, the receiving State must exercise its jurisdiction over those persons in such a manner as not to interfere unduly with the performance of the functions of the mission." Does "those persons" apply to all servants or only to the ones who are not local nationals. If my dinner were being ruined, I would probably argue the former; but since I am merely writing a book, I favor the latter.

70 A LITTLE SMUGGLING: An interesting account is given in Timothy Green's The Smugglers, 1970, pp. 44 et seq.

71 FOREIGN AFFAIRS MANUAL: The consular privileges with regard to excise taxes are stated in FAM, Vol. 2, Section 273.2-2 (b). In fact, Chapter 200 of the Manual is directed to privileges and immunities. Naturally, the greatest emphasis is placed on Federal taxes.

71 KOREAN CONSULAR CONVENTION: The Convention is given in 14 UST 1637 et seq. Article 14 is on page 1647; the next quotation is from the first sentence of Article 10 (3) on page 1645.

71 PROFESSOR BARGHOORN: An account of his arrest is given in Time,

November 22, 1963, p. 27.

72 CONSULAR CONVENTION WITH THE USSR: The Convention is given in 19 UST 5018.

72 UNITED NATIONS: The rights and privileges of representatives to the United Nations are provided for by the Convention on the Privileges and Immunities of the United Nations, 21 UST 1419 et seq. and by the Headquarters Agreement 61 STAT 3725 et seq. (reproduced following 22 USC 287). Domestic American legislation covers all international organizations, 22 USC 288 et seq. The quotation in the text is from 22 USC 288d (b). The Charter of the Organization of American States, 2 UST 2394, has a general provision (Article 104 on page 2435) which reads: "The Representatives of the Governments on the Council of the Organization, the representatives on the organs of the Council, the personnel of their delegations, as well as the Secretary General and the Assistant Secretary General of the Organization, shall enjoy the privileges and immunities necessary for the independent performance of their duties." It is reminiscent of Article 105(2) of the Charter of the United Nations.

72 VISITS OF WARSHIPS: Charles H. Stockton, who was a retired Rear Admiral and therefore particularly qualified to speak on this subject, devotes two complete pages to the subject in his Outlines of International Law, 1914, pp. 164 et seq. On military forces, Moore quotes Hall (apparently with approval) to the effect that the military are generally exempt from local jurisdiction - Moore's Digest, Vol. II, 1906, pp. 559 et seq.

73 STATUS OF FORCES: The agreement is given in 4 UST 1792.

73 GIRARD CASE: The essentials of the case are given in the Supreme Court case referred to in the text, Wilson et al v Girard, 354 US 524 (1957).

74 SHOT THEIR HUSBANDS: Reid v Covert, 354 US 1 (1957).

75 MAY IMPORT DUTY FREE: 4 UST 1812, Article XI, No. 4.

CHAPTER XI
Jurisdiction

TEXTS:

G. Mueller & E.M. Wise, editors, International Criminal Law, 1965.
I. Shearer, Extradition in International Law, 1971.

NOTES:

Page

77   AMERICAN CONSTITUTION: Article I, Section 8, Clause 10.

78   CHILDREN OF DIPLOMATS: Hackworth's Digest, 1942, Vol. 3, p. 12,
     and Whiteman's Digest, 1967, Vol. 8, pp. 122 et seq.

78   ABIDE BYTHE LOCAL LAWS: 2 FAM 225.1. That section states: "A
     diplomatic or consular officer, or other representative of the United
     States, shall not take advantage of the protection afforded by reason of
     his official position nor should he evade the settlement of just obliga-
     tions."

79   LIBEL OR SLANDER: The development of the remedies for libel and
     slander constitutes a fascinating page in English legal history. In
     Pollock and Maitland's classic, The History of English Law before the
     Time of Edward I, 1895, p. 536, the authors give this amusing sidelight
     on early practice: "In the Norman Custumal it is written that the man
     who has falsely called another 'thief' or 'manslayer' must pay damages,
     and, holding his nose with his fingers, must publicly confess himself
     a liar. Shame was keenly felt."

     See also the essay on the subject by Van Vechten Veeder in Select Es-
     says in Anglo-American Legal History, compiled by the Association
     of American Law Schools, 1909, Vol. 3, pp. 446 et seq. Eventually
     a distinction was made between libel (written) and slander (oral), so
     that the latter was not made the subject of criminal prosecutions. Down
     through the reign of Charles I, there was no difference (see page 458).

79   A MEXICAN WAS LIBELLED: The situation is complicated by the fact
     that Mexico claimed the right to punish on the ground that the victim
     was a Mexican. Moore's Digest, 1906, Vol. 2, pp. 228 et seq. has a
     long account of the controversy.

80   CRIME COMMITTED ABOARD: The leading American case on the sub-

ject is Wildenhus's case 120 US 1 (1887), where an American court took jurisdiction over a murder committed on board a Belgian vessel moored to a dock in Jersey City.

80SMOKING OPIUM: United States v Look Chaw, 18 P.I. 573 (1910), summarized by William Bishop, International Law, 1971, p. 609.

80CRIMES COMMITTED ON AN AIRCRAFT: The matter is now the subject of a multilateral convention 20 UST 2941.

80CRIME AGAINST ITS SECURITY: For a good short review of the problems of jurisdiction with respect to offenses committed abroad, the latter part of an essay by Milan Sahović and William Bishop (in Max Sørensen's Manual of Public International Law, 1968, pp. 311 et seq.) is very clear. See, in particular, pp. 353 et seq.

81LOTUS DECISION: P.C.I.J. Ser. A, No. 10 (1927), 2 Hudson, World Court Reports 20 (1935).

82TERRANOVA: Moore's Digest, 1960, Vol. II, p. 622. This case is alluded to by Bailey in his A Diplomatic History of the American People. 1969, p. 305.

82FAR EASTERN HISTORIAN: Nathaniel Peffer, The Far East, 1958, p. 116.

82ADMINISTRATION OF EXTRATERRITORIALITY: The last time provision was made for all four nations was in the Department of State Appropriation Act for the fiscal year ending June 30, 1950 (63 STAT 447 at p. 448). The Act appropriated funds for: "...rent and expenses of maintaining in Egypt, Ethiopia, Morocco, and Muscat institutions for American convicts and persons declared insane by any consular court, and care and transportation of prisoners and persons declared insane..." The final repeal of American laws regarding extraterritoriality, which by then applied only to Morocco, was effected by the Act of August 1, 1956, 70 STAT 773.

84PEREZ JIMENEZ: Perez Jimenez v Aristeguieta, 311 F.2d 547 (1962), summarized in 57 A.J.I.L. 670, 1963. The Department of State summary of the case is given in 49 Department of State Bulletin 364, 1963, and reproduced in 58 A.J.I.L. 185, 1964.

CHAPTER XII
Nationality of Individuals

TEXTS:

H. Van Panhuys, The Role of Nationality in International Law, 1959.

NOTES:

Page

85 SWAIN ISLAND AND AMERICAN SAMOA: As noted by Bishop, International Law, 1971, p. 519.

85 CURRENT LAW: 66 STAT 235.

85 A PERSON BORN OUTSIDE OF THE UNITED STATES: Proof of American citizenship is based upon the certificate of a consular officer, attesting to the registration of the birth of the child. The Department of Justice, however, has indicated that such a certificate is not enough and that a certificate of nationality from the Department of Justice is needed. Under the laws and practice of the Department of State, this is wholly unnecessary and merely inflicts needless trouble on the parents. It is a practice born from the wedlock of Parkinson's Law and the Peter Principle.

86 OR WITH AN INTERNATIONAL ORGANIZATION: The Immigration and Nationality Act of 1952, 66 STAT 163, Sect. 301(a)(7), referred only to service in the Armed Forces. The other language was added by the Act of November 6, 1966,80 STAT 1322. The provisions relating to naturalization likewise form part of the Immigration and Nationality Act, 66 STAT 239.

86 EARLIER LAWS: A short analysis of the earlier laws is given by George G. Wilson, Handbook of International Law, 1939, pp. 132 et seq.

87 EXTRATERRITORIAL COMMUNITY: Moore's Digest, 1906, Vol. III, p. 287.

87 RIGHT OF EXPATRIATION: John Bassett Moore in his The Principles of American Diplomacy, 1918, devotes a chapter to the development of the Doctrine of Expatriation, pp. 270 et seq.

88 READMITTING THEM TO CITIZENSHIP: The legislation readmitting those voting in the Japanese and Italian elections to citizenship, or to

be more exact, providing for their expeditious naturalization, is to be found in 66 STAT 278 and 68 STAT 495, respectively.

88 SEVERAL COURT DECISIONS: The cases involving involuntary loss of citizenship are reviewed in Afroyim v Rusk, 387 US 253 (1967), a five to four decision of the Supreme Court. That case overruled the earlier case of Perez v Brownell, 356 US 44 (1958).

89 ONE WITH SWEDEN: IV Trenwith, Treaties etc., 4656.

89 EFFECTIVE OR DOMINANT NATIONALITY: The case referred to in the text is the Strunsky Mergé case, reported in XIV Reports of International Arbitral Awards 236. (I did not argue the case before the three-men commission as, by that time, I had left Rome. I did however present the initial pleadings.)

90 NANSEN PASSPORT: The Nansen passport was well established by the time the League of Nations was ten years old. According to a volume prepared by the Secretariat of the League, entitled Ten Years of World Co-operation, 1930, by the end of 1929 fifty-one governments had adopted the standard form of identity certificate (Nansen passport) issued by each government to refugees (p. 272).

The Convention relating to the Status of Refugees provides in Article 28 that "The Contracting States shall issue to refugees lawfully staying in their territory travel documents for the purpose of travel outside their territory..." Articles 2 to 34 of the Convention were incorporated by reference in the Protocol Relating to the Status of Refugees, 19 UST 6223. The language quoted appears on page 6274. While it is not inaccurate to think of such travel documents as League or United Nations documents, since they are - or were - sponsored by these organizations, the actual documents are issued by governments.

90 NOTTEBOHM CASE: I.C.J. Reports, 1955, p. 4.

91 FLEGENHEIMER CASE: XIV Reports of International Arbitral Awards 327.

CHAPTER XIII
Nationality of Vessels

TEXTS:

H. Meyers, The Nationality of Ships, 1967.
K. al-Shawi, The Role of the Corporate Entity in International Law, 1957.

NOTES:

Page

92 PARTNERSHIPS AS WELL AS CORPORATIONS: Any discussion as to when a partnership is a legal entity would lead far afield, as the problem is quite complicated and varies according to local law. Its complexity may be realized just by reading Bouvier's Law Dictionary, 1928, pp. 900 et seq.

92 PIERCING THE CORPORATE VEIL: The case is Daimler Co., Ltd. v Continental Tyre and Rubber Co., Ltd., L.R. (1916) 2 A.C. 307, reproduced in its essentials in Fenwick, Cases on International Law, 1951, pp. 194 et seq.

93 BARCELONA TRACTION CASE: I.C.J. Reports, 1970, p. 3, reproduced in 64 A.J.I.L. 653, 1970.

93 OTHER CRITERIA HAVE BEEN SUGGESTED: William Bishop summarizes them in a nutshell in a short editorial note, International Law, 1971, p. 488.

94 LIBERIA STANDS IN FIRST PLACE: According to the World Almanac of 1971, p. 114, Liberia has 30,256 thousand in gross tonnage and 52,-119 thousand in deadweight tonnage. Her nearest rivals are the United Kingdom and Japan. The figures for the former corresponding to the ones for Liberia are 22,237 and 33,133, and for the latter 21,968 and 34,633.

94 TAX ANGLE: I had always been under the impression that flags of convenience were used for commercial vessels. In reading the September 14, 1969 issue of the Italian magazine L'Espresso, I was surprised to see an advertisement of two cabin cruisers, one of which was flying the Liberian flag and the other the Panamanian. What tax dodge will the Italians think of next!

94   GENEVA CONVENTION: 13 UST 2312 (1962) at page 2315.

95   LINK OF NATIONALITY: The whole question of flags of convenience
is thoroughly confused. The Nottebohm case is mentioned many times
by H. Meyers, The Nationality of Ships, 1967 (see index, p. 391). Whiteman's Digest, 1968, Vol. 9, devotes pages 1 et seq. to the nationality
of vessels. The precedents cited do little to clarify the confusion. In
an advisory opinion, the International Court of Justice interpreted the
words "the largest ship-owning nations" in a treaty as including Liberia and Panama, on the basis of registered tonnage (I.C.J. Reports,
1960, p. 150, reproduced 54 A.J.I.L. 884, 1960). In a study on Shipping and the Developing Countries (International Conciliation pamphlet
No. 582, March 1971, by four authors), the statement is made: "The
ownership of shipping tonnage registered under the flags of convenience is difficult to ascertain, but it is known to be controlled by nationals of developed countries. According to the Rochdale Report, 'not
much less than half the tonnage is beneficially owned by U.S. companies
or individuals and a considerable part of the remainder by persons
who have, or once had, Greek nationality.'" (p. 10).

CHAPTERS XIV & XV
The Responsibility of States
The Protection of Nationals

TEXTS:

E. Borchard, Diplomatic Protection of Citizens Abroad, 1915.
C. Eagleton, Responsibility of States in International Law, 1928.
A. Freeman, The International Responsibility of States for Denial of Justice, 1938.
C. Joseph, Nationality and Diplomatic Protection, 1969.
F. Dunn, Protection of Nationals, 1932.

NOTES:

Page

96 HAVING PERMITTED FOREIGNERS: The admission of aliens into the United States is discussed in W.C. Van Vleck, The Administrative Control of Aliens, 1932. This book is not of much help in appraising recent developments, but it gives a good picture of American practice in this field up to 1932.

96 VATTEL: "Le droit des gens ou principes de la loi naturelle," Gregory translation in Carnegie Institution, Classics of International Law, 1916, Book 2, c.6, paragraph 71.

97 I'M ALONE: Vol. II (1929), p. 23 et seq., Foreign Relations of the United States contains the correspondence between the United States and Canada that led to the I'm Alone arbitration. The interim and final reports of the Commissioners are summarized in Hackworth's Digest, 1941, Vol. II, pp. 703 et seq. Bishop, International Law, 1971, p. 492, points out in a footnote that part of the award was given to the widow and children of a French seaman who was on board the Canadian vessel. Bishop, on page 635, quotes from the two reports.

97 JANES CASE: Opinions of Commissioners, General Claims Commission, United States and Mexico (1927), pp. 108 et seq. A.H. Feller, The Mexican Claims Commissions, 1923-1934, 1935, brings out on pages 292 et seq. the exact point I am trying to bring out in somewhat more lurid language.

98 AWARD SHOULD NOT BE MADE TO AN INCOMPETENT: Case of William T. Way, Opinions of Commissioners, General Claims Commission, United States and Mexico (1929), pp. 94 et seq. Actually,

as brought out by Feller (cited supra), the case turned on several issues - pp. 236-237. R.N. Swift, International Law: Current and Classic, 1969, states on page 382 that "...the Mexican government actually argued that it had no responsibility because the one survivor, who was in a mental institution, could feel no distress, mistrust, or lack of safety when Mexico failed to prosecute."

98 RESPONSIBILITY OF STATES: The concept of the responsibility of states is a concept that has been evolving for many decades and has given rise to a substantial literature. Of late, however, the new states have been challenging the full import of that concept. This is brought out quite clearly by S.P. Sinha, New Nations and the Law of Nations, 1967, pp. 91 et seq. On page 91, Sinha cites a large number of the earlier authorities on the subject.

98 NEW ORLEANS: The incident is described in an essay by J.B. Lockey in The American Secretaries of State and their Diplomacy, edited by S.F. Bemis, 1958, Vol. VIII, pp. 146 et seq.

99 PROTECTING AN AMBASSADOR: The United States makes it a particular criminal offense to assault "certain foreign diplomatic and other official personnel." 18 USC 112.

99 REISCHAUER: There is a short account of the attack which took place on March 24, 1964, in Facts on File, 1964, p. 95. As a result of the incident, Home Affairs Minister Hayakawa felt impelled to resign from the cabinet.

99 JOHN GORDON MEIN: On August 28, 1968; this killing is also recorded in Facts on File, 1968, p. 372. Both incidents were also reported in the New York Times and in other newspapers and sources.

99 POLICEMAN ON HIS DAY OFF: The Mallén case, Opinions of Commissioners, General Claims Commission, United States and Mexico (1927), pp. 254 et seq., is particularly revealing, as a deputy constable acted in one instance in a private capacity and in another, in an official capacity.

99 CLAIMS RESULTING FROM CONTRACT: The efforts to restrict such claims are discussed in the next Chapter.

100 UNEXPLODED ATOM BOMBS: The incident is vividly described in Life, February 25, 1966, pp. 106A et seq.

100 A LAW WAS ENACTED: 10 USC 2734.

101 VOLUNTARY PAYMENT: The case was summarized by the American
Agent, Arnold Fraleigh, in 56 A.J.I.L. at p. 424, 1962. The decision
itself is Decision No. 3 of the Commission. It is reproduced in the
Japanese Annual of International Law, No. 5, pp. 51 et seq. (1961).

102 THE PROTECTION OF NATIONALS: The duties of an American Consular Officer, many of which relate to protection, are spelled out in
22 USC 1171 et seq. Some of the provisions, such as the retention of
ship's papers (22 USC 1185) are rather antiquated and have little relation
to the necessities of today. Consular rights are also provided for by
treaty. B. Sen, A Diplomat's Handbook of International Law and Practice, 1965, contains a chapter on Consular Functions (pp. 227 et seq.).

102 CONSULAR CONVENTION WITH JAPAN: 15 UST 768 at p. 793 (Article
16).

104 ARBITRAL TRIBUNALS WITH MEXICO: A. Feller, The Mexican Claims
Commissions, 1935.

104 FOREIGN CLAIMS SETTLEMENT COMMISSION: The legislation on
the Commission is, to say the least, confusing. The portion of the
legislation of relevance to this Chapter is 22 USC 1623. Yet, legislation concerning the Foreign Claims Settlement Commission also appears as 50 Appendix USC 2001 et seq. The 1971 United States Government Organization Manual gives (on page 444) a thumbnail outline of
the purpose of the Commission in these words: "The Commission has
jurisdiction to determine claims of United States nationals against foreign governments for compensation for losses and injuries sustained
by them, pursuant to programs which may be authorized under either
of said acts. Available funds have their sources in international settlements, or liquidation of foreign assets in this country by the Departments of Justice or Treasury, and from public funds when provided by
the Congress."

The provisions concerning claims against Cuba are found in 22 USC
1643.

104 PURCHASE PRICE OF LOUISIANA: The Convention for the Payment of
Sums Due by France to Citizens of the United States, of April 30, 1803,
is the pertinent agreement. It is found in Hunter Miller, Treaties and
Other International Acts of the United States of America, 1931, Vol. 2,
pp. 516 et seq. The agreement had some features in it which differ-
entiate it somewhat from a lump sum agreement of later days. It does
not seem improper, however, to consider it as such.

105 BLOCKADE THE VENEZUELAN COAST: While many historians err in

the interpretation of this event (confusing the claim arbitration with the arbitration of priorities at the Permanent Court of Arbitration), J.H. Latané in his The United States and Latin America, 1929, pp. 249 et seq. gives a very sound account. The Award of the Permanent Court of Arbitration and the awards of the individual commissions are all collected in J.H. Ralston, Venezuelan Arbitrations of 1903, 1904, Senate Document No. 316, 58th Congress, 2d Session.

105   PORFIRIO DIAZ: The chapter on Porfirio Dias in Mexico and its Heritage by E. Gruening, 1928, pp. 55 et seq. is illuminating.

105   COCKROACHES: The Latin American position is clearly stated in paragraph 2 of Article 9 of the Convention on Rights and Duties of States. It reads: "Nationals and foreigners are under the same protection of the law and the national authorities and the foreigners may not claim rights other or more extensive than those of the nationals." 3 Bevans 145 at 148, 1969.

106   LUIS DRAGO: C. Fenwick, International Law, 1965, summarizes the Doctrine on page 354.

106   CARLOS CALVO: Fenwick also summarizes the Calvo Doctrine on page 341.

106   CALVO CLAUSE: The earlier cases are summarized in J. Ralston, The Law and Procedure of International Tribunals, 1926, pp. 58 et seq. The 20th century case usually cited is the one involving the North American Dredging Co., Opinions of Commissioners, General Claims Commission, United States and Mexico, 1927, pp. 21 et seq. There is a book on the subject - Shea, The Calvo Clause, 1955.

107   LATIN AMERICAN STATES: H.B. Jacobini has written A Study of the Philosophy of International Law as seen in Works of Latin American Writers, 1954.

107   INDIAN JURIST: R.P. Anand, "Role of the 'New' Asian-African Countries in the Present International Legal Order," 56 A.J.I.L. 383, 1962, at pp. 388 and 390. More or less in the same tenor is S.N. Guha Roy, "Is the Law of Responsibility of States for Injuries to Aliens a Part of Universal International Law?" 55 A.J.I.L. 863 et seq., 1961.

108   PROVIDING REPATRIATION: A novel twist to this problem has been added by the financial failure of charter lines, resulting in passengers being stranoed abroad.

109   BUSINESS INVESTMENTS: The insurance is provided for by 22 USC 2181.

CHAPTER XVI
Human Rights

TEXTS:

> E. Luard, editor, The International Protection of Human Rights, 1967.
> (This is a series of essays by outstanding authorities.)
> A.H. Robertson, Human Rights in National and International Law, 1968.
> I. Brownlie, editor, Basic Documents on Human Rights, 1971.
> A.L. Del Russo, International Protection of Human Rights, 1971.
> United Nations, Office of Public Information, The United Nations and
> Human Rights, 1968.

NOTES:

Page

110   THE PROTECTION OF HUMAN RIGHTS: The first essay in Evan Luard,
The International Protection of Human Rights, 1967, is devoted to "The
Origins of International Concern over Human Rights."

110   BILL OF RIGHTS: The important passages from the Bill of Rights are
reproduced in Modern Constitutions, 1957, edited by Russell F. Moore,
at pp. 38 et seq.

110   DESPOTIC DOMINATION: The neglect of the poor, the weak and the
distressed in the 18th century is well brought out in a book that appeared
at the end of the last century. In Social England, Vol. V, 1896, edited
by H.D. Traill, a shocking picture is given on pp. 133 et seq. and
again on pp. 386 et seq.

110   ENGLAND ABOLISHED SLAVERY: The Abolition Act of August 28,
1833, initiated the movement (Encyclopedia Britannica, 1971, Vol. 20,
p. 637). The slaves were not, however, set free immediately. Slavery
in Brazil continued until practically the end of the century. England
tried to exercise some influence to modify slavery in Brazil, if not to
eliminate it. David B. Davis in The Problem of Slavery in Western
Culture, 1966, says on page 268: "As late as 1871 Brazilian reformers,
aided by considerable diplomatic pressure from Great Britain, secured
a law compelling masters to emancipate any slave who could pay his
market price..."

110   PERMIT BRITISH WARSHIPS: There is a good short statement on the
subject in the biography of John Quincy Adams by Dexter Perkins - Vol.
IV, pp. 105-106 of The American Secretaries of State and their Diplo-

macy, 1958, edited by Samuel Flagg Bemis.

111   TURKEY WAS FORCED TO AGREE: Luard, The International Protection of Human Rights, 1967, at p. 12.

111   PEACE TREATIES: The term "peace treaties" is used loosely to include the various treaties on minorities forming part of the post-war settlements. See Frank M. Russell, Theories of International Relations, 1936, pp. 391 et seq., and Amos S. Hershey, The Essentials of Public Law and Organization, 1927, pp. 141 et seq. Both sources give copious bibliographic notes.

111   ABOLITION OF SLAVERY: The present slavery treaty is the convention signed at Geneva on September 25, 1926, found in 2 Bevans 607, as supplemented by the general convention of September 7, 1956 (18 UST 3201). The antecedent agreements are summarized in C. Fenwick, International Law, 1965, pp. 508 et seq.

111   NANSEN PASSPORT: See page 90 and corresponding footnote.

112   INTERNATIONAL LABOR ORGANIZATION: The International Labor Organization Conventions on Human Rights are listed up to 1967 in Worldmark Encyclopedia of the Nations, Vol. I, "United Nations," 1967, pp. 134-137. It is an impressive list and gives a picture of the range of ILO activities. Incidentally, this encyclopedia has a good summary of the whole question of human rights on pp. 102 et seq.

112   ITALIAN DIPLOMAT: The parody on the Armenian massacres is taken from Daniele Varè, Laughing Diplomat, 1938, p. 179.

112   THE ATLANTIC CHARTER: The Charter spoke of "Freedom from fear or want" (3 Bevans 686), and the United Nations Declaration said that "...complete victory over their enemies is essential to defend life, liberty, independence and religious freedom, and to preserve human rights and justice in their own lands as well as in other lands..." (p. 697).

112   WHILE SIX MILLION DIED: Written by Arthur D. Morse, 1968.

113   EX POST FACTO BASIS: After almost thirty years, it is impossible for me to remember on what sources I relied. As I recall, there was a series of articles in American law reviews on German criminal law (written by German jurists who had fled Nazi Germany). Since I have never been trained in German law, I could have misinterpreted the situation. The Pentagon, however, to the best of my recollection, never challenged the thesis of responsibility under German criminal law or

asked for a study by German jurists to verify the accuracy of the memorandum. Instead, it became clear that the Pentagon wanted an International War Crimes Tribunal.

113 GENOCIDE CONVENTION: President Nixon submitted the text to the Senate on February 10, 1970 - Department of State Bulletin, 1970, Vol. 62, p. 350.

113 NUREMBERG LAWS: The immense new literature on the subject includes an International Conciliation pamphlet No. 583 of May 1971, The Laws of War 25 Years After Nuremberg, by Tom J. Farer. Bishop, International Law, 1971, has a table on page 1017 showing the indictments and convictions of the major criminals under various counts.

113 RUMANIAN TREATY: 4 Bevans 404.

114 RUMANIA, HUNGARY AND BULGARIA: Interpretation of Peace Treaties with Bulgaria, Hungary and Rumania, Advisory opinion, March 30, 1950, and July 18, 1950 - I.C.J. Reports, 1950, pp. 65 et seq. and pp. 221 et seq. The case is summarized in 12 Whiteman's Digest 1060, 1971.

114 UNIVERSAL DECLARATION: The Declaration is reproduced in Bishop, International Law, 1971, pp. 465 et seq.

114 ONE AMERICAN CASE: Sei Fujii v California, 217 P. 2d 481 (1950), held that a prohibition to own land was in conflict with the United Nations Charter. While the decision was predicated primarily on the Charter, the court did say, "It is incompatible with Article 17 of the Declaration of Human Rights which proclaims the right of everyone to own property."

114 SERIES OF CONVENTIONS: The ILO Conventions have already been alluded to.

114 UNESCO: It is referred to in Luard, The International Protection of Human Rights, 1967, p. 73.

114 GENERAL ASSEMBLY: The proposed conventions are given in the Department of State Bulletin, 1967, Vol. 56, p. 107, along with a statement by Patricia Harris giving the views of the United States.

115 FOREIGN AFFAIRS: William Korey, "Human Rights Treaties: Why is the U.S. Stalling?" Foreign Affairs, 1967, Vol. 45, p. 414. The same author wrote The Key to Human Rights Implementation, International Conciliation pamphlet No. 570 of November 1968.

115 CHIEF JUSTICE WARREN: Department of State Bulletin, 1968, Vol. 59. p. 688

116 MISSOURI V HOLLAND: 252 US 416 (1920).

116 CONVENTION ON ROAD TRAFFIC: 3 UST 3008: Article 17 is on p. 3015.

117 COVENANT ON CIVIL AND POLITICAL RIGHTS: Chicago Today of
     Saturday, August 28, 1971, carried this interesting item: "Charles
     Clark, 71, of Detroit, was unanimously voted $10,000 yesterday by the
     Michigan Senate after he was declared innocent of murder and freed
     after 30 years in prison. The grant, which needs House approval, speci-
     fies the money 'is provided solely out of humanitarian consideration
     for the wrong done by the citizens of the state.'"

     Obviously, Michigan did not consider that Charles Clark had a right to
     compensation. If the Convention were in force, he would have a right
     unless the phrase "compensated according to law" is interpreted narrow-
     ly to mean that the absence of a law precludes compensation. This,
     however, seems much too narrow an interpretation.

     One factor to be considered, however, is that the 11th Amendment pro-
     hibits a suit against a state without its consent. Could the treaty cir-
     cumvent that provision?

117 FEDERAL COURTS: The question of Federal jurisdiction is a very
     difficult one. A district court has original jurisdiction whenever the
     matter in controversy exceeds $10,000 and arises under the Constitu-
     tion, laws or treaties of the United States (28 USC 1331). The matter
     is discussed in C.A. Wright and A.R. Miller, Federal Practice and
     Procedure, 1969, Vol. 5, p. 91, Section 1209. If the amount involved
     is over $10,000 and a treaty is involved, jurisdiction seems clear.
     Moreover, the plaintiff is given the benefit of the doubt as to the value
     of the claim (Seth v British Overseas Airway Corporation, 329 F.2d 302
     1964, certiorari denied 379 US 858, 1964). Furthermore, 28 USC 1343
     gives District Courts jurisdiction over civil rights cases irrespective
     of the amount. Section 1343 refers, however, to Acts of Congress and
     not to treaties - so that technically it might be argued that the $10,000
     limit applies only to civil rights actions arising under a law. It seems
     dubious, however, whether such an argument would prevail.

117 HUMAN RIGHTS COMMISSION: Luard, The International Protection of
     Human Rights, 1967, has a chapter written by A.H. Robertson on "The
     European Convention on Human Rights," appearing on pp. 99 et seq.
     The Lawless case may be found in 56 A.J.I.L. 171, 1962.

CHAPTER XVII
Peaceful Settlement of Disputes

TEXTS:

K.S. Carlston, The Process of International Arbitration, 1946.
J.L. Simpson and H. Fox, International Arbitration: Law and Practice, 1959.
C.W. Jenks, The Prospects of International Adjudiciation, 1964.
Shabtai Rosenne, The Law and Practice of the International Court, 2 Vols., 1965.

NOTES:

Page

118 THEODORE ROOSEVELT: The Roosevelt mediation is described in Chapter 4, p. 56 et seq. of Raymond E. Esthus, Theodore Roosevelt and Japan, 1966.

118 THE ABC POWERS: The ABC mediation is referred to in J. Fred Rippy, The United States and Mexico, 1926, p. 352.

118 KASHMIR: The text of the Tashkent declaration regarding Kashmir is given 3 U.N. Monthly Chronicle 37, April 1966.

119 RUSSO-JAPANESE WAR: The Dogger Bank incident is recounted in chronological form in Appendix L, pp. 468 et seq. of F.E. Smith and N.W. Sibley, International Law as Interpreted during the Russo-Japanese War, 1905. See also pp. 283 et seq.

119 WILLIAM JENNINGS BRYAN: There is an indication that Bryan's proposal for the conciliation treaties made to the diplomatic corps in Washington was not launched under the best of auspices. As related by Robert H. Ferrell in American Diplomacy, a History, 1969, on page 490: "What the hardened members of the corps thought of this proposition is difficult to say. At diplomatic receptions Bryan, a teetotaler, already had mortgaged his credit with Washington diplomats by serving grape juice, and there was talk of milk." Ferrell goes on to recount the zeal with which Bryan pursued his objective.

History records that the general arbitration and conciliation treaties served little purpose. George F. Kennan brings this out in an essay entitled, "Two Planes of International Reality," reproduced in Issues in American Diplomacy, 1965, edited by Armin Rappaport, Vol. 1, at p. 9.

119 ITALY AND THE UNITED STATES: The "arbitration" is discussed by Paul B. Larsen in an article appearing 61 A.J.I.L. 496, 1967.

119 COMMISSIONS ENDEAVOR TO CONCILIATE: Quincy Wright in an article on "Arbitration, International" in the Encyclopedia Americana, 1970, Vol. 2, p. 175, has questioned whether international arbitration is an essentially judicial process.

120 REACH AN AGREEMENT: The case is summarized by my Japanese colleague on the Commission, Ambassador Kumao Nishimura, in an article in the Japanese Annual of International Law, 1962, No. 6, on pp. 47 et seq. (minority shareholders' cases).

120 ALABAMA CLAIMS: The story of the Alabama controversy is recounted in considerable detail in Martin B. Duberman, Charles Francis Adams 1807-1886, 1961, in Chapter 24, pp. 341 et seq. and Chapter 26, pp. 373 et seq. The maneuvering, the legal niceties, and individual idiosyncrasies were extremely complicated. Admittedly the text grossly over-simplifies.

120 ARBITRATION HAD ITS GREAT VOGUE: The early history of American arbitration is given in John B. Moore, The Principles of American Diplomacy, 1918, pp. 306 et seq.

121 FIRST HAGUE CONVENTION: James Brown Scott gave a series of lectures in 1908 on the two Hague Conferences. The lectures, along with a volume of documents, were published as The Hague Peace Conferences of 1899 and 1907, 1909. Chapter V, pp. 188 et seq. of Vol. I, gives the history of arbitration and is an essay that supplements Moore's essay on the subject (cited supra), particularly in giving the history of arbitration before 1794. Chapter VI, pp. 254 et seq., concerns the conventions of 1899 and 1907. Vol. II contains the text of the 1899 Convention on pp. 80 et seq. and the 1907 Convention on pp. 300 et seq. The same treaties may also be found in 1 Bevans 230 et seq. and 577 et seq., respectively.

121 PERMANENT COURT OF ARBITRATION: The initial chapter of Manley O. Hudson, The Permanent Court of International Justice, 1943, discusses the Permanent Court of Arbitration and summarizes the cases before it.

121 PERMANENT COURT OF INTERNATIONAL JUSTICE: See footnote above. Its decisions are given in the official texts of the Court, issued in several series. Conveniently, they are to be found in World Court Reports edited by Manley O. Hudson in four volumes, 1934-1943.

121 AMERICAN DELEGATION: J.B. Scott, The Hague Peace Conferences
      of 1899 and 1907, 1909, Vol. II, pp. 8 et seq.

121 NUMBER OF ARBITRATIONS: I have never been able to find a com-
      prehensive survey of all the inter-war arbitrations. There are, of
      course, reports of decisions of individual commissions. Many are
      referred to in the bibliography to R.B. Lillich and G.A. Christenson,
      International Claims, Their Preparation and Presentation, 1962, appear-
      ing pp. 149 et seq. Moreover, A.M. Stuyt, Survey of International
      Arbitrations 1794-1938, 1939, serves as a convenient index to the cases
      up to 1939. The cases are listed in chronological order. Many of the
      cases likewise appear in other compilations.

122 PERMANENT COURT OF INTERNATIONAL JUSTICE: The story of the
      United States and the Court is given in D.F. Fleming, The United
      States and the World Court, 1945.

122 COURT HAS RENDERED: In a note appended to a letter of October 15,
      1970, Judge Hardy Dillard said, "The Court, since 1946, has dealt with
      51 cases; it has rendered 31 judgments and 13 advisory opinions." These
      were the figures I used. I realize, however, that with each passing
      year the numbers increase.

122 THE TWO LARGEST ARBITRATIONS: They are related to the war
      claims against Italy and Japan, respectively. Some, but not all, of the
      decisions of the two Commissions are given in the United Nations Re-
      ports of International Arbitral Awards, Vol. XIV, pp. 86 et seq. and
      pp. 472 et seq. Reports also carries other documentation concerning
      the arbitrations.

123 IN ADDITION TO THESE ARBITRATIONS: The decision of the French-
      American Tribunal is given in 58 A.J.I.L. 1017, 1964, while the Gut
      Dam Arbitration is discussed by Richard Lillich in a note in 59 A.J.I.L.
      892, 1965. In a recent (June 30, 1971) letter written by the Legal Ad-
      viser to Senator Javits, in answer to some observations I had made,
      it was stated: "In recent years the United States has taken part in the
      following arbitrations; with Italy, under Article 83 of the Peace Treaty
      of 1947; with Japan under Article 15 of the Peace Treaty of 1951; with
      Germany under the Convention of October 23, 1954, on the Settlement
      of Matters Arising out of the War, and under the Agreement on Ger-
      man External Debts, of February 27, 1953; with Spain in the Attilio
      Regolo Case in 1945; with the Netherlands relating to postal sea transit
      charges in 1945; with Italy in the Albanian Gold Case in 1963; with France
      and Italy concerning air transport services; and with Canada with re-
      spect to the Gut Dam claims, under a 1965 agreement."

      It seems to me that the list is somewhat padded.

123 IN JAPAN DIFFERENCES: The quotation in the text that follows is from an essay by Kawashima Takeyoshi in a series of essays edited by Charles A. Moore entitled, The Japanese Mind, 1967, at p. 267.

124 JURISDICTION OF THE COURT: 4 Bevans 140 contains the official text. It is also reproduced innumerable times in case books and other texts.

124 PRINCIPLE OF RECIPROCITY: One of the best, if not the best, critiques of how the Connally Amendment operates in reverse is in an essay by Herbert W. Briggs entitled, "United States v Bulgaria: Domestic Jurisdiction and Sovereign Determinations of Legal Irresponsibility," appearing in Mélanges offerts a Henri Rolin, Paris, 1964, pp. 13 et seq.

124 THEIR OWN LIMITATIONS: A short general survey of the optional clause practice is given in Julius Stone, The International Court and the World Crisis, International Conciliation pamphlet No. 536, January 1962. Not too much has changed since 1962.

124 COMPROMISSARY CLAUSES: A list of compromissary clauses in treaties and agreements to which the United States is a party is contained in C.S. Rhyne, International Law, 1971, pp. 229-230.

124 CHAMBERS: There has been a new and curious development which looks as if the use of Chambers might be approached by the side door. The Argentine, Chile and the United Kingdom entered into an agreement for the arbitration of a boundary dispute between the Argentine and Chile. Instead, however, of referring the question to the Queen of England as was done in an earlier boundary dispute, the agreement provided for a five man arbitration court, all five of whose members happen to be also members of the World Court (International Legal Materials, 1971, Vol. X, No. 6, pp. 1182 et seq.)

125 SOUTH WEST AFRICA CASE: The preliminary and final decisions are reported, respectively, in I.C.J. Reports, 1962, p. 319 and I.C.J. Reports, 1966, p. 6. Ernest Gross comments on the case in Foreign Affairs, 1967, Vol. 45, p. 36.

125 COMPLETELY UNFOUNDED IN LAW: as quoted in 61 A.J.I.L. at 162 1967.

125 BARCELONA TRACTION COMPANY: I.C.J. Reports, 1970, p. 3. Secretary of State Rogers said that the decision "has further eroded confidence in the Court," Proceedings of the American Society of International Law at its Sixty-fourth Annual Meeting, 1970, p. 288. Herbert W. Briggs, however, in an article on the case considered that criticism "ill considered," 65 A.J.I.L. 331, 1971.

125   CONNALLY AMENDMENT CHANGED: In a personal (April 5, 1971)
      letter to me, Senator Javits said: "The resolution adopted by the United
      Nations General Assembly to establish an ad hoc committee to review
      the role and functioning of the International Court of Justice will hope-
      fully make the Senate responsive to the need for reassessing the United
      States policy relating to our submission to the Court's jurisdiction.
      I intend, probably next month, to introduce with Senator Humphrey
      two resolutions, one repealing the Connally reservation, and the other
      attempting to amend it in a way which will diminish the obstacle it pre-
      sents to effective American participation in and support for the World
      Court."

125   BOUNDARY DISPUTES: Rann of Kutch, International Legal Materials,
      1968, Vol. 7, pp. 633 et seq.; Chile and Argentina, 61 A.J.I.L. 1071,
      1967; Lake Lanoux, 53 A.J.I.L. 156, 1959.

125   PERMIT AN INDIVIDUAL: Bishop, International Law, 1971, has a con-
      cise statement on the subject along with copious references, pp. 463
      et seq.

126   THIS PRACTICE: Martin Domke commented on the subject in an ar-
      ticle in 17 Arbitration Journal, 1962, No. 3, pp. 129 et seq., entitled,
      "Arbitration Between Governmental Bodies and Foreign Private Firms."
      One phase of this form of arbitration relates to investment disputes.
      On this, an article by Paul C. Szasz, "The Investment Disputes Con-
      vention and Latin America," in 11 Virginia Journal of International Law
      1971, pp. 256 et seq. is illuminating.

126   COMPTROLLER GENERAL: Decision of January 27, 1953, Decisions
      of the Comptroller General, January 1953, Vol. 32, pp.333 et seq.

CHAPTERS XVIII and XIX
International Agreements
Treaties

TEXTS:

Sir A.D. McNair, The Law of Treaties, 1961.
K. Holloway, Modern Trends in Treaty Law: Constitutional Law, Reservations and the Three Modes of Legislation, 1967.
F.C. Iklé, How Nations Negotiate, 1964.

NOTES:

Page

128 UNITED STATES CODE: 1 USC 112a.

128 AVIATION CONVENTION: 3 Bevans 965.

130 A RESERVATION: Bishop has a concise note on the subject in his International Law, 1971, pp. 124 et seq. The Soviet attitude on reservations is described in J.F. Triska and R.M. Slusser, The Theory, Law and Policy of Soviet Treaties, 1962, pp. 82 et seq.

130 LAW ON TREATIES: The text of the convention appears in 63 A.J.I.L. 875, 1969. Reservations are covered in Articles 19 et seq.

131 CLEAR INTENTION: I should admit at the outset that my views as to the frequency of deliberate ambiguity are not shared by Charles Bevans. Assistant Legal Adviser for Treaty Affairs. Neither are they consistent with the views expressed by Ambassador Winthrop Brown in an article on "The Art of Negotiation," which appeared in the Foreign Service Journal of July 1968, pp. 14 et seq. Nevertheless, I still think I have grounds for my opinion.

131 WAR OF 1812: The Treaty of Ghent is summarized by S.F. Bemis in his A Diplomatic History of the United States, 1965, pp. 164 et seq.

132 AMERICAN DIPLOMATIC HISTORIAN: T.A. Bailey, A Diplomatic History of the American People, 1969, p. 275.

132 M.A.K. MENON: Universal Postal Union, International Conciliation pamphlet No. 552, March 1965, p. 62.

132 A BRITISH LAWYER: Michael Hardy, Modern Diplomatic Law, 1968, p. 16-17.

134 TREATY PROCEDURE: The Department of State Foreign Affairs Manual deals with treaty procedures in Vol. 11, Sections 710 et seq.

136 VIENNA CONVENTION: The article quoted is Article 7 (63 A.J.I.L. 877, 1969).

136 EXECUTIVE AGREEMENT: There is a vast literature on the question of executive agreements. One of the best known studies is E.M. Byrd Jr., Treaties and Executive Agreements in the United States, 1960. An official analysis of the problem is contained in The Constitution of the United States of America, Analysis and Interpretation, prepared by the Legislative Reference Service, 1964, pp. 484 et seq.

136 TREATY OF PEACE WITH JAPAN: The agreement is given in 3 UST 4054 et seq.

137 TEXAS AND HAWAII: 1 Moore's Digest 453 and 509, respectively.

137 TRUE EXECUTIVE AGREEMENTS: Bishop, International Law, 1971, has a note on the subject of executive agreements, pp. 102-104.

137 RULES OF THE HOUSE: Of particular relevance is an early precedent to the effect that an appropriation under a treaty, to pay a claim submitted to arbitration under the treaty, was quite valid. Hinds, Precedents of the House of Representatives, 1907, Vol. 4, p. 426.

137 MODIFIES AN EXISTING STATUTE: The case usually cited as precedent for the proposition that an executive agreement cannot affect a statute is United States v Guy W. Capps, Inc., 204 F.2d 655 (1953).

139 AGREEMENT COMES INTO FORCE: Articles 24 and 25 of the Vienna Convention apply to the entry into force and provisional application of treaties, 63 A.J.I.L. 833, 1969. Articles 42 et seq. relate to the invalidity, termination and suspension of treaties, 63 A.J.I.L. 888, 1969.

139 ITALY HAD REFUSED: Charlton v Kelly, 229 US 447 (1913).

139 TREATY OF UTRECHT: F.L. Israel, Editor, Major Peace Treaties of Modern History, 1648-1967, 1967, Vol. I, pp. 223-224.

140 SPAIN, HOWEVER, HAS NOT ARGUED: The situation with regard to Gibraltar is summarized in Issues Before the 26th General Assembly, International Conciliation pamphlet No. 584, September 1971, at pp. 191-192.

140 REBUS SIC STANTIBUS: Everyone seems to have a slightly different interpretation of that term. Two American law dictionaries give it as

"while things thus stand" and "at this point of affairs, "while H. Kelsen, in his Principles of International Law (edited by R.W. Tucker), 1966, refers to the clause as one "concerning vital change of circumstances."

140 NEW YORK COURT OF APPEALS: Techt v Hughes, 229 N.Y. 222, 128 N.E. 185 (1920).

141 TREATY OF PEACE WITH ITALY: 4 Bevans 325, Article 44.

141 TREATY WITH ISRAEL: 5 UST at p. 574.

142 IN COMMERCIAL TREATIES: The change in American policy that led to the adoption of the unconditional most favored nation clause in commercial treaties is set forth in II Hackworth's Digest 57.

142 IN CONSULAR CONVENTIONS: Precedents in point are referred to in IV Hackworth's Digest 702 et seq.

142 CONVENTION WITH THE SOVIET UNION: The provision granting immunities to consular officers relates to their exemption from criminal jurisdiction. It is Article 19, 19 UST 5031 et seq.

143 LAW OF TREATIES: See page 130 and footnote.

143 ARTICLE 4: 63 A.J.I.L. 877, 1969.

143 ARTICLES 31, 32, 33: Ibid, pp. 885 et seq.

145 STATE SUCCESSION: Ibid, Article 73, p. 898.

146 PROVISIONS OF ITS INTERNAL LAW: Ibid, Article 46, p. 890.

146 BRITISH JURIST: J.G. Starke, Introduction to International Law, 1972, pp. 89-90.

146 FUNDS TO IMPLEMENT A TREATY: In a footnote on page 289 of his A Diplomatic History of the United States, 1965, Professor S.F. Bemis says: "On a number of occasions, but notably in the debates on Jay's Treaty of 1794, on the 'Gadsden Purchase' of 1853, and on the Alaska Treaty with Russia of 1867, vigorous objection was made in the United States House of Representatives to make the appropriations necessary to carry into effect a treaty ratified by the Senate and proclaimed by the President. In no case has the opposition been successful; thus an international issue on such a point has never been precipitated."

146 THE HAGUE ACADEMY: Recueil des cours, Vol. II, 1965, p. 191.

CHAPTER XX
The Law of the Sea

TEXTS:

C.J. Colombos, The International Law of the Sea, 1962.

M.S. McDougal and W.T. Burke, The Public Order of the Oceans - A Contemporary International Law of the Sea, 1962.

W. McFee, The Law of the Sea, 1950.

H. Feiff, The United States and the Treaty Law of the Sea, 1959.

NOTES:

Page

148 IMPERIUM TERRAE FINIRI: The theory of cannon range was first advanced by Cornelius van Bynkershoek in his De Dominio Maris Dissertatio. In the translation of that work (appearing in 1923 as one of the Classics of International Law, edited by James Brown Scott), the pertinent passage appears on page 44. Moreover, J.B. Scott speaks of the development of the theory in the introduction, pp. 17-18.

148 CLAIMS RANGE: On May 8, 1970, the Republics of Argentina, Brazil, Chile, Ecudor, El Salvador, Nicaragua, Panama, Peru and Uruguay adopted the Montevideo Declaration of the Law of the Sea, extending sovereignty "to a distance of 200 nautical miles from the baseline of the territorial sea." (64 A.J.I.L. 1022, 1970). Since a nautical mile is longer than a statutory mile, this means that the territorial sea claimed is just about 230 miles in width - or well over the airline distance from Washington to New York. An interesting article on the subject by an English jurist, J.E.S. Fawcett, is "The Territorial Sea, Theme and Variations," Interplay, January 1971, Vol. 4, No. 1, p. 10. The Department of State published a list as of October 1, 1969, showing the territorial sea claimed by various nations - U.S. Department of State, Sovereignty of the Sea, Geographic Bulletin, No. 3, revised October 1969, p. 28. The list is already somewhat obsolete as more and more nations have extended the limits of the territorial seas.

148 CONTIGUOUS ZONE: W. Bishop, International Law, 1971, points out on page 622 that "the laws of the United States have since 1790 prohibited various acts within 12 miles or 4 leagues of the shore." W.E. Masterson, Jurisdiction in Marginal Seas, 1929, has a detailed account on pp. 175 et seq. of the development of American law. More recent legislation provides for an authority to establish a customs enforcement area that may extend fifty nautical miles beyond customs waters (19 USC 1701).

149 ACT OF OCTOBER 14, 1966: 16 USC 1091. Previous to this legislation, President Truman had issued a proclamation on September 28, 1945, with regard to coastal fisheries - 59 STAT Pt. 2 885.

150 FOUR CONVENTIONS: The four conventions on the sea given in the order of their coming into force in the United States are the ones on:
1. The High Seas, 13 UST 2312.
2. The Continental Shelf, 15 UST 471.
3. The Territorial Sea and the Contiguous Zone, 15 UST 1606.
4. Fishing and Conservation of Living Resources of the High Seas, 17 UST 138.

150 JOHN GUNTHER: There are several editions of Inside Russia Today. In the revised paperback edition (1962) the statement is found on page 201. The same plan is alluded to in an article entitled "Toward International Law - A Report" by William H. Stringer, which appeared in the January/February 1972 issue of Vista (Vol. 7., No. 4, p. 47).

150 RUSSIAN VENTURE: New York Times, May 16, 1971, Section 1, p. 2.

150 DESALINATION: On November 14, 1967, Secretary Rusk, in an address to the Foreign Policy Association, said: "And we and many other countries, including the scientists of the Soviet Union, are now engaged in cooperative studies in the problems of desalting water as a part of the solution." Department of State Bulletin, 1967, Vol. 57, p. 738.

151 PRESIDENT NIXON: Department of State Bulletin, 1971, Vol. 64 at p. 414. The text of the proposed treaty had previously been given in Department of State Bulletin, 1970, Vol. 62, pp. 665 et seq.

151 MALTA SUGGESTED A RESOLUTION: International Conciliation pamphlet No. 569 of September 1968, Issues Before the 23rd General Assembly, p. 52.

151 QUEST FOR A SOLUTION: The continuing search for a solution has generated an enormous literature. The progress of the search in the United Nations can be traced in the International Conciliation pamphlets Nos. 574 (September 1969), 579 (September 1970), and 584 (September 1971), on the Issues Before the 24th, 25th and 26th General Assemblies, respectively. See in particular pages 62, 65, and 79, respectively. Among the innumerable articles on the subject in both legal and technical publications, one of the most interesting is that of the representative of Malta in the United Nations, Ambassador Pardo. His article, entitled "Who will control the Seabed," appeared in Foreign Affairs, 1968, Vol. 47, p. 123. The question of the seabed is one of the problems to be discussed at the forthcoming Law of the Sea Conference in 1973.

In the meantime, the United States has suggested some general principles governing the seabed exploitation (Department of State Bulletin,
1971, Vol. 64, p. 150).

152 NORTH ATLANTIC FISHERIES ARBITRATION: Senate Documents 61st
Congress, 3rd Session, 1910-1911, Volumes 71-82.

152 FUR SEALS: The fur seal arbitration was reported in equal, if not
greater, length. Fortunately, it is given in I Moore's International
Arbitrations pp. 755 et seq. From a diplomatic standpoint, the Bering
Sea controversy is described in the article on James Blaine, written
by James B. Lockey in Vol. VII of The American Secretaries of State
and their Diplomacy, edited by S.F. Bemis, 1958. See in particular
pp. 128 et seq.

152 COOLIE TRADE: There is a good account of the coolie trade and its
horrors in the 11th edition of the Encyclopedia Britannica, 1910, Vol.
VII, p. 77. There is no corresponding article in the present edition.

152 JAW OF PORPOISES: Encyclopedia Britannica, 1971, Vol. 18, p. 252.

152 PRESERVE THE WHALE: Pertinent to whaling are the Conventions for
the Regulation of Whaling (1931) 3 Bevans 26; the International Whaling
Convention (1946) 4 Bevans 248; and the Protocol to the International
Convention for the Regulation of Whaling (1956) 10 UST 952. Over the
years, the International Whaling Commission has expressed considerable concern over the killing of whales. See in particular the Tenth,
Eleventh, and Twelfth Reports of the International Whaling Commission
and especially the Report of the Working Party on Humane and Expeditious Methods of Killing Whales, Appendix V to the Twelfth Report.

152 CONSERVATION HAS NOT BEEN RESTRICTED: Conservation is, of
course, not quite the same thing as humanitarianism. Nevertheless
the preservation of certain species such as the sea otter and the mana-
tee under the Treaty for Nature Protection and Wildlife Preservation
in the Western Hemisphere (3 Bevans 630 at 636) results in humanitarianism. There are also, as noted in the text, many fishing conservation agreements. The agreements are too numerous to enumerate.
They are conveniently listed for each country under the heading "Fisheries" in Treaties in Force.

153 ASSISTANCE AND SALVAGE: 1 Bevans 780.

153 NORTH ATLANTIC ICE PATROL: The Titanic disaster has been described in many publications. Among the best is Walter Lord, A Night
to Remember, 1955. Following the disaster, the American Government

instituted the Ice Patrol Service. Moreover, increasing attention was given over the years to safety at sea. The series of agreements culminating in the presently effective International Convention for the Safety of Life at Sea of June 17, 1960 (16 UST 185) are enumerated in C. Colombos, The International Law of the Sea, 1962, pp. 335 et seq. The actual convention is quite short, but the French and English texts of the regulations, which are made a part of the convention by Article I, cover over 350 pages. The maintenance of the Ice Patrol by the United States is covered by Regulation 6 of Chapter V (16 UST 498). The same regulation also provides for reimbursement. The agreement regarding financial support is found in 7 UST 1969. The American law authorizing the activity is 46 USC 738.

153 LOAD LINES: Load lines are the subject of a specific convention, 18 UST 1857.

153 OIL POLLUTION: The 1954 convention is given in 12 UST 2989. The proposed 1969 conventions are given in 64 A.J.I.L. 471, 1970.

154 THE AMERICAN JOURNAL: Arthur Dean's article appears in 52 A.J. I.L. 607, 1958. He likewise had an article on the 1960 conference in 54 A.J.I.L. 751, 1960.

154 ACCEPTED A TWELVE MILE LIMIT: The Department in a statement of April 15, 1970, said, "With respect to the 12-mile limit on the territorial sea, we have publically indicated our willingness to accept such limit, but only as part of an agreed international treaty also providing for freedom of passage through and over international straits." Department of State Bulletin, 1970, Vol. 62, p. 611.

154 IN 1970 ARGENTINA: 64 A.J.I.L. 1022, 1970.

155 ARTICLE 3: Articles 3 and 4 are found in 15 UST 1609.

156 ARTICLE 15: Ibid, p. 1610.

156 ARTICLE 24: Ibid, p. 1612.

156 NAVAL HOSTILITIES: The Declaration of Panama and the Graf Spee incident are dealt with in VII Hackworth's Digest 702 et seq.

157 I'M ALONE: II Hackworth's Digest 703 et seq. The correspondence that preceded the submission of the case to arbitration is quite interesting. U.S. Department of State, Foreign Relations of the United States, 1929, 1943, Vol. II, pp. 23 et seq.

157 FISHERY DISPUTES: The fishery disputes are becoming more and more complicated. The New York Times has pointed out that the tuna dispute with Ecuador now involves reconciling the positions "taken by the State Department, the Defense Department, the Ecuadorian Government, and the tuna clipper owners." New York Times, January 30, 1972, Section 3, p. 7.

158 PRESIDENT TRUMAN: The proclamation appears in 59 STAT 884.

158 ARTICLE 1: 15 UST 473.

158 INTERNATIONAL COURT OF JUSTICE: I.C.J. Reports, 1969, p. 3; 63 A.J.I.L. 591, 1969.

158 ARTICLE 2: 15 UST 473.

159 SHELLFISH: The argument concerning shellfish crops up periodically. On April 25, 1971, the New York Times, Section 4, p. 4, reported a controversy between Russia and Japan over crabs. The Russians maintained that the crabs belong to the continental shelf and the Japanese the reverse. As far as is known, no one as yet has bothered to conduct an opinion poll among the crabs themselves.

CHAPTER XXI
The Law of Outer Space

TEXTS:

S.H. Lay and H.J. Taubenfeld, The Law Relating to Activities of Man
in Space, 1970.

J.W. Fawcett, International Law & the Uses of Outer Space, 1968.

G. Gal, Space Law, 1969.

D. Johnson, Rights in Air Space, 1965.

Senate Document No. 26, 87th Congress, 1st Session, Legal Problems
of Space Exploration: A Symposium, 1961.

NOTES:

Page

160 WHERE OUTER SPACE BEGINS: 2 Whiteman's Digest 1284.

160 TREATY ON PRINCIPLES: 18 UST 2410.

161 WRECKAGE FROM A SOVIET SPACE VEHICLE: The facts are reported in Facts on File (1969/433/G1-A2).

161 UNITED STATES RETURNED: Ibid, B2.

161 ANOTHER TREATY: 19 UST 757.

161 SECTION 102(2): 42 USC 2451.

161 COMMUNICATIONS SATELLITES: The agreement establishing interim arrangements for a global commercial communications satellite
system entered into force on August 20, 1969 (15 UST 1705). Article 2
has the rather unusual provision that: "Each Party either shall sign
or shall designate a communications entity, public or private, to sign
the Special Agreement which is to be concluded further to this Agreement and which is to be opened for signature at the same time as this
Agreement." The special agreement is, in reality, attached to the
basic agreement (15 UST 1745). In addition there is a supplementary
agreement on arbitration. Curiously enough, that agreement is listed
in Treaties in Force, but the citation (TIAS 5646) is incorrect. See
instead 4 International Legal Materials 735, 1965. There is also an
agreement with Denmark, Norway and Sweden (14 UST 1278).

161 BILATERAL ARRANGEMENTS: The picture is changing so constantly

that it is difficult to document the statement from any printed sources. Hence, I submitted my draft to Professor S. Houston Lay, who is the co-author of one of the texts cited above, and asked him to verify the accuracy of my statement (which, from the beginning, had been largely moulded from information in statements supplied by him).

BIBLIOGRAPHIC GUIDE

The material available on international law and on related fields is enormous. For just one three-month period the American Journal of International Law listed two-and-a-half pages in close print of books received by the American Society of International Law. This does not count the innumerable articles on international law subjects that appear in various legal reviews. Nor does it include judicial decisions, both of international and domestic courts, resolutions of the General Assembly of the United Nations, treaties and other international agreements, the discussions and recommendations of learned societies, and various other documents concerning the law of nations. In all probability it would take an average person a lifetime just to read the material that comes out in one three-month period. Obviously, under the circumstances, it is not possible to prepare a comprehensive bibliography.

Instead an effort will be made to provide a short--or at least relatively short--bibliographic guide to help the student find his way in the maze of available material in the English language. A vast amount is also available in other languages, much of it excellent. Since, however, this is a text primarily for American readers, non-English sources will not be analyzed.

Among the many texts, case books of a general nature and related volumes published in English in relatively recent years are:

Bishop, William W. Jr. International Law-Cases and Materials, 1962 and 1970. (The older edition contains considerable material not available in the later edition.)

Brierly, J.L. The Law of Nations: An Introduction to the International Law of Peace, 1963.

Brownlie, Ian. Principles of Public International Law, 1966.

Chayes, Abram; Ehrlich, Thomas, and Lowenfeld, Andreas F., International Legal Process, Materials for an Introductory Course, 2 vols., 1968; Vol. 3 is a Documentary Supplement.

Collins, Edward, Jr. International Law in a Changing World, 1970.

Fawcett, J.E.S., The Law of Nations, 1968.

Fenwick, Charles G., International Law, 1965.

Friedman, Wolfgang; Lissitzyn, Oliver J.; and Pugh, Richard C. International Law: Cases and Materials, 1969.

Jacobini, H.B. International Law: A Text, 1968.

Jessup, Philip C. Modern Law of Nations: An Introduction, 1968.

Kelsen, Hans, and Tucker, R.W. Principles of International Law, 2nd ed., 1966.

Korowicz, Marek St. Introduction to International Law, 1959.

Lissitzyn, Oliver J. International Law Today & Tomorrow, 1965.

O'Connell, D.P. International Law, 2 Vols., 2nd Edition, 1971.

Oppenheim, Lassa, International Law, 2 Vols. Vol. 1, 1955; Vol. 2, 1952.

Orfield, Lester B., and Re, Edward D. International Law: Cases and Materials, 1965.

Rhyne, Charles S. International Law: The Substance, Processes, Procedures and Institutions for World Peace with Justice, 1971.

Schwarzenberger, Georg. A Manual of International Law, 1967.

Sørensen, Max, ed. Manual of Public International Law, 1968.

Starke, Joseph Gabriel. An Introduction to International Law, 1972.

Svarlien, Oscar. Introduction to the Law of Nations, 1955.

Swift, R.N. International Law: Current and Classic, 1969.

Tung, William L. International Law in an Organizing World, 1968.

Von Glahn, Gerhard, Law Among Nations: An Introduction to Public International Law, 1970.

Whitaker, Urban G., Jr. Politics and Power: A Text in International Law, 1964.

In addition, reference must be made to Charles Chaney Hyde, International Law, Chiefly as Interpreted and Applied by the United States, 1945. This three-volume work, the second edition of which appeared in 1945, is the classic restatement of the law of nations as applied by the United States. Obviously there are many events that have occurred in the quarter of a century since the volumes were published which are naturally not reflected in that work, but up to 1945, it is comprehensive.

Another well documented text which has excellent chapters on the history of international law (Chapters III, IV, and V) is Amos S. Hershey, The Essentials of International Public Law and Organization, 1927.

As will have been noted the bibliography does not include references to texts on special subjects such as the law of the sea, nationality, etc. References to such texts may be found at the beginning of the notes on the individual chapters.

For further information on available books, one can consult a list prepared by the Association of American Law Schools called Law Books Recommended for Libraries: No. 46 International Law, 1968; The Subject Guide to Books in Print published by R.A. Bowker Co. can be very useful. In the 1970 edition there are about five closely written columns on international law with many cross references to other subjects.

The oldest and best known American periodical devoted to international law is the American Journal of International Law published by the American Society of International Law. It began in 1907 and has been published on a quarterly basis ever since. There are three cumulative indexes covering 1907-1920, 1921-1940, and 1941-1960. Since then there has been an annual index appearing at the end of each October issue. The Journal is published in January, April, July, September and October of each year, the September issue containing the Proceedings of the Annual Meeting of the

American Society of International Law. It carries leading articles, editorial comments, book reviews, court decisions, notations to United States practice and official documents. In addition, the American Society of International Law has published since 1962 International Legal Materials to supplement the material carried in the Journal itself. The Society has also published the Annual Proceedings, and has published in the past supplements, such as those which carry a series of proposed codes and commentaries on a large variety of topics from piracy to nationality. Those codes were prepared in the inter-war years by the Harvard Research on International Law which drew on academicians, practicing lawyers, and Department of State officials for help in their preparation.

Since 1966 the International and Comparative Law Section of the American Bar Association has started publishing The International Lawyer, which is a blend of articles and other material on international and comparative law. In addition, a number of law schools publish reviews concerning international law. Among the better known are Harvard International Law Journal, Columbia Journal of Transnational Law, and the Virginia Journal of International Law. One of the most recent, if not the most recent, addition to the field is the California Western International Law Journal.

Articles, notes and other material on International law topics also often appear in law journals not specializing in international law. Reference to at least some of that material can be obtained through the Index to Legal Periodicals and the Harvard Law School Annual Legal Bibliography.

There are international law reviews as well appearing in England and in many of the British Commonwealth countries. It will suffice, however, to mention the British Year Book of International Law and the International and Comparative Law Quarterly, both published in London.

Even in non-English speaking lands, journals, to obtain a wider audience, are sometimes published in English. This is true, for example, of the Japanese Annual of International Law.

Note should be taken of the Recueil des Cours of the Academy of International Law at The Hague. Every summer lectures on various phases of international law are given by outstanding authorities at the Peace Palace. These lectures are subsequently published in a series of volumes that by now includes about 130 volumes. At the beginning the lectures and printed volumes were all in French. Since 1947, however, they have been either in French or English, depending upon the lecturer. An index is available for Vol. 1-101. The lectures include general surveys of international law. In fact, one of the best short surveys of that law known to me is Professor William Bishop's lectures in 1965 which appear in Vol. 115, pp. 151 et seq.

In addition to the general texts, case books and articles, the student can, of course, draw on the digests of international law prepared under the auspices of the Department of State by Judge John Bassett Moore, Judge Green Hackworth, and Dr. Marjorie M. Whitman formerly of the Office of the Legal Adviser. They contain the most complete information available on the precedents of international law as applied by the United States.

More or less they respectively cover the periods up to 1906, from 1906 to the early 1940's, and from the early 1940's to the present. The British Digest of International Law edited by Clyde Parry, plays a similar role in assembling British precedents.

The American student of international law should also know how to use the material available on international agreements, particularly ones involving the United States. Until 1950 treaties and other international agreements were published in the United States in the Statutes at Large. Since the Statutes at Large were so numerous and unwieldy, a collection of treaties in two volumes was made to cover the material up to 1910 by Edmund Malloy entitled Treaties, Conventions, International Acts, Protocols and Agreements between the United States and Other Powers. The collection was continued by a volume edited by Redmond compiling the treaties up to 1923 and by another volume bringing the series up to 1937 edited by Trenwith. The series of four volumes is often collectively referred to as "Malloy's Treaties" even though Malloy edited only the first two volumes.

In 1950 a new official series was started entitled United States and Other International Agreements referred to as UST and the treaties and international agreements were no longer published in the Statutes at Large. All agreements are published in all of the languages in which they are prepared. Within the last few years Mr. Charles Bevans of the Office of the Legal Adviser of the Department of State has been editing a new series which will give all the treaties entered into between the founding of the Republic and 1950, entitled Treaties and Other International Agreements of the United States of America, 1776-1949. When completed, it will, along with the United States Treaty Series, furnish texts of all the treaties and international agreements the United States has entered into up to the present. The Bevans series however gives the agreements in English alone so it is not possible to compare the various language versions, a factor that may be important if there is reason to suspect a variance.

Every year the Department of State issues a list of international treaties and agreements to which the United States is a party in force as of the beginning of that year. The compilers of that list necessarily have to be quite conservative in determining that a treaty or agreement is no longer in effect. Hence some are listed which are of dubious present validity. Just for example, the list makes reference to an arbitration treaty between the United States and Albania. In view of the present relations between the two countries, the relevance of that treaty to contemporary relations is, to say the least, questionable.

As it takes some time to issue a new volume of the UST and, in the meantime, new treaties and agreements have to be consulted, the Department of State issues an individual print of each treaty and agreement in the Treaties and Other International Acts series.

A real problem arises with respect to agreements that are still in the process of being signed or ratified or both. Information as to the status of such agreements as well as their texts may be found in the Department of

State Bulletin to be described later. Admittedly, however, tracking down the exact status of a pending treaty is a laborious and difficult process.

From a historical standpoint, Hunter Miller's Treaties and Other International Acts of the United States of America in seven volumes is quite important, as it gives a good deal of information concerning the background of the treaties. Unfortunately, the Department of State which was publishing the series ran out of energy, or money, or both, around 1942 so the series stops in 1858. Very probably World War II interfered as its prosecution had a higher priority than the preparation of a treaty series.

All treaties registered with the United Nations are published in the United Nations Treaty Series. The League of Nations had published a similar series in the inter-war years. The United Nations publishes (since 1967) an annual compilation called Multilateral Treaties in respect of which the Secretary-General performs Depositary Functions: List of Signatures, Ratifications, Accessions, etc. as at 31 December 19-- (each year). This does not include the treaties themselves, but gives the UNTS citation and the current status of each treaty.

The decisions of the International Court of Justice are published in a voluminous set of records known as the ICJ reports. For anyone wishing a quick survey of the court decisions, a little booklet published by the Information Office of the United Nations entitled The International Court·of Justice is quite useful. Also very useful is J.J.G. Syatauw, Decisions of the International Court of Justice, 1969, which not only summarizes the various cases but gives sources and bibliography.

The jurisprudence of the arbitral courts is collected in a number of volumes. The American decisions up to 1898 are to be found in John Bassett Moore's History and Digest of International Arbitrations to which the United States has been a Party, in six volumes. Moore also published International Adjudications - Ancient and Modern, 1933, also in six volumes. Apparently it was to have been a monumental series that would have incorporated much or all of the material in the earlier digest. Unfortunately, it stopped short with six volumes covering some of the earlier arbitrations to which the United States was a party. Since then they may be found in the reports and decisions of various commissions such as, for example the Opinions of Commissioners, General Claims Commission, United States and Mexico. More recently the reports of arbitral commissions have been appearing in a series published by the United Nations entitled Reports of International Arbitral Awards.

The opinions of the Permanent Court of Arbitration were published by James Brown Scott in a volume entitled The Hague Court Reports, (1916 2nd series 1932). In addition, Sir Hersch Lauterpacht has made a compilation of the decisions of both municipal and international courts which is highly useful. That compilation changed names slightly during the course of the years. It is generally known as The Annual Digest or, in later years, the International Law Reports.

Further recourse to arbitral cases up to World War II can be had through

Stuyt, Survey of International Arbitration, 1939, and through Ralston, The Law and Procedure of International Tribunals, 1926, supplement 1936.

As has been pointed out in the text, the decisions of domestic courts on points of international law are acquiring greater and greater significance. Many of the leading cases, or at least excerpts from them, are reproduced in the various case books previously cited. Others are reproduced in periodical journals. Moreover, a series edited by Francis Deak, American International Law Cases, 1971 is very useful. For complete coverage one has to turn however to the case reports such as the West Publishing Co. series covering the Federal courts and the state courts on a regional basis. The cases are indexed in the American Digest System.

Of great importance to the student of international law are official documents, including treaties in process, statements of the President, the Secretary of State, and lesser officials and, of course, the laws of the United States concerning foreign relations.

Taking the latter first, the laws are published in the Statutes at Large. The laws having a permanent effect, as distinguished from temporary legislation such as an appropriation act appropriating money for one year, are brought together in the United States Code. Title 22 deals with foreign relations. Other provisions affecting foreign policy appear however in other titles.

The West Publishing Co. publishes an annotated edition of the Constitution and the Code which summarizes the salient features of the various cases which interpret particular articles of the Constitution and the Code.

Official documents other than court decisions may range from a short exchange of notes to a sixteen-volume collection of papers relating to the Bering Sea arbitration. (The more important ones are often reproduced in unofficial sources.) All separate documents issued by the government are listed in the Monthly Catalogue of United States Publications which is indexed annually. For the student of international law the Department of State Bulletin issued every week is of particular importance. It is indexed on a semi-annual basis. Material concerning international law may also be found in the series of volumes presently known as the Foreign Relations of the United States published by the Department of State.

In view of the importance of international organizations and particularly the United Nations in the development of international law, the official United Nations documentation cannot be ignored. Unfortunately, there is so much of it, it is hard to tell in a few words how to use it. (One author has estimated that if all United Nations documents prepared in one year were piled one on top of another, the pile would reach twenty miles into the sky.) Fortunately, Brenda Brimmer and others have prepared A Guide to the Use of United Nations Documents Including Reference to the Specialized Agencies and Special U.N. Bodies, 1962.

Before concluding, mention should be made of the volume prepared by the American Law Institute in the Restatement of the Law series called Foreign Relations Law of the United States. A word should also be said of

the International Conciliation pamphlets published on a quarterly basis by
the Carnegie Endowment which contain   many worthwhile studies on international legal topics . Particularly useful is the annual pamphlet published
each fall prior to each General Assembly summarizing issues before that
Assembly, many of which relate to international law in one aspect or another .

Finally, it should be pointed out that in view of the current interest in
international affairs, many articles bearing on international law appear in
non-technical periodicals . The discussion on the law of the sea has produced a whole series of articles in Foreign Affairs, the Saturday Review
and other publications . Access to such articles can be obtained through the
Reader's Guide to Periodical Literature .

SAMPLE EXAMINATION PROBLEMS

Over the course of the years I have given my students a problem in international law based upon wholly fictitous circumstances. I give it to them at the beginning of the term so that they can work on the problem throughout the rest of the term. I realize that this is a departure from the standard approach which consists of giving an examination at the end of the year calling for the solution of hypothetical solutions.

The reason that I prefer a problem to an examination is that it obligates the student to consult a considerable volume of material which he might never look at if he were taking an examination based essentially on the text and the lectures. In preparing the hypothetical problems I have taken considerable liberties with facts in order to establish situations where nice questions of international law would be involved. Thus I have arbitrarily made nations parties to treaties they never dreamt of entering, altered their relationships to one another from the ones in actual life, and changed radically the nature of their obligations under the compulsory jurisdiction clause of the International Court of Justice from what they are in real life. I have even gone so far as to create a rock which as far as I know, does not exist, and moved the Scilly Islands from their actual geographical location. I have also made statements which from a purely scientific standpoint are probably somewhat dubious as, for example, that fish got drunk.

My students have taken all these changes in good spirits and assumed for purposes of discussion the facts as given in the examination rather than as found in actuality.

Since others might be interested in those examinations, I have reproduced them in the pages to follow.

A. INTERNATIONAL LAW EXAMINATION

Margie O'Reen and Pat O'Butter, an attractive, intelligent and energetic Irish couple, had just become engaged. Through their joint efforts they had developed a delicious new dairy product made of various milk ingredients, almond water, and secret formulae, which they called the "Udder Whey." They had had considerable success in marketing that product in Ireland and wanted to expand their markets overseas. Knowing that dairy products, like yogurt, are widely used in the Middle East, they took a trip to that area, visiting the various commercial centers to promote the "Udder Whey."

In addition, Margie had a contract to represent an Irish brassiere company which sold brassieres called "erin-go-bras."

They ended their trip in Teheran in Iran. While there they became quite friendly with the Irish Ambassador and confided to him that they intended to get married as soon as they returned home. The Irish Ambassador suggested the possibility of getting married right away and going home as passengers on a tanker supplying oil from the Persian Gulf to Ireland, thus having a honeymoon en route. He added that he thought he could arrange the passage.

Margie and Pat were very receptive to the suggestion and were, in fact, married by the Irish Consul in Teheran. The Ambassador was as good as his word and did arrange passage on board a tanker which flew the Liberian flag and was registered in Monrovia although owned by a corporation incorporated in Ireland known as the Sinn Sere Oil Corporation. All of the stock in that corporation, however, was owned by Royal Dutch Shell which was controlled by English and Dutch interests. The vessel itself was called the S.S. SHELLDO. The master of the vessel was an Englishman, Captain P.E.T. Roleum. The crew was of mixed nationalities.

After the ship had rounded the Cape of Good Hope and was headed northward on the high seas, Wan Luk, the Chinese cook of the vessel, baked a cake with great pride for the captain's birthday.

Unfortunately, a sailor of Argentine nationality, Juan Roba la Torta, stole the cake and ate it which enraged Wan Luk. Wan Luk got angrier when the sailor was completely unrepentant and, in fact, teased Wan Luk. Wan Luk, who was hot tempered, thereupon took his meat cleaver and chased the sailor around the deck and finally, in the horrified presence of Pat and Margie, killed the sailor with his cleaver.

When the ship arrived in Ireland Wan Luk was taken into custody. The government of Ireland prepared to try him on the ground that the Liberian flag was only a flag of convenience since the vessel had no connections with Liberia and never visited Monrovia. It was alleged that the true nationality of the vessel was Irish as it was owned by an Irish corporation. At this point the Liberian government protested and, realizing that its legal position with regard to the nationality of the vessel might be eroded, expressed willingness to try Wan Luk. The Argentine government asked for the extradition of Wan Luk on the ground that the victim was an Argentinian. Argentina and Ireland have a traditional extradition treaty.

After much diplomatic correspondence the Irish government agreed to submit the question as to what nation had the right to try Wan Luk, which necessarily determined the nationality of the vessel, to the International Court of Justice with Argentina and Liberia being the other parties. The Irish government, the defendant in both cases, since it was the Liberian and Argentine governments who were making demands for the custody of Wan Luk, asked the Court to combine the cases for the sake of speed and economy. It was pointed out that the facts under which the cases arose were the same and the Court could consider them together. The Court in a preliminary hearing agreed to determine whether there should be a merger of cases under the statute of the Court. To complicate matters, since neither Liberia nor Argentina was represented on the Court, each wanted one of its nationals to sit as an ad hoc judge, pointing out that after all they were rival claimants for the custody of Wan Luk and their interests did not coincide.

At this point Panama also asked to be heard since many vessels are registered in Panama and might be considered "flag of convenience vessels" and any decision made by the International Court of Justice might affect its interests.

While the legal moves had been taking place concerning the rule of the International Court of Justice and the procedures to be followed, the Chinese Foreign Office at Taipeh considered the advisability of asking for the extradition of Wan Luk on the ground that he was a Chinese national. The Chief of the Department of Western European Affairs, Hu Niu, asked the opinion of his nephew Hi Niu, who happened to be the Legal Adviser of the Foreign Office. Hi Niu advised that a request could not be made on the double ground that China does not have an extradition treaty with Ireland and that Ireland recognized the Peking government as the true government of China.

In the meantime, Pat and Margie, encouraged by their success in the Middle East, wanted to go abroad again to continue to promote the "Udder Whey." The Irish government told them that they could not leave as they were material witnesses. Since they were fiery, tempestuous and Irish, they told the Court it was none of its business and that the Court could not restrain their travel. They were thereupon placed in preventive detention to make certain they would not leave the country. To make matters worse the prison warden, who had the rather unusual name of Mr. Azure Proboscis, claimed that they were never legally married since the Consul did not have the authority to marry them and therefore they could not be together in detention. After suffering unappetizing jail food, confinement, constraint and separation, Pat and Margie finally gave their word not to leave and put up bond to remain in Ireland. They nevertheless petitioned the European Commission on Human Rights on the ground that the detention violated their rights. At the same time they requested the Irish Foreign Office for a ruling that the Consul had a right to marry them.

Taking all the foregoing facts into consideration, indicate how the International Court of Justice should rule on the preliminary question of the joinder of the cases, the appointments of ad hoc judges, and Panama's request to be heard. Also indicate the proper rulings of the International Court of Justice on the substantive issues, i.e., who should have the right to try Wan Luk.

Also give your opinion as to how the European Commission on Human Rights should rule on the complaint made by Pat and Margie.

Indicate what should be the view of the Foreign Office concerning the validity of the marriage, discussing the scope of a consul's authority under international law. For purposes of this examination you can assume that Irish consuls have the same authority as British consuls. Finally give your opinion on whether Hi Niu's advice was sound.

If the facts as stated are in conflict with actual facts, accept the former as true for purposes of this paper. (For example, Argentina and Ireland may not have an extradition treaty. Assume, however, there is one. Likewise, Ireland may not have recognized Red China as the government of China. Assume, however, that she had.) Otherwise be guided by the various treaties and conventions actually in force between the various parties as well as by international law. Where the treaty or convention is unclear indicate the proper rules of treaty interpretation to apply.

B. INTERNATIONAL LAW EXAMINATION

Private Meek, a member of the American Armed Forces stationed in Hwat Nau, whose capital is Kween Kong, had been harassed and badgered at every turn by his ill-tempered top sergeant, Sergeant Bully. When possible, Private Meek sought refuge from Sergeant Bully by going to the Bar Suds, a local off-base bar frequented by American servicemen. Private Meek usually sat quietly in a corner drinking a bottle of the local brew and writing Chelly Brossom, his new Japanese bride whom he met and married while on leave in Japan and who is still in Japan.

On one particular day Sergeant Bully entered the Bar Suds while Private Meek was sitting there in his customary place. He went up to Private Meek and started casting aspersions on Private Meek's character, courage, fortitude, manhood and good sense. Private Meek tried to contain himself with as much patience as he could muster but when Sergeant Bully started deriding his Japanese bride and questioning her virtue, Private Meek, goaded beyond endurance, picked up a half-full glass of beer and threw it in Sergeant Bully's face.

Sergeant Bully, enraged, seized Private Meek by the throat and started choking him. Hearing the commotion two local Kween Kong policemen passing by on patrol started to come into the Bar Suds. Seeing, however, that it was two Americans who were apparently fighting they decided not to interfere. One of the policemen later testified that his companion said "Why risk getting in that fight; if one of the Americans gets killed, it will be just one less we have to put up with in Kween Kong."

One of the barmaids, Gentyl Thynge, tried to intercede but was violently shoved aside by Sergeant Bully. She fell and broke her wrist on hitting the floor. Gentyl Thynge's intervention did however make Sergeant Bully release his hand from Private Meek's throat. This, nevertheless, made him only angrier so he picked up an empty beer bottle and hit Private Meek over the head killing him.

In the meantime the proprietor of the Bar Suds, Plenty Kash, rushed excitedly out into the street shouting that the Americans were wrecking his bar. A crowd quickly gathered. Among them was a communist agitator, Sabo Tur, who whipped up the feelings of the crowd and started an indignant march on the American Embassy.

The crowd arrived at the Embassy, caught the usual contingent of guards by surprise and forced its way into the Embassy grounds. The doors of the Embassy building, which opened directly on a driveway, were quickly locked. The crowd milled around, becoming more and more enraged by the minute as Sabo Tur stirred up passions. A member of the group, a citizen of Hwat Nau, Ichii Triga, pulled out a revolver and shot into the Embassy severely wounding First Secretary Herbert Mortimer Fairweather Careerman IV who had been incautiously watching from behind a window.

At this point, Phathe Phull Dryva, one of the loyal local employees of the Embassy serving as the Ambassador's chauffeur came from the Embassy garage attracted by the commotion. Being more brave than sensible, feeling a loss of face at the action of his countrymen, and hoping to relieve pressure on the Embassy doors which were beginning to crack under the blows they were receiving, he went back to the garage and brought out one of the Embassy's jeeps used for rough country trips. With this jeep he bore down on the crowd thronging on the driveway in front of the Embassy doors trying to disperse them. Unfortunately in the process, which was fairly successful, he ran down and fatally injured a couple of students taking part in the demonstration. One of them was a citizen of the neighboring state of Laii Lauw who was enrolled in the University of Hwat Nau. As a result when the jeep finally stalled the crowd turned on him, diverting their attention from the Embassy. Fortunately before anything more could happen, police reinforcements arrived.

Who has jurisdiction to try the several offenders involved in the circumstances related?

What international responsibility if any has been incurred by the Government of the United States and to whom? If there is not any responsibility should there be an ex gratia payment? What international responsibility if any has been incurred by the Government of Hwat Nau and to whom? If there is not any responsibility should there be an ex gratia payment? If there is a dispute what judicial methods can be invoked to reach a settlement?

Discuss the problem, or rather problems, in the light of the various sources of international law as set forth in Article 38 of the Statute of the International Court of Justice.

You can assume that the status of American military in Hwat Nau is determined by a Status of Forces agreement that is in all respects parallel to the NATO Status of Forces Agreement.

You can further assume that the interested states are all members of the International Court of Justice, and that all are bound by the compulsory jurisdiction clause, the United States, however, being the only country to attach a "Connally Amendment" to its acceptance of compulsory jurisdiction. In studying the applicability of treaty provisions, take into consideration the customary rules governing the interpretation of treaties.

C. INTERNATIONAL LAW EXAMINATION

Mr. Achilles Helzopopulus was born in the Kingdom of Greece and was a Greek national by birth. At the age of 22 he emigrated to the United States where, in time, he became a naturalized citizen, without, however, losing his Greek nationality. Thenceforward he maintained a residence in the U-nited States, paid his American income taxes and travelled on an American passport. He did, nevertheless, live and travel extensively abroad. He was interested in several large European corporations and particularly in S.A. Mangez Bien, a corporation organized and operated for the manufac-ture and sale of false teeth. S.A. Mangez Bien was incorporated in Switz-erland but had its principal office in Genoa, Italy. It sold its products all through the Mediterranean area. The majority of its bearer shares were held at the time of the events recounted in this problem by West German nationals with the remaining being held by Belgian, Dutch and French na-tionals. Mr. Helzopopulus was its president and directing genius.

In the fall of 1964 Mr. Helzopopulus made a strenuous and exhausting trip to the Middle East. To obtain a little rest he was returning by sea from Beirut to Genoa on board the S.S. Explosion, an American vessel owned by American Extraneous Lines and flying the American flag. Its master was Captain Briney Deap.

Shortly out of Beirut en route to Piraeus the S.S. Explosion rescued some Syrian fishermen whose vessel had been battered by an autumnal Med-iterranean storm and was about to founder. Captain Deap, being a com-passionate mariner, swung his vessel somewhat off course to deposit the fishermen at their native village of Inugo. As he approached the coast he realized from his charts that there were rocks and reefs around Inugo which made it dangerous to approach the shore in the heavy seas that were still running in the wake of the storm. Hence he stood about four marine miles off shore and radioed for the Syrian authorities to come out in a tug to take the fishermen off the S.S. Explosion.

The tug, when it arrived, was accompanied by Major Abdullah Kachem Kwik of the Syrian Police Force. While on deck he noticed Mr. Helzopop-ulus. He at once claimed that Mr. Helzopopulus was an Israeli spy who was badly wanted in Syria for espionage and for participation in the murder of a Syrian national. Despite the strenuous denials of Mr. Helzopopulus and the vigorous protests of Captain Deap, Mr. Helzopopulus was placed in hand-cuffs and taken ashore.

On shore, according to subsequently disclosed evidence, he was badly beaten and given the third degree. He was then tried by a summary court martial and promptly shot.

Notwithstanding the existence of a consular convention between Syria and the United States similar to the U.S.-Korean consular convention, per-tinent excerpts from which are attached, the nearest American consul, who had been advised of the arrest through the protests made by the American Extraneous Lines to the Embassy at Damascus was unable, despite his best efforts, to see Mr. Helzopopulus who was held incommunicado prior to his execution. It is also of record that Mr. Helzopopulus vainly requested to see the American consul.

Following the execution a number of protests were lodged with the Syrian Government. The American Government protested on the general ground of the violation of customary and conventional international law. In addition it lodged a claim for damages on behalf of his wife, Maria Pia Helzopopulus and the minor children of Mr. Helzopopulus, Agamemnon and Clytemnestra Helzopopulus. The children were American nationals, the wife, however was an Italian national. The claims were based on (1) the pain and suffering sustained by the deceased while he was subjected to the third degree treatment and on (2) wrongful death. The Italian government also submitted a claim on the behalf of the widow. The American Extraneous Lines likewise filed a claim through the American Embassy based on the alleged illegal action of the Syrian authorities in effecting the arrest on board the S.S. Explosion. Furthermore the Government of Switzerland interceded on behalf of S.A. Mangez Bien. It seems that a very important meeting had been scheduled in Genoa on the return of Mr. Helzopopulus. It was expected that that meeting would result in an extremely lucrative arrangement with another company for the distribution of false teeth in certain parts of the Orient especially adapted for betel-nut chewing. As a consequence of the death of Mr. Helzopopulus the meeting was never held and the lucrative arrangement never materialized. Moreover the corporation claimed that the loss of its president and guiding genius resulted in a direct loss to the corporation, pointing out that the shares of the company dropped some thirty points following his death.

What principles of international law and practice are applicable to the situation described above? Do you think the protests have been properly made and that the various claims are justified? Have they been brought by the right governments? What are the recourses in each case if Syria fails to give any satisfaction?

You can assume that in each case Syria and the claimant government have accepted the jurisdiction of the International Court of Justice subject to the limitations of a Connally amendment. You can further assume that Syria and the United States are bound by a consular convention such as the one that is in force between Korea and the United States.

CONSULAR CONVENTION

Between the United States of America and the Republic of Korea

ARTICLE 5--Protection of Nationals

(1) A consular officer shall have the right within his district to interview, communicate with, assist, and advise any national of the sending state and, where necessary, arrange for legal assistance for him, provided such national so requests, or comes voluntarily to the consular office, or does not object to inquiry from or visit by the consular officer. The receiving state shall in no way restrict the access of any national of the sending state to its consular establishments.

(2) The appropriate authorities of the receiving state shall, at the request of any national of the sending state who is under arrest or otherwise detained in custody, immediately inform a consular officer of the sending state, who shall be accorded full opportunity to visit and communicate with such a national in order to safeguard his interests.

(3) A consular officer of the sending state shall have the right to visit and communicate with, subject to prison regulations, a national of the sending state who is serving a sentence of imprisonment.

(4) For the purposes of the provisions of paragraphs (1) and (2) of this Article, the phrase "national of the sending state" shall be deemed to apply also to any person employed on a vessel or aircraft of the sending state, who is not a national of the receiving state.

ARTICLE 16--Settlement of Disputes

Any dispute concerning the interpretation or application of the permanent Convention which is not settled by negotiation may be referred, at the option of either party, to the International Court of Justice for decision, provided (1) that matters falling within the discretion of either party under the Convention shall not be subject to the Court's jurisdiction, and (2) that neither party may refer a dispute to the Court until it has exhausted its legal remedies in the territory of the other Party, in the same manner as would a private person claiming rights, exemptions, and immunities under local law and regulations.

D. INTERNATIONAL LAW EXAMINATION

Pierre l'Aventurier, an engaging and adventuresome French officer in love with wine, women and song and the good things of this earth, was stationed with a unit of the French fleet in Tahiti. He had earned a six weeks leave and decided he would spend that time scuba diving in the Arafura Sea on the Continental Shelf north of Australia where the pearl oysters cluster, guarded by the lurking sharks. He enlisted on this venture some other companions who were similarly minded, including an American tourist in Tahiti with considerable experience in diving, whose name was Downey Goes, and the German Consul in Tahiti, Herr Brusch. The group went to Western Samoa where Pierre visited his inamorata, Petal Pusha, who lived in the mountains high above the sea. With her help they purchased a small boat with a powerful motor which was registered and continued to be registered under the Western Samoan flag. Loaded with adequate supplies for a fairly lengthy voyage, they went to Northern Australia and then out to the Arafura Sea. About fifteen miles off shore above a ledge about thirty feet deep, Pierre put on his scuba suit and started diving. While still on the surface, he had noticed not far away, another small vessel flying a Japanese flag, but had paid little attention to it.

Pierre, at the bottom of the sea started to look around and found a whole row of oysters symmetrically arranged. They looked as if they were the type that produced pearls. He started to pick several up when another diver approached him. It appeared that the other diver was a Japanese national, Omizu San, and that the oysters had been deliberately planted by his employers in a row to be cultivated in the benign waters of the Arafura Sea. Omizu San, naturally took a prejudiced view of any interlopers gathering the oysters and lunged at Pierre. Pierre took out his shark knife and, in the scuffle that followed, Omizu San was stabbed to death.

Pierre realized what he had done and made haste to return to his boat which departed immediately for fear of retaliation by the Japanese. Unfortunately, on his return to Tahiti the story of the adventure spread as a result of a drunken indiscretion by Downey Goes who had indulged too freely at the Bar Ber, one of the local bars.

The French naval and local authorities in Tahiti learned about the homicide but did nothing to discipline Pierre. In fact they quietly permitted Pierre to leave for the Argentine until the scandal blew over.

The circumstances just related started a whole series of demands and counterdemands. Pierre was traced to the Argentine and demands for his extradition were made by the Japanese, Western Samoan and Australian governments. The Japanese claimed jurisdiction on the ground that the victim was a Japanese national; the Western Samoans on the ground that Pierre was a member of the crew of a Western Samoan vessel and the Australians on the ground that their criminal jurisdiction extended over the Continental

Shelf. Moreover, the French authorities, urged by Paris, belatedly decided that they had better try Pierre themselves to avoid international criticism and prevent Pierre's trial by a third state. Hence, France also made a claim for extradition on the ground that Pierre was a French national.

The Argentine had extradition treaties with Japan, France and Australia similar to the one attached as Annex A while Western Samoa does not have any treaty at all with the Argentine.

The French authorities also decided to try Herr Brusch and Downey Goes as accessories to the alleged crime. Both denied French jurisdiction. Herr Brusch, moreover, claimed immunity on the grounds that he was a consular officer. In addition, the Japanese government brought an international claim against France on behalf of the widow and minor children of Omizu San, on the basis that Pierre was an officer of the French Navy for whose actions France was responsible and that in any event France had assumed responsibility by permitting his escape to the Argentine.

Moreover, the scandal forcibly brought to the attention of the Australians that the Japanese were using the Continental Shelf. In a diplomatic note to the Japanese Foreign Office, the Australian government claimed exclusive jurisdiction and insisted that the pearl cultivating operations cease. The Japanese denied the claim of the Australian government on the grounds that the Australian's control extended only to the natural riches of the Continental Shelf and did not include any oyster farm specifically cultivated by man and that in any event oysters were not part of the Continental Shelf. The Japanese government claimed further that the operation had been carried on for some twenty years with the tacit acquiescence of the local Australian authorities.

Unable to reach an agreement, the Australians and Japanese decided to submit the latter question to arbitration. There was likewise disagreement with regard to the extradition of Pierre, the Argentine refusing to permit extradition in view of the several conflicting claims. The four nations, i.e. Japan, France, Australia and Western Samoa presented a joint case to the International Court of Justice to determine their respective rights vis-a-vis the Argentine. Japan and France also disagreed among themselves on the pecuniary liability of France and that question as well was submitted to the International Court of Justice.

Assume that France and the Argentine have accepted the compulsory jurisdiction of the court without reservation, Japan and Western Samoa subject to a "Connally type" reservation, and Australia is merely a member of the court by virtue of being a member of the United Nations.

Analyze the above situation from the legal and factual viewpoint.

Indicate the best type of arbitral tribunal that should be established to determine the dispute between Australia and Japan concerning the Continental Shelf and give an indication as to how that Tribunal should function.

Discuss the decision that should be rendered by the Tribunal.

Discuss likewise the cases before the International Court of Justice, analyzing the jurisdiction of the court; and assuming that the Court has jurisdiction, indicate the substantive nature of the decisions that should be rendered.

Determine whether a joinder of the parties is permitted under the statute and rules of the court or whether separate cases should have been brought by each nation. What effect does a joinder have on jurisdiction? What effect does it have on the appointment of national judges?

BRAZIL

Extradition

Treaty and additional protocol signed at Rio de Janeiro January 13, 1961 and
June 18, 1962, respectively;
Ratification advised by the Senate of the United States of America May 16,
1961, and October 22, 1963, respectively;
Ratified by the President of the United States of America May 29, 1961, and
October 29, 1963, respectively;
Ratified by Brazil August 25, 1964;
Ratifications exchanged at Washington November 17, 1964;
Proclaimed by the President of the United States of America November 20,
1964;
Entered into force December 17, 1964.

By the President of the United States of America

A PROCLAMATION

Whereas a treaty of extradition between the United States of America
and the United States of Brazil was signed at Rio de Janeiro on January 13,
1961 and an additional protocol thereto was signed at Rio de Janeiro on June
18, 1962, the originals of which treaty and additional protocol, being in the
English and Portuguese languages, are word for word as follows:

TREATY OF EXTRADITION BETWEEN THE UNITED STATES OF AMERICA AND THE UNITED STATES OF BRAZIL

The United States of America and the United States of Brazil, desiring
to make more effective the cooperation of their respective countries in the
repression of crime, have resolved to conclude a treaty of extradition and
for this purpose have appointed the following Plenipotentiaries:

The President of the United States of America: His Excellency John
Moors Cabot, Ambassador of the United States of America to Brazil, and
The President of the United States of Brazil: His Excellency Horacio
Lafer, Minister of State for External Relations,
Who, having communicated to each other their respective full powers,
found to be in good and due form, agree as follows:

Article I

Each Contracting State agrees, under the conditions established by the present Treaty and each in accordance with the legal formalities in force in its own country, to deliver up, reciprocally, persons found in its territory who have been charged with or convicted of any of the crimes or offenses specified in Article II of the present Treaty and committed within the territorial jurisdiction of the other, or outside thereof under the conditions specified in Article IV of the present Treaty; provided that such surrender shall take place only upon such evidence of criminality as, according to the laws of the place where the fugitive or person so charged shall be found, would justify his commitment for trial if the crime or offense had been there committed.

Article II

Persons shall be delivered up according to the provisions of the present Treaty for prosecution when they have been charged with, or to undergo sentence when they have been convicted of, any of the following crimes or offenses:

1. Murder (including crimes designated as parricide, poisoning, and infanticide, when provided for as separate crimes); manslaughter when voluntary.
2. Rape; abortion; carnal knowledge of (or violation of) a girl under the age specified by law in such cases in both the requesting and requested States.
3. Malicious wounding; willful assault resulting in grievous bodily harm.
4. Abduction, detention, deprivation of liberty, or enslavement of women or girls for immoral purposes.
5. Kidnapping or abduction of minors or adults for the purpose of extorting money from them or their families or any other person or persons, or for any other unlawful end.
6. Bigamy.
7. Arson.
8. The malicious and unlawful damaging of railways, trains, vessels, aircraft, bridges, vehicles, and other means of travel or of public or private buildings, or other structures, when the act committed shall endanger human life.
9. Piracy, by the law of nations; mutiny on board a vessel or an aircraft for the purpose of rebelling against the authority of the Captain or Commander of such vessel or aircraft; or by fraud or violence taking possession of such vessel or aircraft.
10. Burglary, defined to be the breaking into or entering either in day or night time, a house, office, or other building of a government, corporation, or private person, with intent to commit a felony therein; housebreaking.
11. Robbery.

12. Forgery or the utterance of forged papers.

13. The forgery, falsification, theft or destruction of the official acts or public records of the government or public authority, including Courts of Justice, or the uttering or fraudulent use of the same.

14. The fabrication or the utterance, circulation or fraudulent use of any of the following objects: counterfeit money, whether coin or paper; counterfeit titles or coupons of public debt, created by national, state, provincial, territorial, local or municipal governments; counterfeit bank notes or other instruments of public credit; and counterfeit seals, stamps, dies, and marks of State or public administration.

15. The introduction of instruments for the fabrication of counterfeit coins or bank notes or other paper currency as money.

16. Embezzlement by any person or persons hired, salaried or employed, to the detriment of their employers or principals.

17. Larceny.

18. Obtaining money, valuable securities or other property by false pretenses, or by threats of injury.

19. Receiving any money, valuable securities or other property knowing the same to have been unlawfully obtained.

20. Fraud or breach of trust by a bailee, banker, factor, trustee, executor, administrator, guardian, director or officer of any company or corporation or by anyone in any fiduciary capacity.

21. Willful non-support or willful abandonment of a minor or other dependent person when death or serious bodily injury results therefrom.

22. Perjury (including willfully false expert testimony); subordination of perjury.

23. Soliciting, receiving, or offering bribes.

24. The following offenses when committed by public officials: extortion; embezzlement.

25. Crimes or offenses against the bankruptcy laws.

26. Crimes or offenses against the laws of both countries for the suppression of slavery and slave trading.

27. Crimes or offenses against the laws relating to the traffic in, use of, or production or manufacture of, narcotic drugs or cannabis.

28. Crimes or offenses against the laws relating to the illicit manufacture of or traffic in substances injurious to health, or poisonous chemicals.

29. Smuggling, defined to be the act of willfully and knowingly violating the customs laws with intent to defraud the revenue by international traffic in merchandise subject to duty.

30. Aiding the escape of a prisoner by force of arms.

31. Use of explosives so as to endanger human life or property.

32. Procuration, defined as the procuring or transporting of a woman or girl under age, even with her consent, for immoral purposes, or of a woman or girl over age, by fraud, threats, or compulsion, for such purposes with a view in either case to gratifying the passions of another person; profiting from the prostitution of another.

33. The attempt to commit any of the above crimes or offenses, when such attempt is made a separate offense by the laws of the Contracting States.

34. Participation in any of the above crimes or offenses.

Article III

Except as otherwise provided in the present Treaty, the requested State shall extradite a person accused or convicted of any crime or offense enumerated in Article II only when both of the following conditions exist:

1. The law of the requesting State, in force when the crime or offense was committed, provides a possible penalty of deprivation of liberty for a period of more than one year; and

2. The law in force in the requested State generally provides a possible penalty of deprivation of liberty for a period of more than one year which would be applicable if the crime or offense were committed in the territory of the requested State.

Article IV

When the crime or offense has been committed outside the territorial jurisdiction of the requesting State, the request for extradition need not be honored unless the laws of the requesting State and those of the requested State authorize punishment of such crime or offense in this circumstance.

The words "territorial jurisdiction" as used in this Article and in Article I of the present Treaty mean: territory, including territorial waters, and the airspace thereover, belonging to or under the control of one of the Contracting States; and vessels and aircraft belonging to one of the Contracting States or to a citizen or corporation thereof when such vessel is on the high seas or such aircraft is over the high seas.

Article V

Extradition shall not be granted in any of the following circumstances:

1. When the requested State is competent, according to its laws, to prosecute the person whose surrender is sought for the crime or offense for which that person's extradition is requested and the requested State intends to exercise its jurisdiction.

2. When the person whose surrender is sought has already been or is at the time of the request being prosecuted in the requested State for the crime or offense for which his extradition is requested.

3. When the legal proceedings or the enforcement of the penalty for the crime or offense committed has become barred by limitation according to the laws of either the requesting State or the requested State.

4. When the person sought would have to appear, in the requesting State, before an extraordinary tribunal or court.

5. When the crime or offense for which the person's extradition is requested is of a political character. Nevertheless

a. The allegation by the person sought of political purpose or motive for the request for his extradition will not preclude that person's surrender if the crime or offense for which his extradition is requested is primarily an infraction of the ordinary penal law. In such case the delivery of the person being extradited will be dependent on an undertaking on the part of the requesting State that the political purpose or motive will not contribute toward making the penalty more severe.

b. Criminal acts which constitute clear manifestations of anarchism or envisage the overthrow of the bases of all political organizations will not be classed as political crimes or offenses.

c. The determination of the character of the crime or offense will fall exclusively to the authorities of the requested State.

Article VI

When the commission of the crime or offense for which the extradition of the person is sought is punishable by death under the laws of the requesting State and the laws of the requested State do not permit this punishment, the requested State shall not be obligated to grant the extradition unless the requesting State provides assurances satisfactory to the requested State that the death penalty will not be imposed on such person.

Article VII

There is no obligation upon the requested State to grant the extradition of a person who is a national of the requested State, but the executive authority of the requested State shall, subject to the appropriate laws of that State, have the power to surrender a national of that State if, in its discretion, it be deemed proper to do so.

Article VIII

The Contracting States may request, one from the other, through the channel of their respective diplomatic or consular agents, the provisional arrest of a fugitive as well as the seizure of articles relating to the crime or offense.

The request for provisional arrest shall be granted provided that the crime or offense for which the extradition of the fugitive is sought is one for which extradition shall be granted under the present Treaty and provided that the request contains:

1. A statement of the crime or offense of which the fugitive is accused or

convicted.

2. A description of the person sought for the purpose of identification;

3. A statement of the probable whereabouts of the fugitive, if known; and

4. A declaration that there exist and will be forthcoming the relevant documents required by Article IX of the present Treaty.

If, within a maximum period of 60 days from the date of the provisional arrest of the fugitive in accordance with this Article, the requesting State does not present the formal request for his extradition, duly supported, the person detained will be set at liberty and a new request for his extradition will be accepted only when accompanied by the relevant documents required by Article IX of the present Treaty.

Article IX

The request for extradition shall be made through diplomatic channels or, exceptionally, in the absence of diplomatic agents, it may be made by a consular officer, and shall be supported by the following documents:

1. In the case of a person who has been convicted of the crime or offense for which his extradition is sought: a duly certified or authenticated copy of the final sentence of the competent court.

2. In the case of a person who is merely charged with the crime or offense for which his extradition is sought: a duly certified or authenticated copy of the warrant of arrest or other order of detention issued by the competent authorities of the requesting State, together with the depositions upon which such warrant or order may have been issued and such other evidence or proof as may be deemed competent in the case.

The documents specified in this Article must contain a precise statement of the criminal act of which the person sought is charged or convicted, the place and date of the commission of the criminal act, and they must be accompanied by an authenticated copy of the texts of the applicable laws of the requesting State including the laws relating to the limitation of the legal proceedings or the enforcement of the penalty for the crime or offense for which the extradition of the person is sought, and data or records which will prove the identity of the person sought.

The documents in support of the request for extradition shall be accompanied by a duly certified translation thereof into the language of the requested State.

Article X

When the extradition of a person has been requested by more than one State, action thereon will be taken as follows:

1. If the requests deal with the same criminal act, preference will be given to the request of the State in whose territory the act was performed.

2. If the requests deal with different criminal acts, preference will be given to the request of the State in whose territory the most serious crime

or offense, in the opinion of the requested State, has been committed.
3. If the requests deal with different criminal acts, but which the requested State regards as of equal gravity, the preference will be determined by the priority of the requests.

Article XI

The determination that extradition based upon the request therefor should or should not be granted shall be made in accordance with the domestic law of the requested State, and the person whose extradition is desired shall have the right to use such remedies and recourses as are authorized by such law.

Article XII

If at the time the appropriate authorities of the requested State shall consider the documents submitted by the requesting State, as required in Article IX of the present Treaty, in support of its request for the extradition of the person sought, it shall appear that such documents do not constitute evidence sufficient to warrant extradition under the provisions of the present Treaty of the person sought, such person shall be set at liberty unless the requested State or the proper tribunal thereof shall, in conformity with its own laws, order an extension of time for the submission by the requesting State of additional evidence.

Article XIII

Extradition having been granted, the surrendering State shall communicate promptly to the requesting State that the person to be extradited is held at its disposition.

If, within 60 days counting from such communication--except when rendered impossible by force majeure or by some act of the person being extradited or the surrender of the person is deferred pursuant to Articles XIV or XV of the present Treaty--such person has not been delivered up and conveyed out of the jurisdiction of the requested State, the person shall be set at liberty.

Article XIV

When the person whose extradition is requested is being prosecuted or is serving a sentence in the requested State, the surrender of that person under the provisions of the present Treaty shall be deferred until the person is entitled to be set at liberty, on account of the crime or offense for which he is being prosecuted or is serving a sentence, for any of the following reasons: dismissal of the prosecution, acquittal, expiration of the term of the sentence or the term to which such sentence may have been commuted, pardon, parole, or amnesty.

Article XV

When, in the opinion of competent medical authority, duly sworn to, the person whose extradition is requested cannot be transported from the requested State to the requesting State without serious danger to his life due to his grave illness, the surrender of the person under the provisions of the present Treaty shall be deferred until such time as the danger, in the opinion of the competent medical authority, has been sufficiently mitigated.

Article XVI

The requesting State may send to the requested State one or more duly authorized agents, either to aid in the identification of the person sought or to receive his surrender and to convey him out of the territory of the requested State.

Such agents, when in the territory of the requested State, shall be subject to the applicable laws of the requested State, but the expenses which they incur shall be for the account of the State which has sent them.

Article XVII

Expenses related to the transportation of the person extradited shall be paid by the requesting State. The appropriate legal officers of the country in which the extradition proceedings take place shall, by all legal means within their power, assist the officers of the requesting State before the respective judges and magistrates. No pecuniary claim, arising out of the arrest, detention, examination and surrender of fugitives under the terms of the present Treaty, shall be made of the requested State against the requesting State other than as specified in the second paragraph of this Article and other than for the lodging, maintenance, and board of the person being extradited prior to his surrender.

The legal officers, other officers of the requested State and court stenographers in the requested State who shall, in the usual course of their duty, give assistance and who receive no salary or compensation other than specific fees for the services performed, shall be entitled to receive from the requesting State the usual payment for such acts or services performed by them in the same manner and to the same amount as though such acts or services had been performed in ordinary criminal proceedings under the laws of the country of which they are officers.

Article XVIII

A person who, after surrender by either of the Contracting States to the other under the terms of the present Treaty, succeeds in escaping from the requesting State and takes refuge in the territory of the State which has surrendered him, or passes through it in transit, will be detained, upon simple diplomatic request, and surrendered anew, without other formalities, to the State to which his extradition was granted.

Article XIX

Transit through the territory of one of the Contracting States of a person in the custody of an agent of the other Contracting State, and surrendered to the latter by a third State, and who is not of the nationality of the country of transit, shall, subject to the provisions of the second paragraph of this Article, be permitted, independently of any judicial formalities, when requested through diplomatic channels and accompanied by the presentation in original or in authenticated copy of the document by which the State of refuge has granted the extradition. In the United States of America, the authority of the Secretary of State of the United States of America shall be first obtained.

The permission provided for in this Article may nevertheless be refused if the criminal act which has given rise to the extradition does not constitute a crime or offense enumerated in Article II of the present Treaty, or when grave reasons of public order are opposed to the transit.

Article XX

Subject to the rights of third parties, which shall be duly respected:

1. All articles, valuables, or documents which relate to the crime or offense and, at the time of arrest, have been found in the possession of the person sought or otherwise found in the requested State shall be surrendered, with him, to the requesting State.

2. The articles and valuables which may be found in the possession of third parties and which likewise are related to the crime or offense shall also be seized, but may be surrendered only after the rights with regard thereto asserted by such third parties have been determined.

Article XXI

A person extradited by virtue of the present Treaty may not be tried or punished by the requesting State for any crime or offense committed prior to the request for his extradition, other than that which gave rise to the request, nor may he be re-extradited by the requesting State to a third country which claims him, unless the surrendering State so agrees or unless the person extradited, having been set at liberty within the requesting State, remains voluntarily in the requesting State for more than 30 days from the date on which he was released. Upon such release, he shall be informed of the consequences to which his stay in the territory of the requesting State would subject him.

Article XXII

The present Treaty shall be ratified and the ratifications thereof shall be exchanged at Washington, as soon as possible.

The present Treaty shall enter into force one month after the date of exchange ratifications. It may be terminated at any time by either Contracting State giving notice of termination to the other Contracting State, and the termination shall be effective six months after the date of such notice.

IN WITNESS WHEREOF the respective Plenipotentiaries have signed the present Treaty and have affixed hereunto their seals.

DONE in duplicate, in the English and Portuguese languages, both equally authentic, at Rio de Janeiro, this thirteenth day of January, one thousand nine hundred sixty-one.

(seal)   John M. Cabot

(seal)   Horacio Lafer

ADDITIONAL PROTOCOL TO THE TREATY OF EXTRADITION
OF JANUARY 13, 1961, BETWEEN THE UNITED STATES
OF AMERICA AND THE UNITED STATES OF BRAZIL

The United States of America and the United States of Brazil,

Having concluded at Rio de Janeiro, on January 13, 1961, a Treaty of Extradition for the purpose of making more effective the cooperation between the two countries in the repression of crime,

And desiring to make clear that their respective nationals will be subject to extradition only if the constitutional and legal provisions in force in their territories permit it,

Have resolved to sign an Additional Protocol to the aforementioned Treaty of Extradition and, to this end, have appointed the following Plenipotentiaries:

The President of the United States of America: His Excellency Lincoln Gordon, Ambassador Extraordinary and Plenipotentiary to Brazil, and

The President of the Republic of the United States of Brazil: His excellency Francisco Clementino de San Tiango Dantas, Minister of State for External Relations,

Who, having communicated to each other their respective full powers, found to be in good and due form, agree as follows:

Article I

Article VII of the Treaty of Extradition concluded between the two countries at Rio de Janeiro, on January 13, 1961, shall be interpreted as follows:

"The Contracting Parties are not obliged by this Treaty to grant extradition of their nationals. However, if the Constitution and laws of the requested State do not prohibit it, its executive authority shall have the power to surrender a national if, in its discretion, it be deemed proper to do so."

Article II

The present Protocol shall enter into force on the same date as the Treaty of Extradition of January 13, 1961, and shall cease to be effective on the date of the termination of the Treaty.

IN WITNESS HEREOF, the respective Plenipotentiaries have signed the present Additional Protocol and have fixed hereunto their seals.

DONE in duplicate, in the English and Portuguese languages, both e-qually authentic, at Rio de Janeiro, on this eighteenth day of June, one thousand nine hundred sixty-two.

LINCOLN GORDON

F C de San Tiago Dantas

(Seal)

TIAS 5691

E. INTERNATIONAL LAW EXAMINATION

On a clear, calm, and sunny day the good ship Tory Stronghold carrying a cargo of Algerian wine in bulk ran aground on a rock, known as Stupid Rock, geologically connected to the neighboring Scilly Islands. Stupid Rock is located thirteen miles from the main English coast and eleven miles from the nearest point on the Scilly Islands. It is submerged at high tide but at low tide it protrudes a meter or so above the sea. At the time of the collision the tide was changing so that the rock was barely visible.

Stupid Rock is plainly marked on all the standard navigation charts and is well known to mariners. Hence the only explanation for the collision was that the Master had been grossly negligent. The Tory Stronghold was flying the Liberian flag and claiming Monrovia as its home port. It was owned by a corporation known as U-Floatem, Inc. The corporation was incorporated in Liechtenstein and all its shares were owned by the Principality of Liechtenstein. Its head office was in Paris, France. At the time of the collision the vessel was on bareboat charter to an Algerian corporation engaged in the transportation of wine known as Bibulous Bubbles, S.A. The Master, Captain Scaloppini di Vitello, and most, although by no means all, of the crew were Italian nationals. The ship was proceeding from Algiers to Liverpool where its contents were intended to gladden the hearts of those depressed by the austerity measures of Mr. Wilson.

The collision between the vessel and the rock created a large hole in the bow. The sea water flowed through that hole trapping and drowning a seaman. The seaman, whose name was Jacques Tarre had been born in England of a French father and mother. He was consequently a French national through the application of the jus sanguinis and a British subject by the application of the jus soli. Nevertheless, despite his dual nationality he considered himself French. He traveled on French travel documents and was married to a French national. He and Madame Tarre had a cottage in Northern France in the little seacoast village of Pernod-sur-les-Rochers.

The collision and pounding of the waves caused further leaks in the hull and the wine poured out into the sea. Unfortunately Stupid Rock was a favorite gathering place for a large school of mackerel. The mackerel, unaccustomed to anything more powerful than sea water, promptly became inebriated and were swept helplessly by the tide to the fashionable seaside resort of What-ho-by-the-Beach which was then at the height of its short summer season. The mackerel were thrown by the waves on the beach by the thousand and proceeded to decompose before arrangements could be made for their removal. In view of the stench, virtually all of the guests departed leaving the hotel and innkeepers to face a severe financial loss.

The ship was finally floated from the rock but sank as it was being towed to shore. The captain and crew were, however, removed in plenty of time and taken to Plymouth. After appropriate inquiry the British authorities arrested Captain di Vitello and charged him with negligence resulting in the death of a British subject. Captain di Vitello, through his barrister, Sir Devious Wiles, Q.C., claimed that even if the charges of negligence were proved, the British courts lacked jurisdiction to try the case under either British or International law.

In the meantime, the Ritz Charlatan, Ltd. Hotel chain which operated a hotel in What-ho-by-the-Beach sought the advice of the well-known firm of solicitors, Messrs. Obfuscate and Complicate as to possible remedies. They were told that it would be hopeless to sue for damages in England as neither U-Floatem, Inc., or Bibulous Bubbles, S.A. had any agent in the United Kingdom on whom process could be served or any assets against which a possible in rem suit could be brought. It was suggested, however, that since Captain di Vitello was the servant and agent of Bibulous Bubbles, S.A. with home offices in Algiers, it might be possible to sue that company in Algiers. The Ritz Charlatan, Ltd., which was incorporated in England although most of its stockholders were American nationals, took that advice and a suit was brought in the Algerian courts. The lower court rendered a judgment in a substantial amount for the plaintiffs, and that judgment was affirmed by an intermediate court. On appeal to the Supreme Court, the decision was reversed by a three to four vote. The plaintiffs learned that one of the judges, Judge Suleiman Ben Baksheesh had accepted a sizeable bribe from the defendants to vote in their favor. They were able to prove the bribery through Baksheesh's secretary, Fatima Wata Lulu, who had fallen in love with the plaintiff's attorney and was indignant at the corruption of the judge.

The plaintiff brought the matter to the attention of the British Embassy in Algiers, which in turn complained to the Algerian Foreign Office. The British complaint was rejected on the ground that international liability had not been established and that in any event Ritz Charlatan, Ltd. had not any right to invoke diplomatic interposition. The latter argument was predicated on the fact that Ritz Charlatan, Ltd., which also operated a hotel in Algiers overlooking the picturesque Wadi-U-No had renounced its right to invoke diplomatic protection in return for a concession to establish and operate a hotel in Algiers.

The British Government then brought the case before the International Court of Justice, both Algeria and the United Kingdom having previously submitted themselves to the compulsory jurisdiction of the court. At this point the Algerian government revoked the concession of Ritz Charlatan, Ltd. to operate a hotel in Algiers predicating its action on a clause in the concession contract which provided that the Algerian government could cancel the concession in the event Ritz Charlatan, Ltd. invoked diplomatic interposition. The British government promptly amended its pleadings in the pending case to include and protest against the alleged illegality of the action of the Algerian government in effecting such a revocation.

While the above-described litigation was going on, Madame Tarre instituted suit in a French Court against U-Floatem, Inc. for damages resulting from the death of her husband . U-Floatem, Inc . raised the point that the French courts lacked jurisdiction on the ground that U-Floatem, Inc . was a corporation wholly owned by the Government of Liechtenstein, and therefore entitled to sovereign immunity.

What should be the decisions of the British Courts, the International Court of Justice, and the French Courts? Explain fully, giving precedents and authorities . Were there any other remedies available to the injured parties or other defenses to the respective defendants? If so, specify their nature .

F. INTERNATIONAL LAW EXAMINATION

Senator Ripley "Rip" Snorter from Missibama is an important and high-ly influential member of the Senate Foreign Relations Committee. During World War II he had been with the O.S.S. in Sweden. Later he became the representative in Sweden of the Pan Demonium Air Lines. While in that country he met and married a Swedish national, Miss Smorgasbored.

The Snorters had a child born in Sweden, Charles "Short" Snorter, who was both a Swedish and American national at birth. The family returned to the United States when Charles was two. Aside from occasional trips abroad they lived continuously in the United States from then on. Two or three times they spent summers in Sweden visiting Charles' grandparents, permitting him to become fluent in Swedish.

To the Senator's disappointment, Charles took little interest in poli-tics. Instead he developed into somewhat of a musical genius and became a member of a well known chamber music quartet known as the Haydn Seek-ers. Before becoming a professional musician he performed his military service in the intelligence branch of the American army.

While on tour in Paris he happened to attend a performance of a dancing troupe from the Mongolian People's Republic. He was enchanted by one of the dancers, Ting-a-Ling. He managed to obtain an introduction and took her out to dinner several times at the famous restaurant "La puce qui saute." Unfortunately for the budding romance the dancing troupe had to return to Mongolia. Charles, who had fallen in love, was in despair and decided he had to follow Ting-a-Ling. He thought that it might be easier for him to go to Mongolia on a Swedish passport rather than an American one since the United States does not recognize the Mongolian People's Republic. Hence he went to Sweden where he obtained a Swedish passport on the basis of his Swedish nationality.

He next went to the capital of Mongolia, Ulan Bator, via the Soviet Union. Unfortunately, the local police discovered that Charles was also an Ameri-can national who had been in the Army Intelligence service and whose father had been in the O.S.S. and suspected him of espionage. They promptly put him in jail and his jailer, Wang Bang, subjected him to harsh treatment --insufficient and poor food, a cold and filthy cell, repeated and prolonged questionings, solitary confinement, etc. Through another foreigner then in Ulan Bator, word of his plight reached his father who immediately re-quested the Department of State to effect his release. The Department could not approach the Mongolian People's Republic directly. Fortunately, the request came at a time when the Soviet government wanted some minor concessions from the United States so they agreed to intercede with the Mongolian People's Republic to try to obtain his release.

The attempt was successful and Charles was released after having been in jail some six months. On his way back to the United States he stopped to recuperate with his grandparents in Sweden. While in Sweden he was, greatly to his surprise, drafted into the Swedish Army.

He wrote at length to his father complaining about his induction and giving a detailed account of his sufferings in Mongolia.

Senator Snorter immediately called on the Secretary of State and insistently requested (1) that the Department of State effect his release from the Swedish army and (2) demand compensation from the Mongolian People's Republic.

In view of Senator Snorter's importance, the Department of State proceeded to investigate promptly. Through the Soviet Embassy in Washington, it was ascertained that the Mongolian Foreign Minister, Yummygin Tennisball, adamantly refused compensation, saying that the Outer Mongolians had good grounds for suspicion and that the treatment afforded was not any different from that given other prisoners in jail.

Nevertheless, Tennisball surprisingly suggested arbitration. Apparently the suggestion was motivated by the thought that the entry of the United States into an arbitral agreement with the Mongolian People's Republic might constitute recognition, which would be a feather in his cap.

Assume that you are the Legal Adviser of the Department.

Prepare a detailed memorandum for the Secretary analyzing the issues and recommending a feasible and desirable course of action. Among other factors take into consideration whether Charles is entitled to any protection from the United States vis-a-vis Outer Mongolia since he was travelling on a foreign passport. Also consider whether Charles has any claim that could be maintained successfully against the Mongolian People's Republic. Is there in reality a substantive claim? Is the United States government entitled to press his claim since he was a Swedish national? Was he also an American national or had he lost that nationality? Even if it is decided by the appropriate American authorities that he is an American national, can an arbitral tribunal interpret the American nationality laws in a contrary sense?

Discuss also the possible consequences of establishing an arbitral tribunal with Mongolia on American relations with that state.

For the Secretary's information give him your thoughts as to how an arbitral tribunal should be constituted in case he decides to proceed to arbitration.

Furthermore, indicate what, if anything, can be done to obtain Charles' release from the Swedish army, giving reasons for your views. Take into consideration pertinent treaty provisions, if any. If a pertinent provision is found but it is ambiguous, follow the usual rules of treaty interpretation to determine its meaning.

While Charles was enduring his misadventures, poor Ting-a-Ling was harried and questioned by the Mongolian police, who suspected that her affair with Charles was not all romance. Finally, having good cause to fear arrest and possibly death, she sought refuge in the British Embassy, which she managed to enter through a side door that had been left unwatched by the Mongolian police.

Sir Launcelot Goodhearte, the British Ambassador, was sympathetic to Ting-a-Ling and gave her asylum. On learning of her flight to the British Embassy, the Mongolian Foreign Office immediately protested, claiming that the British Embassy had no right to grant asylum to Ting-a-Ling. The British government, which had been subjected to pressure through innumerable letters to the London Times sympathizing with Ting-a-Ling, offered to submit the dispute to the International Court of Justice.

The Outer Mongolian government, thinking it had a good case and seeing no other way out of the impasse, reluctantly agreed. What would be the decision of the Court and why?

INDEX

260